DO NOT REMOVE
CARDS FROM POCKET

*The Plato Cult and Other Philosophical Follies*

*To my friend John Brown
of Treachery Headland
to whom it is due that the part of Australia
which means most to me
is still, in 1990,
much as it was in 1937,
this book is gratefully dedicated*

# The Plato Cult and Other Philosophical Follies

David Stove

Basil Blackwell

Copyright © David C. Stove 1991

First published 1991
Allen County Public Library
Ft. Wayne, Indiana

Basil Blackwell Ltd
108 Cowley Road, Oxford, OX4 1JF, UK

Basil Blackwell, Inc.
3 Cambridge Center
Cambridge, Massachusetts 02142, USA

*British Library Cataloguing in Publication Data*

A CIP catalogue record for this book is available from the British Library.

*Library of Congress Cataloging in Publication Data*

Stove, D. C. (David Charles)
    The Plato cult and other philosophical follies / David Stove.
      p. cm.
    Includes bibliographical references and index.
    ISBN 0-631-17709-4
    1. Philosophy. I. Title.
B29.S815   1991                      90-42130
100--dc20                             CIP

Typeset in 11 on 12½pt Sabon
by Photo·graphics Ltd, Honiton, Devon
Printed in Great Britain by T.J. Press Ltd, Padstow, Cornwall

# Contents

Acknowledgements     vi

Preface     vii

1   Cole Porter and Karl Popper: the Jazz Age in the Philosophy of Science     1

2   Philosophy and Lunacy: Nelson Goodman and the Omnipotence of Words     27

3   'Always apologize, always explain': Robert Nozick's War Wounds     43

4   'I only am escaped alone to tell thee': Epistemology and the Ishmael Effect     61

5   Idealism: a Victorian Horror-story (Part One)     83

6   Idealism: a Victorian Horror-story (Part Two)     135

7   What is Wrong with Our Thoughts? A Neo-Positivist Credo     179

Index     207

# Acknowledgements

The only part of this book which has been published before is the first essay in it. This appeared in the magazine *Encounter* in June 1985. I thank the editor, Mr Melvin Lasky, for his permission to re-publish it here. But I have taken the opportunity to reverse certain minor changes which Mr Lasky had made to the text.

I thank Miss Rae Langton (formerly an undergraduate at the University of Sydney, now a graduate student at Princeton University) for some bibliographical information about Kant which I make use of in Essay 5.

Mrs Anthea Bankoff, secretary to the Department of Traditional and Modern Philosophy in the University of Sydney, typed most of the essays which make up this book. I thank her for the cheerfulness, speed, and accuracy with which she typed them. She pleased me even more by enjoying most of them.

D.C.S.

# Preface

This is a book of philosophy, written by a philosopher. It consists of a number of essays. Each essay, except the last, is about some particular philosophy; the last is about philosophy itself. The essays are independent of one another, except that the two about idealism are intended to be read in the order in which they are printed here.

But the book has certain unifying threads. One is, that all the philosophies discussed at any length in it are ones of which my opinion is low. Another is, that all the essays exemplify a certain view of philosophy: a view which, if it needed to be described in one word, would be best called positivistic. In fact, of course, more than one word is necessary to describe any view of philosophy. Yet the few pages of this preface will be sufficient to make clear what my view is, and even, I believe, to justify it. What its consequences are, will be best seen in the last of the essays which follow.

Philosophy is not history, or psychology either, and it is not even the history, or the psychology, of philosophers. All the same, a philosophy often owes much to the historical circumstances of its author, or to his individual psychology. No student of the history of philosophy will dispute this.

In some parts of this book, however, I give an amount of attention which may be thought improper, to the historical circumstances of the philosophers whom I discuss. For example, I describe modern idealism as a part of the religious reaction of the nineteenth century against the Enlightenment of the century before. In another essay I point out that Professor Popper's philosophy of science bears the unmistakable impress of the Jazz Age in which it was born. Again, I say that Professor Nozick's philosophy of philosophy could only have arisen in the period of American history which followed that country's defeat in Vietnam. In one case I even attach explanatory importance to a certain biographical detail: the fact that Professor Goodman is, or at least was for a long time, a dealer in modern art.

Is there anything improper in a philosophy book containing such material? One or more of my historical or biographical assertions may be mistaken, of course, but that possibility is irrelevant, as well as being trivial. The question is, is it wrong for a philosopher to refer in a philosophical book to the historical circumstances, or to the individual lives, of the philosophers whom he discusses? I have never so much as heard of anyone who does think it wrong. Yet the difficulties which I have encountered, in trying to publish this book, seem to prove that at least some people do think so.

It is indeed wrong to let the historical question, how a philosopher came to believe p, supplant or take precedence over the question whether p is true. Precisely this is, of course, one of the intellectual vices of our time. For Marxists, the first and only question is, what 'class interests' are served by a philosopher's believing p? For Freudians, the first and only question is, what early trauma or misdirection of his sexuality lies behind a philosopher's believing p? But there is no instance in this book of that kind of thing, and in fact there is no intellectual vice which is less attractive to philosophers than that one. Philosophers have other and better things to think about: first, and mainly, the question whether p is true.

At least, that is part of the official ethics of philosophy. If there were a Hippocratic oath for philosophers, it would say: 'Attend first and mainly to the question whether what a philosopher says is true.' But in the actual practice of our profession it is, and always has been, impossible to live up to this rule in every case. We are often absolutely compelled to seek some historical or psychological explanation of a philosopher's holding a certain opinion, rather than to consider whether that opinion is true. And the reason is, that philosophers often believe – or at any rate they *say*, with every sign of sincerity – things which are uniquely bizarre, and which even they themselves know to be false. If this seems a shocking accusation, a few examples will suffice to remind any philosophical reader that it is not only true, but perfectly well known to him.

Parmenides said that nothing can move. Yet he travelled, and knew he travelled, around Greece and southern Italy, defending this opinion; and he defended it, of course, by moving his tongue and lips. So, what in the name of God, or sanity, or whatever you value most, is to be made of his theory? Was Parmenides mad? Was he, perhaps, insincere, and merely seeking notoriety? This case is, indeed, such a desperate one that even a hypothesis about infantile psychology – say, of a yearning for the security of the mother's womb – is for once, perhaps, not altogether despicable. Anyway, no one will deny that here *some* extra-philosophical explanation is necessary; and therefore is permissible.

Berkeley held that there are no physical objects: that there was no right hand behind his ideas of his right hand, no wig behind his ideas of his wig, and so on. Indeed, he said, there is nothing at all behind any of our ideas of physical objects, except the will of God that we should *have* those ideas when we do. Yet Berkeley was a physical object himself, after all – born of a certain woman, author of certain printed books, and so forth – and he knew it. So here again, as with Parmenides, we are *compelled* to seek some historical or psychological explanation of a philosopher's holding a certain opinion. In this case, however (unlike that of Parmenides), the explanation is obvious enough, and Berkeley himself was always perfectly explicit about it. His philosophy was an attempt, however eccentric, to defend the Christian religion against the attacks of 'infidels, sceptics', and the like.

Even if this is not the true explanation of Berkeley's *bizarreries*, it will at least be admitted to be a permissible one. And if it is, then it is also permissible for me to advance an historical explanation which is of the same general kind, when Popper says bizarre things about science, or Nozick says bizarre things about philosophy.

Plato held that no particular thing can be *really* white, or round, or human, or whatever: that only whiteness is really white, only roundness truly round, only humanness actually human. In another and better world, he said, such 'universals' exist on their own, unmixed with space, time, or each other. They form a club, like Herman Melville's 'paradise of bachelors', though For Universals Only, which no new member can ever join, and of which no member ever ages or dies. Yet Plato was a particular thing himself, of course, and was human too; and furthermore he knew both those facts. So, again, how can we *avoid* seeking a non-philosophical explanation of this philosophy? A plausible biographical explanation has sometimes been advanced, that Plato had a constitutional aversion to *change*: that he disliked particulars because they are prone to that habit, and liked universals because they are free from it. Whether true or not, this suggestion is at least a permissible one. And if it is, then it is also permissible for me to make the biographical suggestion that Goodman's *bizarreries* (far more extreme, incidentally, than Plato's) owe something to his long-standing interest in modern art.

Philosophers' theories, then, are often so exceedingly strange that we are obliged to postulate some non-rational cause, in order to explain the philosophers' believing them. Indeed, to say that they are 'often' so is to understate the case grievously. Berkeley, Plato, and Parmenides are *paradigm*-philosophers. That there are no physical objects, that no particular thing can really have any property, that nothing can move: it is impossible to deny (however embarrassing it may be to admit) that these are *typical* philosophical theories.

There is not, and never has been, anything else in the world like typical philosophical theories. In particular, and contrary to what is nowadays often supposed, there is nothing like them in the history of science. A new scientific theory can, of course, give people a violent intellectual and emotional shock. The Copernican theory did so in 1543, and so did Darwin's theory in 1859. But there is a world of difference between scientific theories and philosophical ones. Recall how little was really at stake even in the two cases just mentioned, which set off the most tremendous of all scientific revolutions so far. In the Copernican case, all that was at stake was the physical 'geography' of the solar system. In Darwin's case, all that was at stake was the history of terrestrial organisms. Such theories are, at the worst, initially surprising: no more. They do not, and cannot, do what philosophical theories typically do: assail the very fabric of our minds, and threaten to overwhelm us with madness. In philosophy, but nowhere else, we typically must resort, if only in defence of our sanity, to some extraneous and non-rational explanation of a man's believing what he does.

That Parmenides travelled, that Plato was a particular human being, that Berkeley was himself a physical object: these are undisputed historical facts. They are also extremely precious facts, because it is largely by reminding ourselves of such facts as these that we preserve our sanity when we are reading the philosophies of these men. But then, *what of those men themselves, and their theories?* Berkeley (as I said) *knew* he had a mother, Plato knew he was a particular man, Parmenides knew he travelled: these too are undisputed historical facts. Yet these men also believed theories which were obviously incompatible with this knowledge that they had, and which were, at the same time, typical philosophical theories.

These facts, taken together, do not merely suggest – they *prove* – that *there is something fearfully wrong with typical philosophical theories.* But this conclusion is Positivism, or at any rate the basic proposition of Positivism.

From this point of view, what a spectacle of nightmare-irrationality is the history of philosophy! Think, for example, of the reverence which has been accorded to Plato. It began during his life and has continued, with some fluctuations, for nearly 2400 years. Soon after his death in 347 BC, a story was current at Athens that Plato was actually divine: born of a virgin, and a son of Apollo. Diogenes Laertius knew of this story from three sources contemporary with Plato's death, and at least one of these sources was a very credible one: the philosopher Speusippus, who was Plato's nephew, and his successor as head of the Academy. Diogenes does not say whether Speusippus believed this stupid story, or whether Plato himself did. It is possible that Plato had started the story without believing it: he was not at all averse, as we know from the *Republic*, to disseminating beliefs which he knew to be false but considered to be good for people. But even if no one believed in Plato's divinity at the time of his death, many others did later. Some neo-Platonist philosophers worshipped him as a god.

They might easily have chosen a worse man to worship, of

course. It is even possible that the worship of Plato is the highest point to which religion has ever risen. As Samuel Butler said, 'an honest God's the noblest work of man', and Plato's honesty, while not unblemished, was certainly far in advance of that of the average god. Still, to worship him was also, surely, a low point in the history of philosophy.

How could any rational person ever need to be reminded that philosophers, whether great or small, are human beings? Some of them are men of genius, certainly, but all alike are but 'poor forked creatures'. And it deserves to be noticed that men of philosophical genius, while they far exceed us ordinary people in force of intellect, are very often not less but *more* the slaves of their passions than the rest of us are. For example, who can fail to detect, in Berkeley's philosophy, a mystic's overwhelming passion for the divine energy which, he believes, courses through all things at every instant? Who can fail to detect a *love* of immobility in Parmenides?

The great Renaissance revival of Platonism in Italy, which was begun by the Greek philosopher George Gemistus (c. 1355–1452), included the revival of the cult of Plato. Gemistus changed his name to Pletho, in honour of the god, when he decided that he was not only the chief priest, but a reincarnation, of Plato: a form of ecclesiastical pluralism which might have embarrassed a saner man. Among the seventeenth century Cambridge Platonists, there was probably no actual worship of Plato: otherwise their Calvinist or Anglican enemies would have let us know of it. But they certainly kept alive the fervid Renaissance piety towards him. Thomas Taylor, who died in 1835, is the most recent philosopher, as far as I know, who believed in the divinity of Plato. But it would be the height of rashness to call him the last, in view of the apparent indestructibility of the cult.

The case of Plato is not at all unique, merely extreme. In fact, *all* great philosophers attract a reverence which is far stronger and more widespread than that which, by any rational estimate, they are entitled to. The idolatry of Aristotle, for four hundred years after the revival of his philosophy in the twelfth century, is a stock example. But Kant, similarly, has enjoyed for two hundred years a reputation as a philosopher which is ridiculously exaggerated; as is the odour of Enlightenment-sanctity which surrounds his life. Hegel's philosophy is now as much respected as it deserves to be despised, and even his most prosaic (not to say sordid) political adjustments are represented, in retrospect, as Absolute Spirit working itself out in history. And so on.

There is, it is clear, some powerful force at work, especially among philosophers though not only among them, disposing people to overvalue great philosophers, or those who are taken to be such. This force is so strong, and so undiscriminating, that it has even bestowed semi-divine status on such an unlikely candidate as Karl Marx: a man distinguished less by intellectual gifts than by his undisguised impatience for the widespread homicide which he predicted and promoted, but did not live to enjoy.

This force has always been a mystery to me, and I have never felt the reverence for great philosophers to which it disposes so many other people. As there is certainly too much of that reverence, I would gladly see it lessened, and I hope that this book will do something to lessen it. But the contest is such an extremely unequal one, that this result is evidently something rather to be hoped for than expected.

Mulgoa
New South Wales

# 1

## Cole Porter and Karl Popper: the Jazz Age in the Philosophy of Science

The world has gone mad to-day,
And good's bad to-day . . .

> Cole Porter, 'Anything Goes'

Irrefutability is not a virtue of a theory, (as people often think) but a vice.

> Karl Popper, 'Science: Conjectures and Refutations', in his
> *Conjectures and Refutations: the Growth of Scientific
> Knowledge*

## I

I have heard a Marxist 'explain' Darwin's theory of sexual selection as being just a 'reflection' of middle-class Victorian courtship practices. Nowadays, of course, this kind of thing is all the rage: I mean, pretending to explain the currency of a scientific theory, or a philosophy, by reference just to the historical circumstances of its origin, especially the 'class-origins' of its propounder or adherents.

It is a stupid and discreditable business. To talk about Darwin as though he were some simple mechanical toy is discreditable, unless your mental powers happen to be much superior to his: a condition seldom satisfied by anyone, and never, one may safely say, by Marxists. In this particular case the business was so stupid as to be embarrassing, since it is well known that other middle-class Victorian naturalists, including some of the most Darwinian, denied the very existence of sexual selection. But the stupidity which is common to all such 'explanations' is, of course, simply that of proceeding as though the *merits* of a theory – such things as truth, or probability, or explanatory power – could not possibly be among the reasons for its currency.

Sometimes, of course, and to some extent, you *do* need to refer to social circumstances, in order to explain the currency or the origin of a theory. You are more likely to need to do so, obviously, the less merit the theory has. Lysenko's biology is a conspicuous case in science. And you are more likely to need to do so for a philosophy than for a scientific theory. Hegel's political philosophy is an obvious example. In either of these two instances, it would be absurd to deny that social circumstances had a great deal to do with the origin, and the currency, of the theory.

A similar instance is Sir Karl Popper's philosophy of science.

We have from Popper's own hand a brief but illuminating account of the social circumstances in which his philosophy was born.[1] The place was Vienna, where Popper was a university student. The time was that great watershed of our century, the years immediately after the first world war. The social circumstances were – well, 'the world turned upside down'.

In Austria the defeat of the central powers brought about the overturning of authority in almost every form: political authority, moral and religious authority, financial authority. As the old structures dissolved almost overnight, Marxism, Anarchism, Freudianism, Dadaism – any-ism, so long as it promised a Great Reversal – competed, not only for the minds of the young, but for government. A bewildered bohemian, who had never controlled so much as a horse in his life, might wake to find the reins of office in his hands. Nor was the Austro-Hungarian empire the only one to crack up at this time. For the mind of the young Popper, the fall of another and far more soundly based empire was no less formative: I mean the Newtonian empire in physics. In art, Western Europe found that its anti-academy had become its academy 'even in the twinkling of an eye'. The galleries were suddenly full of the art of African societies formerly the most despised. Victorian architecture was all at once the object of a universal detestation, or rather horror. Black music began its long and excruciating revenge on the white man. The Jazz Age, in short, had arrived.

Cole Porter's words 'Anything goes' are not quite right for this situation, though; for they suggest *random* change, or anarchy. He is nearer the mark with 'day's night to-day', 'good's bad to-day', and so on; for these words convey the idea of *reversal* rather than of random change. Of course it is often not easy to keep the two ideas separated in one's mind. Even the prophet Isaiah, when he says that 'every valley shall be exalted, and every mountain and hill made low', is open to the suspicion of being not quite clear in his own mind as to whether he is promising us a plain, or only new mountains where valleys were before. Still, the two ideas really are distinct, and it is the idea of reversal, rather than that of random change, which is the key to the Jazz Age. It is also the key to Popper's philosophy of science.

The difference between the propositions of science, on the one hand, and the speculations of philosophy, religion, and pseudo-science on the other, has always been felt strongly enough. But what exactly is the difference? According to long-standing philosophical tradition (as also according to common sense), the difference is that the propositions of science are *verifiable*. On this point even the Logical Positivists, who were certainly revolutionary enough in other respects (and who came to constitute Popper's main philosophical environment), agreed with everyone else. Very well then: Popper would say that the distinguishing mark of scientific propositions is that they are *falsifiable*.

The main stream of philosophy, at least since Bacon, had always maintained (and here again the Logical Positivists agreed) that the method of science is essentially *inductive*. We infer the future from the past, the unobserved (and perhaps unobservable) from what is observed, and in general the unknown from the known. Very well: Popper would maintain that we do not and cannot infer the unobserved from the observed; that in science we always infer the known from the unknown; that the method of science is entirely *deductive*.

*Caution* is of the essence of science, everyone used to say. So Popper said that *audacity* is of the essence of science, and that, of two theories equal in other respects, the bolder is the better.

Science was supposed to be distinguished from guesswork, and from everyday opinion, by the fact that its conclusions are *certain*, final, irrefutable. Newton's boast that he never meddled with hypotheses – '*Hypotheses non fingo*' – was supposed to express the scientific ideal. Well then, Popper would say that the conclusions of science are never more than guesswork, hypotheses, conjectures; that not meddling with hypotheses is an ideal impossible to achieve and pernicious even to aim at; and (as in the epigraph above) that irrefutability is *not a virtue but a vice* in a theory.

Conventional philosophy of science, in a more cautious variant, said that scientific conclusions are never actually certain, but have a vast preponderance of *probability* in their favour. So Popper said that no scientific conclusion can ever be probable; that no theory ever becomes even *more* probable, when evidence in its favour is discovered, than it was beforehand; and indeed that every scientific theory not only begins by being, but must always remain, *infinitely improbable*.

It would be easy to give still more examples, but the foregoing will probably suffice as a sample of central early-Popper opinions. In any case the reader, even if he was previously ignorant of Popperism, will by now have grasped its implicit rule, and can churn out other examples for himself, and for as long as that kind of thing amuses him. A Freudian might see, or imagine he sees, something more than adolescent revolt, something actually obsessive, in Popper's compulsion to *reverse* things. But at present I merely point out that the central parts of Popper's philosophy do all in fact exhibit this pattern. And I say nothing, here or elsewhere in this essay, about any part of Popper's philosophy which is either later or less central than the parts which have just been mentioned. My concern is only with central and early Popperism; for it was by that that 'the West was won.'

And won it was, with ridiculous ease. Indeed, the reception of a philosophy so congenial to the Jazz Age could never have been in doubt. Popper began to publish it in 1934, and his shocking reversals of received ideas were greedily taken up by an entire generation, almost faster than he could write them down. His own career flourished almost equally quickly. Having left Europe as a refugee a little before the second world war, he was by the end of the war a Reader in, soon Professor of, Logic and Scientific Method at the University of London. By 1950 he was easily the most influential philosopher of science in the West. Thousands had undergone at his hands a 'transvaluation of all values' which turned their inherited ideas of scientific virtues into vices, and vice versa: just as Cole Porter's song says.

Nor was it only philosophers who underwent the Popperite conversion experience. Far from it: a gospel so much in keeping with the spirit of the age could never have been confined to that tiny audience. Popper's philosophy of science reached almost the entire educated public. Most striking of all, it reached scientists themselves. Scientists almost always find what philosophers write about science either incomprehensible, or superficial, or ridiculous. But Popper's philosophy of science was modelled so closely on the history of science, and in particular on its twentieth-century history, that many scientists, on reading it, felt an agreeable 'shock of recognition'. Science as they knew it from the inside was far more like a series of 'conjectures and refutations' than like that accumulation of certainties which was implied by the textbooks, and by old-fashioned histories of science. As a result, Popper's most ardent admirers came to include a number of Nobel prize winners in science, and even at the present day, if you scratch a scientist of middle age or older, you are almost certain to meet with a philosophy of science which consists of half-remembered scraps of Popperism. (The idea that a theory is not scientific unless it is 'refutable', is an especial favourite.) This is true fame, and other philosophers of science can only mournfully envy it.

Since 1950 Popper's fame has done nothing but increase. In philosophy he is now the acknowledged grand old man in Britain; the recipient of academic honours innumerable; a knight, a Companion of Honour, etc., etc. His pen has lost nothing of its former facility: if anything, the reverse. Gigantic volumes, interspersed with *petits riens*, still pour from his desk, and publishers, who know a good thing when they see it, will crawl over broken bottles to get their hands on them. No philosophical writer could possibly expect to arrive, in his own lifetime, at a situation more agreeable.

But that is only socially speaking. Intellectually speaking – that is, in the philosophy of science itself – the present situation must seem to Popper to be, as indeed it is, a 'city of dreadful night'. The reason is, that old story about Pandora's box, or the genie who refuses to go back into his bottle. It is one thing to start a revolution, in philosophy or anywhere else, and quite another to control it. The Jazz Age turned out to possess a hideous strength, which no one had foreseen, in philosophy as well as in music. And in the one case as in the other, the beginnings seem now to belong to an age of innocence almost inconceivably remote.

## II

One of the few topics on which Popper did not see his way to a reversal of conventional opinions was mathematics. There, at least, the 'accumulation-of-certainties' story seemed to be just plain right, and Popper had had to reconcile himself to agreeing, for once, with the Logical Positivists. In consequence, he had never had much to say about mathematics.

It was a bolt from the blue, therefore, though a very pleasant one, when one of his disciples appeared to extend the Popperite sway to this previously unconquered province. This was Imré Lakatos, who in 1963–4 published a long series of articles in which he documented, in microscopic detail, the vicissitudes which a particular geometrical proposition had undergone in the eighteenth and nineteenth centuries: vicissitudes of refutation, qualification, refutation again, re-interpretation, refutation yet again. . . . [2] The effect of these articles was sensational at first. Mathematics, it turned out, was just as much a matter of 'conjectures and refutations' as empirical science! It must have been music to Popper's ears. What master could resist an industrious apprentice who showed that he was even more right, or right over an even wider area, than he himself had realized? In 1969, when the time came for Popper to retire from the London chair, Lakatos got the job.

Yet his gift to Popper was but a Greek one after all, and might have been detected as such even at the time. The propositions of mathematics are of a fundamentally different nature from those of empirical science, and are known in a different way: so most philosophers have always believed, and so most of them found themselves still believing, when the initial impact of Lakatos's articles had worn off. If the *history* of mathematics is not basically different from the *history* of empirical science, then that only shows – this was the longer-term reaction, and was bound to be so – that history is one thing, and philosophy, whether of mathematical or empirical science, is quite another. Popper's crit- ics had all along accused him, and with good cause, of drowning the philosophy in the *history* of science: of pretending to resolve questions of *logical value* by appealing to matters of *historical fact*. The sole long-term effect, therefore, of Lakatos's rash venture into mathematics was to add irresistible weight to this old criti- cism. It was the Sicilian Expedition of Popperism: intended to add a mighty new province to the empire, it fatally recoiled on the seat of empire itself.

Popper was not long in concluding that, both intellectually and personally, he had taken a viper to his bosom. Once safely installed in his chair, Lakatos turned his attention to empirical science, and did not leave his master's doctrine there undisturbed. He did not deny – no one has ever denied – the elementary asymmetry which Popper, with 'a damnable iteration', had insisted upon: that while 'All crows are black', say, cannot be verified by any number of black crows, a single crow of any other colour suffices to falsify it. Lakatos merely insisted – and *Popper* was in no position to question the relevance of this – that in the history of actual science, such neat and decisive falsifications never in fact occur. Nor could they, Lakatos argued. Popper had said that Marxism, Freudianism, astrology, etc. are pseudo- sciences, because their central propositions are 'unfalsifiable': that is, consistent with *every* report of an actual or possible obser- vation. But then, Lakatos pointed out, Newtonian physics too is unfalsifiable in that sense; and so is every other typical scientific theory.

This is true, and it was 'a very palpable hit'. But it also left Lakatos with a daunting task, by way of reconstructing Popperite philosophy of science. For Lakatos, it must be understood, remained at bottom a loyal enough Popperite. (I do not mean loyal enough to satisfy Popper: no one is that.) He could never bring himself to question the basic tenets of the school, such as the worthlessness of induction. He was also resolved, again like Popper, to model his philosophy of science on the actual history of science; only he would be more faithful to history than Popper had been. Within these two Popperite constraints – fidelity to 'hypothetico-deductivism' and to the history of science – Lakatos faced the task of distinguishing good science from bad: but even before that, and more urgently, he faced the task of distinguishing between science and non-science. For without this there would be, obviously, nothing to distinguish a Karl Popperish philosophy of science from a Cole Porterish one, according to which anything goes.

The result was Lakatos's theory of research programmes. I will not enter into any details about this. When every allowance has been made for its author's early death, it must be said that, as an answer to either of the two questions which Lakatos had set himself, this theory is extraordinarily unconvincing. It does not appear to have convinced even Lakatos himself. To the question, 'What distinguishes science from other things?', Popper had given an answer which, however wide of the mark, was at least definite. Lakatos's answer is hopelessly indefinite, or rather he gives no answer at all. The question is a philosophical one, but Lakatos, in his attempt to answer it, loses both himself and his readers in impenetrable thickets of detailed history of science. Worse still, he confesses that in some instances he has simply made up the historical details himself: a proceeding which manages to be scandalous and pointless at the same time.

Not that it would have mattered much anyway; for even while he wrote, Lakatos had been outflanked on the philosophical left by an historian of science far more formidable than himself. Thomas Kuhn is an American who made a great reputation by his early study of the Copernican revolution in astronomy. He was never a Popperite *dévot*. (Popperism is almost exclusively a, or rather the, *British* disease in philosophy.) He simply picked up from the surrounding air a sufficiently lethal dose of Popperite radiation, as others have done who are 'as the sands of the sea for multitude'. We have Kuhn's own testimony in print to his agreement with 'anti-inductivism' and other central points of Popperism. When he turned philosopher of science in his own right, in *The Structure of Scientific Revolutions*,[3] the effect was enormous. This book had sold, some time ago, half a million copies in the English edition alone, and has been translated into almost every other language. Even among philosophers, who are a notably resistant strain of people, not a few have succumbed, or (if the jargon of my profession can be permitted) 'gone Kuhn'. In the intellectual slums, where resistance of any kind is weak – among sociologists, educationists, anthropologists, and the like – the execution done by this book has been simply terrific. What is more important, the book has been and still is being read, with the effects to be expected, by scientists in their thousands.

Kuhn claims to have detected a certain cycle in the history of science. First there is a 'pre-paradigm' stage, when a chaos of facts overwhelms all students, theories proliferate but no theory wins, one man's solution is another man's problem, and so on. Then a paradigm, some acknowledged model of how things should be done, emerges. It is usually, though not necessarily, a book, such as Darwin's *Origin*, Newton's *Principia*, or Copernicus's *De Revolutionibus*. The paradigm imposes an intelligible order on the welter of known facts, solves some problems decisively, and indicates the lines along which many others will be able to be solved. Guided by the paradigm, scientists mop up the problem areas: this is the period of what Kuhn calls 'normal science'. Sooner or later, however, difficulties accumulate on the successful paradigm, like barnacles and weed on a ship's hull: 'anomalies' multiply. When this process has reached a sufficiently serious point, then if, though only if, a new paradigm offers itself, you have a period of 'paradigm-shift' and 'revolutionary science'. Young scientists desert the old paradigm for the new, like rats deserting a ship which, though it is not yet actually sinking, they somehow know is doomed. The new paradigm triumphs, a new period of normal science begins, and . . . away we go again.

Now you could, of course, take all this just as an account of the history of science, and find more or less of value in it, according as you consider it more or less accurate history. But that is not at all how it is intended to be taken, or how Kuhn

himself takes it. He takes it as a sufficient reason to accept a
certain *philosophy* of science, and a philosophy of the most
uncompromisingly relativist kind. He will not talk himself, or let
you talk if he can help it, of *truth* in science, or (and this
galls the Popperites even more) of falsity: he claims he cannot
understand that class of talk. (You have to be very learned indeed
to find things as hard to understand as Kuhn does.) As for
'knowledge', 'discovery', 'progess': why, all that, of course, is no
more than the language which the partisans of *any* paradigm will
apply to their own activities. It is no more to be taken at face
value than is talk about 'reforms' in politics: after all, whenever
*your* bunch gets its way on some political point, you call the
result a 'reform'. Or as Kuhn puts it in his more demure way, all
such talk is 'paradigm-relative'. There is nothing *rational* about
paradigm-shift in science, according to Kuhn. He constantly com-
pares it to what psychologists call 'gestalt-switch': that non-
rational process by which a drawing of an ascending flight of
stairs is suddenly seen as a descending one, or what just before
seemed only some shrubbery is seen as a human face. *That*
kind of thing is what the history of science comes down to,
notwithstanding all the Whiggish rhetoric of the past few centuries
about progress and enlightenment.

Kuhn in his turn has been outflanked by a philosopher in whom
the Jazz Age has finally come to full fruition: P. K. Feyerabend.
He was at one stage a convert to Popperism, but got de-converted,
and now exhibits something of the animus of the ex-seminarian:
insults the London philosophers (and even Popper's wife!) in
print, calls for their dismissal, etc. His loss of faith was helped
by the work of Kuhn and Lakatos, but even more by his own
increasing sense of the authoritarianism of Popper: not just the
style but the stuff. Feyerabend calls himself a 'Dadaist' and his
philosophy 'epistemological anarchism'. He maintains that science
knows, and should know, *no* rules of method, no logic – inductive,
deductive, or whatever. And for his slogan he actually chose, and
still defends against all comers, Cole Porter's old title 'Anything
Goes'.

Feyerabend's main manifesto is a book called *Against Method*.[4]
Of all the productions of the human mind in any age, this must
rank as one of the most curious. It is impossible to convey briefly

the unique absurdity of the book, but one or two of the author's foibles may be mentioned. Feyerabend says – not as a joke or schoolboyish pun on the word 'laws', but in all seriousness – that scientific laws ought to be decided in the way that other laws are decided in an open society: by a democratic vote. He is also a sturdy partisan of the claims of witchcraft, voodoo, and astrology, and does not refuse his countenance even to the vulgar charlatan who writes the 'Don Juan' books. Feyerabend is a professor in – it is almost too pat to be true, but it *is* true – California, and is one of the highest-paid philosophers in the world. His collected papers are now being published by Cambridge University: the university of Newton and Darwin.

It is these three writers, Lakatos, Kuhn, and Feyerabend, who now dominate the scene in the philosophy of science. Thus, if we take a representative recent textbook, such as A. Chalmers's *What is This Thing Called Science?*,[5] we find that it is these three writers who engage the author's interest almost exclusively. Popper is often mentioned, but he figures chiefly as a worthy if insufferable forerunner to these three, worth perhaps six out of ten for trying. The very title of this book speaks volumes. It has the true Feyerabendian ring: a combination of levity and menace. (Even the drawing of a kitten on the paperback cover has, for Feyerabend-adepts, a meaning.) The title also brings us back, of course, to Cole Porter again: 'What is this Thing Called Love?' And these conjunctures are, as the Marxists say, no accident: deep calls to deep here, as it always will.

Popper (as I intimated before) regards the philosophy of Lakatos, Kuhn, and Feyerabend in the way that anyone should: with hatred, ridicule, and contempt. Any suggestion that he himself might be, for all that, the begetter of it, he rejects with boundless indignation.[6] But then, of course, this is a form of blindness exceedingly common in fathers. Dostoevsky's Verhovensky *père* could not for the life of him see how he could have been responsible for Verhovensky *fils*. But other people can see a short and simple causal chain when it is before their eyes, and in the present case Popper's paternity cannot seriously be disputed.

Lakatos, Kuhn, and Feyerabend are all philosophers, like Popper himself, in the broad main stream of *empiricism*: they all agree that we cannot learn anything about the actual universe except by experience. Who was it who taught them, then, that we cannot learn anything about the actual universe *even by* experience – that is, that induction is worthless? Popper, of course. You have only to put these two propositions together, to reach the conclusion that we cannot learn anything about the actual universe at all. Yet when Lakatos, Kuhn, and Feyerabend arrive (whether gleefully or otherwise) at the same conclusion, Popper is outraged. This is understandable enough in one way, and even does his heart some credit; but where does it leave his head? No: Popper had it (as they say) coming to him, if ever a man did.

## III

Few philosophers would now dispute this: the nihilist or irrationalist nature of Popperite philosophy of science is by now pretty much an open secret. But how was the secret kept for so long? For nearly forty years, after all, Popperism succeeded in passing for something very different, and Popper himself, in par- ticular, passed for the *arch-enemy* of irrationalism. How did this extraordinary deception come about?

Not, of course, deliberately; philosophers are not like that. They do not produce delusions in others, without first being in the grip of them themselves. The deception I speak of was brought about by a certain abuse of language which Popper and his followers engaged in on an enormous scale.[7] The abuse undoubt- edly imposed on the writers themselves, as well as on their readers; though it would have been of no importance, of course, had it imposed only on the writers.

Some words are *success*-words, and others are not. 'Seek', for example, is not: you can seek something unsuccessfully, and you can even seek what does not exist. 'Find', on the other hand, is a success-word: you cannot find something unsuccessfully, and you can find only what exists. Again, 'prove' is a success-word, while 'believe', for example, is not: you can prove only what is true, but you can believe what is not true. 'Refuted' (the verb) is a success-word, since it means 'proved the falsity of'; 'denied' is not, since it means only 'asserted the falsity of'. And so on.

But a success-word can be used in such a way, or in such a context, that its implication of success is cancelled or 'neutralized'. One way to neutralize a success-word is to put inverted commas around it: as in, say, 'The minister "refuted" allegations that he had misled Parliament.' Another way is *bald*-neutralizing: just using a success-word *as though* it had no implication of success. Where this is done conspicuously and deliberately, the result is usually a joke: as in Mark Twain's objection to a certain young man, which was 'not so much all the things he don't know, as all the things he do know, that ain't so'. But bald-neutralizing is usually done unconsciously, through ignorance, forgetfulness, or disregard of the meaning of the success-word. It is through mere ignorance, for example, that Australian or American journalists often bald-neutralize the success-word 'refuted'. They will write 'The minister refuted the allegations', when all they really mean is that he denied the allegations.

'Knowledge', of course, is a success-word: you can know only what is true. So is 'discovery': you can discover only what exists. So is 'explanation': you cannot explain the sun's rising in the west, for example, or explain anything except what is the case. These are facts, trivial in themselves, about the meanings of some words. They are no more important in themselves than the fact that you can be married only to your spouse.

But 'knowledge', 'discovery', and the like, *are* important words, in fact absolutely indispensable, if you want to write about the history or the philosophy of science. Imagine trying to write on these subjects without ever using these or other success-words! It would be ridiculous: everyone would just laugh at you, and rightly. You could easily, in fact very easily, do without success-words if you were writing about, say, the Procession of the Holy Ghost; but not if you are writing about the precession of the equinoxes. You do not need such words in writing the history of palmistry; in writing the history of chemistry, you do. Very well: Popper and the Popperites were obliged to use these words as freely as everyone else does who writes on the history or the philosophy of science. But then there was a problem: these words are *success*-words, while Popperite philosophy abhors the very idea of scientific success, and implies that there never has been, or could be, any knowledge or discovery at all. Solution: as you cannot do without the old success-words, use them indeed, but *neutralize* them.

And this is what Popper, and Lakatos, Kuhn, and Feyerabend following him, duly did. Not absolutely all the time, of course: that would have drawn the readers' attention, and their own, to the abuse of language which was going on. But they do it often enough to make neutralized occurrences of words like 'knowledge' and 'discovery' their unfailing literary trademark.

The quotation-mark was Lakatos's main weapon for abolishing scientific success. He nearly always writes ' "proof" ' for 'proof', ' "fact" ' for 'fact', and so on. Popper and the others do a certain amount of this, but they rely more on bald-neutralizing. Thus Kuhn, for example, has Galileo *discovering* things which Kuhn tells us in the same sentence do not exist. But Popper is the master of this art, as he was the teacher of it to the others. Take for example the phrase 'conjectural knowledge', a coinage of his own to which he attaches great importance. The phrase is mere nonsense, of course, since knowledge is of something known to be true, while something is conjectural only if it is not known to be true. Never mind: how many readers nowadays are capable of recognizing a solecism when they meet one? Even if they do recognize it, how many citizens of the Jazz Age will dare to object to it? Anything goes. And a writer, once he has got his readers to submit to such a phrase as this one, can be confident of getting away with anything after that. The phrase 'conjectural knowledge', Popper tell us, contains in a nutshell the 'solution to the problem of induction'. Well, no doubt it does, in a way, and the solution of every other problem too. For what problem could there be, so hard as not to dissolve in a sufficiently strong solution of nonsense?

By using the old Whiggish success-words, you conciliate the optimistic delusions of your readers (and yourself) about science; while by neutralizing those words, you undermine those delusions. Nothing could have been better suited to Popperite purposes, therefore, than the process of neutralizing success-words in writing about science. Much more than that, however: it was out of an instance of this very process that Popper's philosophy first arose.

It arose, as Popper himself tells us, from a new insight into the nature of scientific propositions: that the mark of a non-scientific proposition is unfalsifiability. By this new word, 'unfalsifiable', he meant, as he said from the start, 'consistent with every observation-statement'. But, also from the start, he more often expressed his new insight by speaking (as in the epigraph at the beginning of this essay) of *irrefutability*, rather than of unfalsifiability. He has always written, in fact, as though 'irrefutable' means the same, or near enough the same, as 'unfalsifiable'.

But of course it does not. 'Irrefutable' is a success-word. It means 'indisputable', 'incontrovertible', 'certain' in the sense of 'known for certain': it therefore entails 'true'. But 'unfalsifiable' does not entail 'true': a fact which Popper himself emphasized. (A proposition can easily be consistent with every observation-statement, yet not true: for example, 'Fairies exist.') Hence to use 'irrefutable' as Popper does, as though it meant the same as 'unfalsifiable', is to neutralize the success-word 'irrefutable'.

And this instance of neutralization was absolutely indispensable to Popper. The germ from which his entire philosophy of science grew was, not the dictum that unfalsifiability is a vice not a virtue in a theory, but the dictum which I have used as an epigraph: that *irrefutability* is a vice not a virtue in a theory. People might not have been convinced by being told that unfalsifiability is a vice not a virtue, but at any rate they could not possibly have been *shocked*. For no one before Popper had ever thought at all about that property, of being consistent with every observation-statement. (The property is, indeed, a very uninteresting one, being common to almost all propositions.) But tell people instead that *irrefutability* is a vice not a virtue in a theory, and you have at once the element of shocking reversal which the Jazz Age demanded, and which Popper never failed to supply. And this element is due, of course, to one of the strongest success-words, 'irrefutable', being baldly, or rather, violently, neutralized.

It is an understatement, of course, to say that 'irrefutable' and 'unfalsifiable' do not mean the same. Since the former means 'known for certain' and the latter means 'consistent with every observation-statement', there is in fact, quite obviously, no connection between the meanings of the two words. They are no more related in meaning than, say, 'weighty', in 'weighty thinker', and 'overweight'. Someone who identified weighty thinkers with overweight thinkers, and took himself to have gained a new insight into the nature of thinkers, would be guilty of a stupid enough pun. Someone who identifies irrefutable propositions with unfalsifiable ones, and takes himself to have gained a new insight into the nature of scientific propositions, is guilty of something no better.

Ignorant people suppose that a philosopher rises to fame by having deep thoughts, but the case of Popper shows that, at least in the Jazz Age, there are other routes which will do quite as well. One is, pitiless repetition of a stupid pun, and a general willingness to use words with a brutal disregard for their meaning.

(The things I have been speaking of were done by Popper in German, of course, before they were done in English. But there is no problem about that. You can neutralize success-words in any language. Mark Twain's little joke, for example, is obviously fully translatable into German. In fact, the abuses of language in which philosophers engage are hardly ever of so delicate a nature as not to survive translation into another language.)

How can anyone ever have mistaken 'unfalsifiable' and 'irrefutable' for synonyms? Well, 'unfalsifiable' was a new word, and it is often hard to keep a firm grip on what a new word means, even if it has been carefully explained. But the reason, I suspect, lay more at the other end, with 'irrefutable'. During the Jazz Age, people's grip on the meaning of this word and of others like it has been loosened, by a process which I call 'ironization'.

Some words are born ironic: for example, the colloquial-English 'know-all' ('know-it-all' in American). For this word means, of course, and always has meant, a person who does *not* know everything, but thinks or tends to think he does. What I call ironization is a word's *becoming* ironic. 'Enthusiast' is an example. This word means literally, and originally meant, one who is possessed by a god or by God; but by the middle of the eighteenth century it had come to mean one who mistakenly believes himself to be so possessed. (The word changed its meaning again, of course, after that.)

There are plenty of similar cases. 'Sanctimonious', for example, originally meant 'saintly'. When the process of ironization has gone some way but not all the way, you get a 'smile-word', such as 'respectable' is with us now. When it has gone all the way, 'F' has come to mean 'not F but believed (by so-and-so) to be F'. The word has then grown invisible quotation-marks around it, and it is no longer in our power to remove them.

Among us, most of the fully ironized words are connected with religion, and the reason is obvious. Few of us now believe in the existence of gods, but in the past almost everyone did, and there are many others who still do. We want to be able to talk about these beliefs of theirs without having to resort to tiresome periphrases, and without constantly drawing attention to our disagreement with them. The best way to do this is to keep the religious words, but to ironize them; and this is the solution which, quite unconsciously, we have adopted. With us, a word such as 'sacred' is fully ironized. 'Sacred' now means 'not sacred but believed (by so-and-so) to be sacred'. And it is not in our power, even if our lives depended on it, to mean anything more than this when we use the word.

Now, suppose that you had undergone an analogous 'loss of faith' about science. You have come to believe that nothing in science is known for certain; but almost everyone else remains convinced that there is much in science which *is* certain. You will want to be able to talk about this common opinion (and if you want to write about the history or philosophy of science, you will have to do so); and you will want to be able to talk about it without periphrases, and without constantly drawing attention to your disagreement with it. It will then be natural to keep the words which connote certainty, such as 'irrefutable'; but, just as disbelief in gods tends inevitably to the ironization of religious words, your disbelief in certainty will inevitably tend to the ironization of words connoting certainty. In your usage, 'irrefutable', for example, will tend to acquire invisible quotation-marks; it will start to mean 'not irrefutable but believed (by so-and-so) to be irrefutable'.

And this, of course, was exactly Popper's case. Newton's 'laws' of mechanics and gravitation had been believed for two hundred years to be known for certain, yet they were not so. Popper and many others concluded that, since Newtonian physics is not certain, nothing is. It was therefore inevitable that words like 'irrefutable' should begin, in their usage, to be ironized.

This is why I say that, even when Popper began to write, people's grip had been loosened on the meaning of 'irrefutable' and of words like it. Since then, the ironization of words such as 'irrefutable' does not seem to have gone much further, as far as *general* usage is concerned: 'irrefutable' has clearly not gone the way of 'sacred', or even of 'respectable'. Among philosophers, on the other hand, the ironized or Popperite use of the word has spread like wildfire. At present, even philosophers who are otherwise uninfluenced by Popper often use 'irrefutable' as a smile-word. And, as I know from experience, it is uphill work to get them to realize what they are doing.

Still, it is not quite impossible. Some of them can still be got to see that while it is, *of course*, a vice not a virtue that a theory which is not irrefutable should be believed to be so, still, irrefutability, as distinct from 'irrefutability', is *a virtue not a vice* in a theory. The unconscious ironization which has overtaken this word, that is to say, can sometimes even now be brought to consciousness. To this extent, the Popperite transvaluation of all values has proved to be not entirely irreversible.

# IV

Philosophies, although they should be judged by intellectual standards, are not purely intellectual productions, but always have their roots in powerful feelings of some kind. If a philosopher systematically abuses language, therefore, it is always for some 'reason of the heart'. We have seen here something of what Popper's abuses of language were; but what was the emotional fuel for them?

Partly, of course, it was the sort of thing which was felt by the fox in Aesop, about the grapes he could not reach. We citizens of the Jazz Age can now neither remember nor imagine the confidence which Western civilization had for two hundred years invested in the finality of Newtonian physics, but it is scarcely possible to exaggerate it. The shock of disillusion, when it came, was correspondingly great. To philosophers like Popper, the moral was obvious: such excessive confidence in a scientific theory must never be allowed to build up again. The most 'irrefutable' of all such theories has turned out to be not irrefutable at all: very well then, Popper will say, like the fox in the fable, that irrefutability, even if our theories could achieve it, would be a bad thing anyway. The parallel would be complete if the fox, having concluded that neither he nor anyone else could ever succeed in tasting grapes, should nevertheless proceed to write many large books about the progress of viticulture.

This ingredient of the emotional soil of Popperism, the consuming anxiety lest Newtonian *hubris* should ever have a sequel, is obvious: it lies quite close to the surface in Popper's writings. But the most marked peculiarity of his philosophy of science, the impulse to reverse every commonplace of the subject, suggests some feeling deeper than the 'sour grapes' one, and something more characteristic of the Jazz Age as a whole. I think it was a case of *horror victorianorum*. I mean by this, that horror which even nowadays is felt, at least to a slight degree, by almost everyone who visits a display of Victorian stuffed birds under glass, for example, or of Victorian dolls and dolls' clothes. Such things as these, of course, now communicate at most the *quality* of the horror. They cannot convey anything like the intensity with which it was felt fifty or sixty years ago, or the historical importance of this feeling.

Among literary objects of this horror – the literary counterparts of stuffed birds – the novels of Dickens were always pre-eminent. For countless people, a single volume of Dickens used to be enough to cause uneasiness, especially if it had old illustrations; a house containing a complete set of Dickens, as millions of houses did, was a nightmare. Evelyn Waugh, with unerring instinct, distilled this particular nightmare into the second-last chapter of *A Handful of Dust* (1934): a chapter which, to many people who first read it forty years ago or more, is so horrible that they will not re-read it even now.

But the original classic expression in literature of *horror victorianorum* was, of course, Samuel Butler's *The Way of All Flesh*.

This book was, as Malcolm Muggeridge said, the first hand-grenade thrown over the Victorian garden wall, before the Freudian heavy artillery came up, and its curious fate shows indirectly the strength of the horror when it finally arrived. Butler never in his life succeeded in getting any of his many books published, except at his own expense. But twenty years after his death in 1902, this posthumous book became a best-seller, and the bible of a generation. It was, in fact, one of those books which succeed so completely that they make themselves superfluous. Accordingly, few young people nowadays have heard of the book; but then, they do not need to, since it is already in their blood. Samuel Butler, it is worth adding, is one of Popper's enthusiasms.

But literature itself is only one expression of the enormous revolution in feeling which divides the Jazz Age from the pre-war world. Obviously, I cannot do justice here to that revolution. But I will mention one other expression of it, and one the historical importance of which no one will dispute: modern architecture.

It is now impossible, and has been impossible for over fifty years, for anyone to make a building which is beautiful or even agreeable. Whatever may be the reason for it, this is simply an historical fact; like the impossibility of travelling abroad nowadays without a passport, or the fact that no one could make a television set in the twelfth century. No one likes to look at a modern building, let alone live or work in it, and hardly anyone even pretends nowadays that they do like to. That this long-kept secret is now out, is thanks in part to Tom Wolfe's *From Bauhaus to Our House*.[8] But Wolfe, besides making unwarranted exceptions to his condemnation (in favour, for example, of the embarrassing Frank Lloyd Wright), is altogether unsatisfactory on one basic point. He has not a word to say in explanation of how modern architecture came to be successfully sold to the world in the first place. It was not under totalitarian governments, after all, that this architecture triumphed: it must therefore have had *something* to offer that people wanted, something, in fact, which they seized on with the energy of desperation. What this was, Wolfe is perhaps too young to have known first-hand, but no one over fifty can possibly be in doubt for one moment as to what it was. It was escape from *horror victorianorum*.

To go back to the *quale* (as philosophers say) of this horror:

it is somewhat as follows. A sensation of darkness, stillness, enclosure, and, above all, of weight or pressure: some indefinite but massive incubus is pressing down on us, and we are about to suffocate. 'For God's sake *let the air in and me out!*', is the most prominent element in the sufferer's reaction.

Many of us, of course, feel this kind of horror concerning 'relics' of any period, and of any kind, at least after a little while. Even this is a very recent thing, and largely confined to the West even so. Medieval pilgrims underwent untold hardships in order to visit religious relics (Jesus's foreskin, luckily preserved at five different places, etc., etc.), which most modern men would pay to avoid visiting even, or rather especially, if they believed the relics to be genuine. It is no different with secular relics: many of us cannot look at such things for long without stifling. 'These people are all *dead*!' is our strangled cry. 'Let the dead bury their dead: I have a life to live!' This *generalized* horror of relics is not quite confined, perhaps, to the present century: it is evident, for example, late last century, in Mark Twain. But with the arrival of the Jazz Age, and focused especially on Victorian relics, whether literary, architectural, or whatever, it suddenly became 'an universal shout'.

My suggestion is, then, that the main emotional source of Popper's philosophy was *horror victorianorum*. That, I think, is what lay behind his compulsion to turn upside-down every single commonplace which he found standing in the old philosophy of science.

If it was so, then I for one cannot, after all, refuse Popper a large measure of sympathy. For Victorian writing about science – and that means, in practice, writing up to about 1920–is suffocating enough, in all conscience, to give any citizen of the Jazz Age the horrors. Why, even I, even now, cannot read Humboldt, or Whewell, or Mill, or Huxley, or Mach, or Jevons, or Duhem, not to mention the legion of less original and therefore more representative writers of the period, without feeling at least some twinges of the horror of which I have been speaking. Yet this is 1985, and I was born in 1927 in a remote colony of the Western world. If, as I suppose, Popper felt the same horror at its height and at the centre, how much more intense must it have been!

What makes Victorian writing about science so peculiarly oppressive? Mainly, it seems to me, three things.

One is, that it never lets you forget for long the nightmare which is Victorian Christianity. Think of the case of Darwin. The discreditable outcry which greeted *The Origin of Species* in 1859 came partly, of course, from reverends and right reverends without number, right up to Samuel Wilberforce, Bishop of Oxford. But it came also, and more importantly, from distinguished scientists with Christian convictions, such as Owen and Sedgwick. The real offence which Darwin had given these people was, of course, that his theory, for all its many defects, was at least an obvious improvement on their own brilliant one: that each species originated in a special act of the Divine Will. But they hardly ever said this. What they chose principally to say instead was that Darwin had 'deserted the true method of induction', 'abandoned the slow but sure Baconian path'; and *this* they said – as Darwin's son Francis later wrote – *ad nauseam*. Now, would not a prolonged diet of this stuff make a Popperite out of anyone? *Ad nauseam* indeed: what a sickening crew! But the Darwinians themselves are scarcely more attractive. They liked to call Wilberforce, behind his back, 'Soapy Sam', but for any Jazz Age stomach they are saponaceous enough themselves. They, for example, must have Darwin buried in Westminster Abbey, forsooth. Never mind that this was against his family's wishes, and presumably his own. Never mind that they thereby involved the Dean of Westminster in a scandalous dereliction of his duty, in consenting to the burial there of a person who made no profession of Christian, or of any, religious belief. And the cream of the jest is that their instinct was entirely sound. By 1882 Darwin was in fact a *part* of the Christian religion, or at least a part of that 'peculiar institution', the Church of England. Samuel Butler's bitter scoff at Darwin, or at least at the nauseous quality of his fame, is perfectly just: that in him, 'Science was made flesh, and dwelt among us.'

The second thing which oppresses the modern reader of Victorian writers on science is their almost unvarying tone of Whiggery. History is over; the long reign of ignorance and superstition is at an end; the writer, in short, knows everything.

Third, Victorian writing about science is almost always semi-popular, and accordingly superficial. The nineteenth century regarded the eighteenth as the century of superficiality, but in fact, in the philosophy of science at least, no one in the nineteenth century took matters as deep as Hume had taken them a hundred years before. Even Mill, who goes as far into the logic of science as almost any of them, published little even in his *Logic* (1843) which could not as easily have appeared in the *Westminster Review*. The same goes for almost all Victorian writing on science. Almost none of it is *bad*; almost all of it is good, as far as it goes. But it goes very little way, at enormous length. Jazz Age stomachs find it intolerably insipid: an ocean of boiled rice pudding.

When I try to analyse the *horror victorianorum* as it applies to the literature of science, these three components seem to me to be the main ones: Christianity, Whiggery, and superficiality. These, I think, are the main things which we of the Jazz Age have against the writings of the preceding century about science.

If they are, however, then it is we who are in the wrong. If these are our main complaints, then our complaints are frivolous: it is the Victorians who are the responsible adults, and we their irresponsible children, 'disdaining to be pleased'.

The first of the three complaints is manifestly frivolous. Since about AD 400, after all, scarcely any department of intellectual life has been free from the influence of the Christian religion. We must, therefore, simply 'divide through' for Christianity.

Then, as to Whiggery. It is true, of course, that to hear Macaulay on Bacon, say, or Brougham on optics (or on anything), is to endure no pleasing sound: brass tongue, brass head, brass lungs. But these are mere 'individual variations' (as the Darwinians say), and in any case are errors on the right side. Much of what the 'modern nervous' reader finds abrasive, in nineteenth-century writers, is no more than a masculine and admirable directness. And, when you come right down to it, there simply is *no* non-Whiggish way of writing, about science or any subject. It is entirely pointless for an author to indulge in *general* acknowledgements of his liability to error and ignorance; while he cannot, on obvious logical grounds, point out to us *specifically* where he errs or is ignorant. He could, of course, conciliate modern nervousness by putting 'It seems to me that ...' in front of everything he wishes to say. But that is a proceeding equally pointless and vexatious, as well as generating a regress ('It seems to me that it seems to me that . . . ') which will prevent him from ever saying anything at all.

Finally, as to superficiality. Well, the history of Western science has been, since about 1600, almost entirely a *success*-story. This is hard luck for Popperites and other bohemian enemies of success, but that is how it is. But not only have we learnt much. We have learnt something even more imporant: *how to learn*. This is a unique achievement of the West, and is the secret of its peculiar dynamism: the Moslem, Buddhist, Marxist, astrologer, etc. are as far as ever from learning it. But the odd thing is that, once you *have* learnt how to learn, there is hardly anything to it. Almost any drongo (if an Australianism can be permitted) can do 'normal science'. Scientific method really does pretty well reduce, as Bacon said it would, 'all wits to a level'. And a consequence is that all the essentials of a sound *philosophy* of science really are, after all, rather obvious and superficial. It is no wonder, then, that the Victorians got them right. Ordinary intelligence, playing on as much concrete scientific achievement as there was by (say) 1850, was bound to see them through to a basically sound philosophy of science.

For these reasons I cannot help concluding that, where the literature of science is concerned, *horror victorianorum*, my own or Popper's or anyone's, springs from a fundamental levity. In the old commonplaces of the philosophy of science, such as those which were mentioned in section I above, there is much truth, and scarcely any falsity. They merely require, like any other commonplace wisdom, to be applied in practice with tact. You can, of course, always go deeper if you want to, but someone who wishes, as Popper wished, simply to *reverse* them all, is doomed from the outset. He will simply be wrong on the main issues, and his wish is nothing more than the wish of the adolescent to escape the burden of adult knowledge and responsibilities. Jazz Age man, as I said, hath said in his heart, 'Let the dead bury their dead.' But since the dead cannot bury anything, while someone has to bury the dead, the words which St Matthew attributes to Jesus are but foolish and irresponsible words after all.

But it is not only Victorian ideas *about* science which weigh on

Jazz Age man like a nightmare: there is the burden of *accumulated scientific knowledge itself*. *That* great inheritance from the past, like every other, Jazz Age man would put off if he could: 'Let the dead bury their dead.' And he has, in every other respect, come far closer to achieving this ideal than would have been possible in any earlier age. He inherits, and can inherit, nothing or next to nothing of money or property, of family tradition, of social status, of morality or religion, and he can live, if he wants to, as though there never had been such things in the past. But he cannot live as though there had never been any accumulation of scientific knowledge. He cannot subsist for twenty-four hours, without drawing on the fruits of scientific knowledge for his food, light, transport, and all the rest.

This last and most inescapable burden, too, Popper's philosophy was expressly designed to rid us of. For one theory is better than another, Popper says, other things equal, if it is more easy to refute than the other; and what is this but to put a premium, in science as in shavers, on disposability? The best scientific theory is that one which enables us to avoid most easily the burden of belief which it threatens to impose on us: so says our Jazz Age philosopher. And just so, the Jazz Age says, the best family policy is that one which enables us to avoid most easily the burdens which our parents, and our spouses, those other horrifying relics of the past, threaten to impose on us.


It has often been noticed that Popper's philosophy of science appealed, among scientists, to theoretical physicists especially. It is not often noticed, but it is also a fact, that in the Jazz Age these scientists are distinguished from all others by their degree of levity. (They are anxious to convey, as chemists for example are not, that if it's not *fun*, it's not physics; they love to borrow words, like 'quark', from such anti-Victorian heroes as James Joyce; and so on.) No doubt this is partly to be explained by the remoteness of their work from everyday applications, and by the extreme strangeness of the theories which they are constantly being obliged to entertain. But both the Popperism and the levity of theoretical physicists would be further explained, if I am right in tracing Popper's philosophy back, through *horror victoriano-*

*rum*, to a kind of levity which is characteristic of the Jazz Age as a whole.

## Notes

1   The best short account by Popper of his philosophy of science is an article first published in 1957 but later re-published, under the title 'Science: conjectures and refutations', in his book *Conjectures and Refutations: the Growth of Scientific Knowledge* (Routledge and Kegan Paul, London, 1963). This article also contains the brief autobiographical account mentioned in the text above. The book by which Popper first made his mark was *Logik der Forschung* (Vienna, 1934, although the title-page says 1935), translated into English as *The Logic of Scientific Discovery* (Hutchinson, London, 1959).

2   Lakatos published no book, but his 1963–4 articles on mathematics were posthumously published as a book: *Proofs and Refutations* (Cambridge University Press, 1976). For his philosophy of empirical science, see *The Methodology of Scientific Research Programmes*, which is vol. I of his *Philosophical Papers*, ed. J. Worrall and G. Currie (Cambridge University Press, 1978).

3   T. S. Kuhn's *The Structure of Scientific Revolutions* (Chicago University Press) was first published in 1962. What is nowadays usually seen is the 2nd edn, enlarged, of 1970.

4   P. K. Feyerabend's *Against Method* (New Left Books, London) was published in 1975.

5   A. F. Chalmers, *What is This Thing Called Science?* (University of Queensland Press, St. Lucia, Queensland, 1976).

6   Feyerabend, Kuhn, Lakatos, and Popper can all be found, discussing their agreements but still more (naturally) their disagreements, in *Criticism and the Growth of Knowledge*, ed. I. Lakatos and A. Musgrave (Cambridge University Press, 1970).

7   On the use of language by these philosophers, see my *Popper and After: Four Modern Irrationalists* (Pergamon Press, Oxford, 1982). Part of section II above is also drawn from my article, 'How Popper's philosophy began', *Philosophy*, 57 (1982), pp. 381–7.

8   Tom Wolfe, *From Bauhaus to Our House* (Farrar, Straus & Giroux, New York, 1981).

# 2

## *Philosophy and Lunacy: Nelson Goodman and the Omnipotence of Words*

When people talk about the history of philosophy, they often employ a curious manner of speaking, of which the following are some examples. 'Descartes' theory made animals mere automata.' 'Hobbes resolves all social ties into self-interest.' 'Hume dissolved the self into a succession of perceptions.' 'Leibniz's monads made interaction between things impossible.' 'Berkeley's philosophy abolishes the physical universe.' 'Kant gave man back the soul of which the French materialists had robbed him.' 'Marxism reduced all social phenomena to their economic base.' 'Meinong bestows a kind of existence on the non-existent, and even on the impossible.' 'In *Language, Truth and Logic* (1935), Ayer had constructed material objects out of sense-impressions.' 'Australian materialism makes mental states indentical with brain-states.'

Of course none of these statements, and no statement like these, is literally true. Descartes' theory did not make animals – anything. The physical universe is not abolished, Berkeley's philosophy notwithstanding. Hume never dissolved anything, except sugar in his tea, and the like. Material objects were not constructed by Ayer in 1935. Marxism never reduced anything to anything, except, indirectly, most people who came under its influence to terror and poverty. And so on.

Everyone knows this. No one takes literally the manner of speaking which I have illustrated. Everyone knows that all that is meant is, for example, that Descartes *said*, or implied, that animals are mere automata; that Hume *said* the self is only a succession of perceptions; and so on. People saying things: that is all that the history of philosophy is, and everyone knows it. But it is tiresome to be always saying that so-and-so said that such-and-such. Even writers of fiction have to find devices for avoiding too much 'he said' and 'she said'. The need for such devices is even more pressing when we talk about the history of philosophy, because we then have nothing *but* sayings to talk about. The manner of speaking that I began with is simply one of these devices. It is one of the more vulgar ones, but it saves words, and no one is misled by it.

Statements like those I mentioned, if taken literally, are not only not true: they are incomprehensible. Animals may be mere automata, or not, but either way it does not make sense to say, literally, that Descartes' theory made them mere automata. That the physical universe should be abolished by Berkeley's philosophy simply defies understanding, taken literally. Ayer not only did not construct material objects out of sense-impressions in 1935, he could not possibly have done so. And so on.

Where a statement 'p' is impossible to understand if taken literally, it will also be impossible to understand the statement, 'So-and-so believes that p', taken literally. If you could understand the statement that knowledge is literally a poached egg, then you could understand the statement that Smith literally believes that knowledge is a poached egg; but since you can't understand the former, you can't understand the latter either.

No one, therefore, could literally believe any such statements as those with which I began. If, *per impossibile*, someone did take such statements literally, and believed them, he would be believing – what? Well, he would be believing, for example, that Descartes, by saying that animals are mere automata, made them so. Or, he would be believing that the self is only a succession of perceptions because Hume said that the self is only a succession of perceptions. And so on. In short, he would be believing in something like the omnipotence of words.

The qualification, 'something like', is essential. To say that words are omnipotent is at least as unintelligible as to say that Descartes made animals mere automata by saying they are so. It is therefore also unintelligible to ascribe to anyone belief in the omnipotence of words. To believe in *something like* the omnipotence of words, on the other hand, is something we can understand. We can, because we all do, at certain times, believe in something like the omnipotence of words. We do so, in fact, whenever what Hume called 'the calm sunshine of the mind' is absent: in infancy, in dreams, in the theatre, in delirium, in danger, in religion. At the age when we first heard 'God said, Let there be light, and there was light', it seemed fair enough.

And this understanding can be of use to us. The statement, for example, 'He believes in something like a plot of the prime numbers against him', might be of use to us, as being the best explanation of a lunatic's words and actions, even though, since 'The prime numbers are plotting against him' is unintelligible, we cannot intelligibly ascribe to anyone a belief that the prime numbers are plotting against him. Just so, although you cannot intelligibly ascribe to anyone belief in the omnipotence of words, because 'Words are omnipotent' is unintelligible, still, the sayings of a philosopher or a lunatic might be such that the best explanation of them was 'He believes in something like the omnipotence of words.'

This explanation is not needed, of course, for sayings like those from which I began. As I said, everyone knows how to paraphrase-out of those sayings the lunatic suggestion of the omnipotence of words: 'Descartes' theory made animals mere automata' really just means 'Descartes said or implied that animals are mere automata', and so on. But are not other things sometimes said, which imply something like the omnipotence of words, and which *are* meant literally by the people who say them?

Well, it is true that nowadays there are many people like the modish historian who recently said in print that 'the Pacific is in reality a European artifact', 'a construct of the European mind'.[1] The existence of such persons is no doubt a historical portent, but, except as historical portents, they are not worth talking about. Probably they do not mean literally what they say, but even if they do, they do not deserve the attention of philosophers; nor is such attention at all likely to do them any good. If the writer just quoted were to be dropped midway between Valparaiso and Dunedin, say, and asked afterwards whether he still thinks the Pacific is a construct of the European mind, *that* might do; though probably it would not. All of this goes, too, for those so-called 'sociologists of knowledge' who, by their talk of 'the social construction of reality', avow, clearly enough, a belief in something like the omnipotence of words; or avow it, at any rate, as clearly as their literary disabilities allow them to avow anything.

Nelson Goodman, however, is an entirely different matter. He is a most unusual man: a successful art-dealer, as well as a distinguished philosopher. His *Fact, Fiction and Forecast* (1954)[2] left a deep mark on recent philosophy, and deserved to; at least, the bit in it about 'grue' did. But his later book, *Ways of World-making* (1978),[3] is the most emphatic avowal possible of belief in something like the omnipotence of words. Goodman says here that worlds can be made with words, and he spares no effort to ensure that his readers do not mistake this for a metaphorical saying. He even claims to know of many people who have made worlds with words already.

Words are not even the only materials with which you can make worlds, according to Goodman. He says, for example, that Igor Stravinsky made worlds with sounds, and that Mondrian made worlds with colours and shapes; and the book is dedicated to 'K.S.G., who makes worlds with watercolours'. Whether less genteel artists, such as tattooists or cake-decorators, share in the privilege of being able to make worlds, Goodman does not say; but his ontology is certainly very democratic.

Anyway, he definitely does believe that you can make worlds with words, as well as in other ways; at least, he says he believes it, and , if only as a matter of common courtesy, we would believe him, if we could. Only, we can't, for the sort of reason mentioned before. The statement that worlds can be made with words, if not metaphorical, is incomprehensible, and so the statement, 'Goodman believes that worlds can be made with words', is incomprehensible too. We cannot believe what we cannot even comprehend. So all his words are wasted on us. In fact, 'Ways of Wordwasting' would have been a more accurate title for the book. Of course, it would not have been so good a way of salesmaking; whereas the actual title is admirably adapted to catch the trendy vote, as well as the lunatic one. And not only those votes: the catalogue of Sydney University library lists a second copy of *Ways of Worldmaking* as having been bought for the library of the Department of Geography.

The trendies and the 'sociologists of knowledge', I said, are both beneath philosophical notice and unlikely to benefit from it. The first of these things is certainly not true of Goodman. Is the second? There is a long-standing joke in the profession according to which it is, but I do not know whether or not the joke is a fair one. What I do know is that, apart from details, Goodman need fear no philosophical criticism whatever of *Ways of Worldmaking*. What criticism need one philosopher fear from others, when a statement which they would regard as the most terrific *reductio ad absurdum* imaginable, if it turned up as a remote consequence of his starting-points, he calmly takes *as* a starting-point? Criticism is disarmed in such a case. And that is how it is with Goodman, and the statement that worlds can be made with words: a statement which, as Hume said of the doctrine of the real presence, 'is so absurd, that it eludes the force of all argument'.[4]

Of course, if you purchase exemption from criticism in this way, you pay by exposing yourself, if not to neglect, then to ridicule. No book of Goodman's is in any danger of neglect, but this one is a strong temptation to satire. The book belongs to, and indeed brings to a climax, the American philosophical tradition of self-indulgence, or to give it its usual name, pragmatism. This is that tradition which William James began when he learnt how to stop worrying about the non-existence of God and start living, and set out to preach what he well named 'the gospel of relaxation', the right of 'the will to believe', and that truth is what works. O unworthy non-pioneers! It must be a poor satirist who could not make something out of a hundred years of this inglorious national heritage.

I therefore wonder whether it was wise of Goodman to give prominence in *Ways of Worldmaking* to Woody Allen. Not that Allen is formidable, but others are, and there is such a thing as begging for trouble. The news might reach Tom Wolfe's ears, for example, that the young at Harvard are taught that you can make worlds with your mouth, and Goodman could find himself the subject of a best-seller. His earnest devotion to Stravinsky, James Joyce, and all the other grisly objects of middlebrow piety, would probably also get a bit of rough handling in the process.

Philosophers have no field-work to do, or laboratory-work, or studio-work. They occupy themselves exclusively with words. As everyone is apt to overestimate the importance of his own occupation, delusions about the power of words are an occupational hazard with philosophers. In fact that is putting it much too mildly. The truth is that a difficulty in distinguishing words from the world, or from God or God's words, is a weakness to which philosophers as a class are peculiarly and painfully prone. Nowadays, of course, almost anyone with a university degree is likely to say 'sociological' when what he means is 'social', 'mythological' when he means 'mythical', and so on. But it is only philosophers among whom that kind of confusion corresponds to something deeply rooted in the mind. If this fact gives philosophy a deep affinity with lunacy, I am sorry for it, but it cannot be helped.

That the world is, or embodies, or is ruled by, or was created by, a *sentence-like* entity, a 'logos', is an idea almost as old as Western philosophy itself. Where the Bible says 'The Word was made flesh', biblical scholars safely conclude at once that some *philosopher* has meddled with the text (and not so as to improve it). Talking-To-Itself is what Hegel thought the universe is doing, or rather, is. In my own hearing, Professor John Anderson maintained, while awake, what with G. E. Moore was no more than a nightmare he once had, that tables and chairs and all the rest are propositions.[5] So it has always gone on. In fact St John's Gospel, when it says 'In the beginning was the Word, and the Word was with God, and the Word was God', sums up pretty accurately one of the most perennial, as well as most lunatic, strands in philosophy. (The passage is also of interest as proving that two statements can be inconsistent without either being intelligible.)

While the distinction between words on the one hand, and the world or God or God's words on the other, is always apt to be a source of difficulty for philosophers, some philosophers find it especially difficult to make these distinctions where *their own* words are concerned. This is why so much of the literature of philosophy consists of megalomaniac autobiography, lightly disguised. Comte is the most obvious example. No bishop of Rome ever claimed for himself a hundredth part of the power claimed by the self-appointed Supreme Pontiff of the Religion of Humanity.[6] But the lust for universal dominion is evident in philosophers who are far more revered than Comte. In that respect, Plato is the Comte of the fourth century BC; though you are not supposed to say so. Compared with Hegel, however, Plato and Comte are sane and modest men. When Hegel writes that logic forbids this, or that logic requires that, he uses the word 'logic' sometimes to mean (a) the structure of the universe, and sometimes to mean (b) a certain book he had written, entitled *Logic*. He just couldn't tell the difference between (a) and (b).

Still, if you take the past as a whole, making worlds with words was a privilege accorded to only a very few persons. Not counting ordinary lunatics, it was confined to philosophers, and most of them were restrained, of course, by not being lunatics, from thinking that words can make worlds. William James, however, by the twentieth-century dawn's early light, could see that this bastion of privilege could not survive, any more than any other. Hence the revolutionary gospel which he dimly foreshadowed, and which Goodman has now published: that, subject of course to commonsense qualifications, such as a certain amount of intelligence, effort, and training, *anyone* can make worlds with words.

Now this was too bad: in fact, democratic fallacy at its worst. Lunacy or megalomania are good things in Hegel and Plato and a few others, of course, and we can never honour those men too much. But it by no means follows that the same things are good in all men. What it is good for some to have, need not be good for all to have. Indeed, it can easily happen that it is logically impossible for something, contingently true of some, to be true of all. Some competitors in a race may finish behind others, but it is logically impossible that they all should do so. Here, as usual, the logic of the satirists has been better than that of the professed logicians. Descartes, for example, thought that, since our senses sometimes deceive us, it must be logically possible that they always do: but W. S. Gilbert knew that when everybody's somebody then no one's anybody.

As it is not even false, but simple nonsense, to talk of making worlds, the James-Goodman promise, that everyone can make worlds, is even more fraudulent than most of the promises that are made, to distribute among all a privilege previously confined to a few. Disappointment is absolutely guaranteed. James's 'will to believe' doctrine was intended to relieve, and did relieve, Christians under intellectual siege. But the Christians, though of course grateful at first, themselves reported afterwards that the doctrine had merely produced a frightening atrophy of their ability to believe in anything.[7] This was truly pathetic, and should serve as a warning to all against accepting lifts from philosophical strangers. Similarly, any who at first expand under Goodman's flattering assurance that they too can make worlds, are sure to demand their money back later on. For the 'cash-value' (as James liked to say) of this assurance turns out to be only that, if they want to, they can paint in watercolours, etc. Well, they knew that before: what a sell!

When a privileged upper house proves too obstructive, the king or the president, in a constitutional government, does not shoot or remove members of that house. On the contrary, he *increases* their numbers: the upper house is 'stacked' with as many new 'lords', of the desired political complexion, as may be needed. New lords are lucky people, obviously. Still, any of them who feel a need to justify their situation intellectually are not much to be envied. For they face the problem of shutting the flood-gates *behind them*: well known to be no easy task. The bicameral system will collapse, obviously, if too many people come in, or if the stacking gambit is resorted to too freely. But what principle can the lucky ones appeal to, in order to prevent too many other people from getting lucky? Religion is out of the question, and no principle of personal morality covers such a case. The arbitrary will of the king or president is not available as a principle here. Few will defend, as an unqualified rule, even the will of the popular house. What is left, except an appeal to constitutional precedent and practice? But that, alas, coming from new lords, would be altogether too reminiscent of the boy who murdered both his parents and then demanded the mercy of the court as an orphan. Precedent, if it excluded anyone, would exclude the new lords themselves. An appeal by them to precedent, therefore, as it does not exclude themselves, really excludes nothing.

There is no known solution to this problem in constitutional theory, and in philosophy James and Goodman face an insoluble problem which is almost exactly the same. They are not *new* lords, of course, because, being philosophers, they belong by right of birth to the old privileged house of worldmakers. But, since they stand in that house for the proposition that everyone can make worlds, they *are* revolutionary lords. At the same time, their common sense and prudence, as well as their old exclusive instincts, tell them that, with the enunciation of the general principle, democracy has gone far enough, and that the clear and *present* danger is less from entrenched philosophical reaction than from an unrestrained ontological democracy. Goodman, being the later writer, is naturally far more apprehensive of this danger than James was, and in fact he is a bundle of nerves. He is always returning to the theme that what is required for progress and peace in our time is *liberty not licence* in worldmaking.[8] So then, while of course everyone *can* make worlds, still, some are better at it than others, and Goodman thinks it will be best, on the whole, if worldmaking, in science or art or philosophy, is left in the hands of the responsible authorities.

And what rule is to guide the authorities, in any of these spheres? Why, says Goodman, practice. (Naturally: he *is* a pragmatist.) But of course the appeal to practice, coming from him, is fatally reminiscent, again, of the self-made orphan's defence. If *practice* had been the prevailing rule in the past, where would all the revolutionaries be? Where would Copernicus be? Where Stravinsky? Where would Goodman himself be? As his rule of practice evidently does not exclude them, it really excludes nothing. When revolutionary lords, or new lords, turn grave, and start to talk constitutional precedent, sensible people just laugh at them, or wink.

This kind of thing is the nemesis of pragmatism: it always does nothing or too much. An appeal to practice could do nothing to guide us, obviously, if the practice being appealed to were past *or future* practice: it must be just *past* practice that is meant. But past practice, unless by a miracle it happens to be perfect and complete, will include some old bad things, or omit some future good ones; and then, clearly, the appeal to practice will do too much.

It may be worthwhile to illustrate this, by reference to what Goodman says here about logic. This part of the book[9] is entirely independent of the 'worldmaking' business, and is in fact essentially what was said about logic in *Fact, Fiction and Forecast*. It is pragmatism, but pragmatism without ontological pretensions. Goodman's summary is this: 'inductive like deductive validity consists of conformity with principles that codify practice.'[10] It is past inferential practice, then, which determines validity. If you want to know whether a given inference is a valid one or not, Goodman's test is this. Elicit from past inferential practice the principles to which it conforms, or the principles which codify it: then see whether the given inference conforms to those principles. If it does it is valid, otherwise not.

This is not a test which could often be applied in real life with much rational confidence. You can't tell what principles an inference conformed to, unless you know what inference it was; you don't know what inference it was, unless you know what all of its premises were; and in real life you seldom do know what all the premises of an inference were. A man may seem, for example, to infer 'A' just from 'If A then B' and 'B'. Silly people are then likely to start talking about popular fallacies, 'guilt by association', etc. Well, the man *may* have committed a fallacy, but equally he may have been reasoning from more premises than we gave him credit for, and his other premises may have included, for example, 'If B then A'. This kind of possibility can hardly ever be excluded with much confidence. The inferrer's own intro-spection is no infallible guide; *asking* people to identify all their premises sets up perturbations of its own, quite apart from being unrealistic in itself; and brain-scans of the kind that might settle the matter are mere science fiction.

But Goodman's test for validity is not only almost useless in practice; it is futile in principle. To search for *the* principles to which past inferential practice has conformed, or for *the* principles which codify it, is necessarily to search in vain. In empirical science, all the observations which have been made up to any given time will always 'conform' to indefinitely-many contrary hypotheses about the unobserved part of nature. And just so, inferential practice up to any given time will always conform to indefinitely-many contrary logical principles of codification. Has past inferential practice conformed to the principle, 'From "p" and "If p then q", infer "q"'? If it has, then it has also conformed to the principle, 'From "p" and "If p then q" infer "q", if inferring before 2000; otherwise don't.' It has also conformed to the prin-ciple, 'From "p" and "If p then q" infer "q", up to 2000; after that, infer "not-q".' And so on. An inference in 2001, therefore, from 'A' and 'If A then B', to 'not-B', as it conforms to a principle which codifies past practice, is valid by Goodman's test. So too, obviously, is every other possible inference, however invalid.

Goodman must be the last person in the world who needs to be taught about 'grue'. No doubt this is why the quotation on page 35 refers, not to *the* principles which codify inferential practice, but just to 'principles' which do so. But then, of course, every possible inference conforms to *some* principle which codifies practice, and indeed to many contrary principles which do so, so that you have the familiar gruesome result. Goodman's test for validity in fact excludes nothing, and the past, despite the authority apparently ascribed to it by that test, draws no line at all between the valid and the invalid inferences.

Of course, if, *per impossibile*, every inference conformed to just one principle, and if, contrary to fact, we knew concerning each past inference *which* principle it conformed to: why then, indeed, the past would be invested by Goodman's test with a real authority, and would draw a line between valid and invalid inferences. All too real, in fact, since the line would then be drawn, failing a miracle, in the wrong place. For his test would then say that an inference is not valid unless it conforms, and conforms only, to a principle already hallowed by use, and is valid so long as the principle it conforms to is so hallowed. But we are not yet such complete logicians that an inference is absolutely damned as invalid if it conforms only to a principle which is new to us. And equally, our logical beliefs *may* be imperfect even as far as they go: an inference might conform only to our most hallowed principle, and be invalid for all that. Established error is a possibility in logic, as it is elsewhere.

Some philosophers have lately seemed disposed to deny the latter possibility. They seem to think that departures from logicality, or at least gross departures, cannot be or ever have been widespread. Their optimism is engaging, but it flies in the face of common sense and common knowledge.

Take the question, where the most intelligent things are to be found. It is common knowledge that for more than twenty years a search for evidence of extra-terrestrial intelligence has been vigorously prosecuted by both American and Russian scientists, and also that this search has not turned up a single thing, any more than did the earlier and more amateurish searches for such evidence. It is even commoner knowledge that, as far as terrestrial beings go, all the evidence points, and always has pointed, to the conclusion that man is the cleverest. Consequently, if someone were to believe that there is something cleverer than man, he would believe it not only in the absence of evidence, but in defiance of all the evidence; and to believe something in defiance of all the evidence is grossly illogical. Yet nearly every religion asserts the existence of something cleverer than man, and nearly every human being in the past believed in one or other of the religions which do assert this. Such belief is common even now. Scarcely any human being, consequently, has been in the past free from gross illogicality, and multitudes still are not.

And religious beliefs appear, at least, to be at bottom the conclusions, precisely, of bad or unreasonable *inferences*. Not all of them are, of course. Many of them are, quite obviously, the conclusions of perfectly reasonable inferences, from premises which were false to begin with. But bad reasoning from true premises seems to be the basic religious case. It is, as far as we can tell, from perfectly genuine observations of happenings in the sky, the sea, on or under the ground, that religious beliefs are inferred in the first place. I take it that it was from true premises about the sea and seafaring, for example, that people at first inferred the existence of something like Poseidon. If so, then the propositions which people thought were reasons for believing in Poseidon were true enough. They just weren't reasons for believing in Poseidon, that's all.

If this strikes you as too harsh a verdict on human rationality on its strictly inferential side, then by all means embrace the alternative. That must be to explain religious delusions, not as the result of bad inference from good premises, but as the result of good inference from bad premises. But since religious delusions are, on any view, almost universal, bad premises will then have to be almost universal too, and the implied verdict, on human rationality in a broad sense, will be as harsh as before. Man is, indeed, the cleverest thing we know of; but he is also inveterately religious, and there is no way in which his religion can be reconciled with the idea that his rationality is complete, or even perfect as far as it goes.

When I say that the basic religious inferences are bad or

unreasonable, I hope no one will think I say this because the conclusions are false and the premises true. The conclusions *are* false and the premises true, but since I am not a deductivist, I do not think that that is enough to make the inferences unreasonable ones. Australia's famous contribution to logical and biological science, the black swan, prompted J. S. Mill to write that the inference from the whiteness of European swans to the whiteness of all 'cannot have been a good induction, since the conclusion has turned out erroneous'.[11] But this is just Mill doing us his usual service, of making important mistakes *clearly*. A proposition may be false though it is rational for us to believe it, and a proposition may be true which we have no reason to believe.

To prevent this kind of misunderstanding, then, let us suppose that the voodoo religion, say, is in fact true. There really are exactly 712 deities, or whatever, and their haunts and habits are exactly as laid down in the voodoo manuals. The voodoo religion is true, then; but this does not affect my argument at all. For it is also true that there is not and never has been the smallest reason to believe it. And this truth, along with the facts of life in Haiti these past several hundred years, is sufficient to establish the existence of gross and widespread illogicality among humans.

With the arrival of the Jazz Age, a religion which had previously been confined to a tiny minority, and which even with them was no more than about seventy years old, suddenly swept over the Western world: the religion of art. Ever since then, this religion, or more accurately this cult, has gone from strength to strength. In the second century, the most successful practitioners of imposture and self-glorification were magicians; in the twentieth, they are artists. What department of human life have the missionaries of this religion not claimed as their own? We have had education through art: health through art; the city revitalized through art; 'the family of man' united, at last, through art . . . It is a wonder if there is a wooden leg or broken heart left in the world. Occasionally a man of sense, such as Jacques Barzun, has protested against the all-enveloping and ceaseless roar of art-propaganda:[12] in vain. The mere scientists succumbed completely to this propaganda long ago. Your physicist or biologist may be something of a heretic in his own subject, but he could not, if his life depended on it, think an impious thought about Picasso, say, or Joyce, and if he hears anyone else utter such a thought, he suddenly rediscovers what the word 'blasphemy' means. Books which have been published in the last ten years make it sadly clear that this propaganda has finally taken its toll even on philosophers. The reader of Feyerabend's *Against Method*[13] was expected, amid all his other afflictions, to digest a whole chapter centred on Greek pots, with copious illustrations. The reader of *Ways of Worldmaking* sinks under a hail of references, again with illustrations, to paintings, music, ballet, literature. The philosophy book which has 3-D pop-up reproductions cannot be long delayed. Resistance is overdue.

Let art be as important as its greatest devotee now thinks. Still, the verdict of 2500 years of experience, *expériences nombreuses et funestes*, is this: that what philosophers write about art is not worth reading. Aesthetics in general was from the start, and has remained, the most 'maimed and abortive' member of the philosophic litter; and as to art in particular, it has absolutely refused to yield up the least of its secrets to philosophers. Whether this fact is owing to the poverty of philosophy, or to the richness of art, or to both or neither, I do not pretend to decide, but it is in any case a fact. It should be unnecessary to say, since it is a trivial logical truth to say, that things *may* be different in the future. But at any rate the pages which are devoted to art in Goodman's book, or in Feyerabend's, are no exception to the rule. It is very clear that the writers think a good deal the better of themselves on account of these pages. But the reader is merely oppressed and distracted by them, and all the brow-beating is to no purpose.

That is how things are, even on the supposition that art, and even modern art, is as important as it could be. In fact, of course, scarcely anything in modern art is worth a moment's attention, from philosophers or anyone else. Even if it were otherwise, many of us could fairly plead that we have served our sentences already. In common with many others, I threw away a considerable part of my youth on Joyce, Picasso, and the rest, and take it a little hard to find myself, forty years on and as a philosopher, put to school again to those masters. As for being told, as we are told by Goodman in *Ways of Worldmaking*, that we must make room in our *metaphysics* for all the 'worlds' made by these public benefactors . . . ! Hazlitt says somewhere that, in the Britain of 1825, Sir Walter Scott's feudalism was, like the old armour and weapons in his house, only 'auctioneers' stuff' after all. Well, it is certainly silly to take your politics from auctioneers or their suppliers. But how silly would you have to be to take your metaphysics from dealers in modern art, or their suppliers?

Philosophies usually have their roots in strong feelings, but in Goodman's case I cannot myself detect any deeper source than a certain impatience with what he calls, in reply to a critic of this book, 'flatfooted philosophy'.[14] The same feeling surfaces in an injunction to the reader[15] which Goodman distils from a long quotation from Woody Allen. It is this: 'never mind mind, essence is not essential, and matter doesn't matter.' As you can see, this is the gospel of relaxation, with a vengeance; and there is no passage in the book which is more heartfelt than this one.

But suppose we embrace this gospel, and obey the injunction. If we go so far in cultivating (in Hume's words) 'carelessness and inattention', as distinct from flatfooted philosophy, why will we not go further? Mind, for example, is at least an intelligible subject, and it is one which, as we are the most intelligent things we know of, is naturally interesting to us. If we agree to give up our interest in mind, it will be, if we are rational, in favour of something else, which we find more interesting or rewarding: fishing, perhaps, or crime, or whatever. At any rate it will certainly not be in favour of things so little interesting, or even intelligible, as Goodman's 'worlds'.

How can Goodman himself retain any appetite for his ontological smorgasbord, especially when he knows that every pitiful potter, poet, etc., is busy every moment adding to the delights which are in store for him? The Christian religion was justly derided, by Celsus and others in the second century, for drawing its adherents mainly from people labouring under some natural or acquired intellectual disadvantage: slaves, the poor, women, children, and so on. The twentieth-century art-religion likewise draws both its priests and their followers mainly from people who are, though from different causes, intellectually disadvantaged. What is Goodman, of all people in the world, doing cultivating these unfortunates, let alone taking his metaphysics from their still more unhappy productions on canvas, etc.?

I suppose that part of the answer must be the old commonplace: that Americans don't really know how to relax, but will always turn even self-indulgence into a penitential exercise. At any rate it will be obvious that an *Australian* gospel of relaxation, if it went as far as Goodman's, would go a great deal further still.


## Notes

1  *New York Review of Books*, 13 October 1983, p. 31.
2  N. Goodman, *Fact, Fiction and Forecast* (University of London/Athlone Press, London, 1954). The part about 'grue' is on pp. 73–83.
3  N. Goodman, *Ways of Worldmaking* (Hackett Publishing, Indianapolis, 1978).
4  *The Natural History of Religion*, in *David Hume: The Philosophical Works*, ed. T. H. Green and T. H. Grose (Longman's, Green, London, 1882), vol. 4, p. 343.
5  See J. M. Keynes, *Essays and Sketches in Biography* (Meridian Books, New York, 1956), p. 25.
6  See, for example, J. S. Mill, *Auguste Comte and Positivism* (Routledge, London, n.d.), pp. 125ff.
7  See J. M. Robertson, *Christianity and Mythology* (2nd imp., 1936, of 2nd edn, Watts, London, 1910), p. 434.
8  See Goodman, *Ways of Worldmaking*, pp. 97, 107, for example.
9  Ibid., pp. 125–9.
10  Ibid., p. 126.
11  J. S. Mill, *A System of Logic* (1941 imp. of 8th edn, Longmans, London, n.d.), bk III, ch. III, sect. 3, p. 205.
12  J. Barzun, *The House of Intellect* (Harper, New York, 1959), pp. 17ff.
13  P. K. Feyerabend, *Against Method* (New Left Books, London, 1975).
14  N. Goodman, *Synthese* 45 (1980), 215.
15  N. Goodman, *Ways of Worldmaking*, p. 96.

# 3

# 'Always apologize, always explain': Robert Nozick's War Wounds

An unprecedented expansion of communism took place immediately after the second world war. For the next twenty-odd years, any possibility of resistance to communist expansion depended almost entirely upon America: no other country possessed both the requisite military capacity and the willingness to use it. But the outcome of the Vietnam war showed that, while America's capacity for such resistance remained intact, her willingness did not. For that war was lost, not through defeat of American armies in the field, nor yet through treachery among them, but through a massive sedition at home. The nation showed that it had become utterly opposed to any further armed resistance to communism.

So great a revolution in national sentiment, effected in a few years, could not fail to be reflected in American intellectual life, and even in so remote a branch of intellectual life as philosophy. It is reflected nowhere more faithfully than in Professor Robert Nozick's book, *Philosophical Explanations*.[1]

Nozick is a professor at Harvard, but in his student days he was one of those who agitated with so much success 'against the war', as such people used to say: this being their favourite euphemism for 'against the anti-communist side in the war'. Whether Nozick's political ideas were then pro-communist ones, I do not know. If they were, they soon changed, because his political-philosophy book, *Anarchy, State, and Utopia*, published in 1974,[2] is the reverse of sympathetic either to communist practice or to communist theory. *Philosophical Explanations*, however, is not a work of political philosophy. The bulk of the book is devoted to certain mainstream philosophical topics, such as personal identity, scepticism, and the meaning of life. It may

therefore not be obvious at once to the reader of the book, and
perhaps was not obvious to the writer, what a perfect political
period-piece it is. But then a literary self-portrait, like a photo-
graphic one, is all the more likely to be accurate and revealing,
the more unconsciously it has been produced. And in fact this
book is a largely unwitting self-portrait of American philosophy
in the period when America became, of its own volition, an ex-
world-power. This is true of the body of the book, into the details
of which I will not enter at all, but even more true of the long
and very arresting Introduction. Here the author speaks from the
heart, and admits us to the inmost recesses of his philosophy of
philosophy.

The result is a display, as in a war museum, of the gruesome
and disabling wounds which were inflicted on American life, and
on American intellectual life in particular, by the defeat in Vietnam. Not that this is at all how the author sees it, quite the
reverse. The whole book in fact breathes self-satisfaction, because
in Nozick's eyes every war wound is a symptom of health and
strength, and one of the signs that we have entered into a new
and better era. This may appear anomalous, but it should not:
such self-deception is entirely characteristic of the period. Suicide
as a *military* power, America explained to itself, is the supreme
exercise of *moral* power; and Watergate, a fatal wound to the
legitimacy of American government, was received with rapture,
as the exemplary triumph of a free press. Such things are no
accident: an ex-world-power must perforce be content to make
imaginary victories out of real defeats.

The completeness of Nozick's composition is remarkable: he
touches somewhere in the book, however lightly, almost every
note on the keyboard of American decadence. Gandhi is there.[3]
The necesssary deference to feminism is there.[4] The necessary
reproof to 'racism' is there.[5] Carlos Castaneda is there,[6] referred
to as though he were a thinker, which he is not; he is not referred
to as the writer of best-sellers which encouraged the taking of
hallucinogenic drugs, which he is. Drugs of course are there, and
in no unfavourable light: drugs may have their place, Nozick
thinks, in 'the treatment for philosophical parochialism'.[7] Has he
left anything out? Is there anyone in post-Vietnam American
who needs to be placated, whom he has not placated? This was

obviously a worry, and there is a nervous catch-all reference to 'children's rights, the treatment of animals, domination, and ecological awareness'.[8] But nothing human is perfect, and Nozick, for all his care, has forgotten the homosexuals. No doubt this omission will be repaired in a second edition.

But he did not forget sex. Consider the following passage. 'At no point is the person forced to accept anything. He moves along gently, exploring his own and the author's thoughts. He explores together with the author, moving only when ready; then he stops. Perhaps at a later time . . . , he will move further.'[9] This is Nozick on the joy of reading philosophy when philosophy is read as it should be. But who can possibly fail to recognize here the accents of Dr Alex Comfort in *The Joy of Sex*? In fact only two words would need to be changed to make it absolutely impossible for anyone to tell that the quotation did not actually come from that book: put 'partner' for 'author', and 'body' for 'thoughts'.

Nor is there any doubt that here at least Nozick knew what he was doing, and meant his book to sound like some contemporary sexual *vade-mecum*. For his Introduction reaches its climax with the last paragraph, where he returns to the joy of philosophy, and having asked, 'Can any pleasure compare to that of a new idea, a new question?', answers as follows:

> There is sexual experience, of course, not dissimilar, with its own playfulness and possibilities, its focused freedom, its depth, its sharp pleasures and its gentle ones, its ecstasies. What is the mind's excitement and sensuality? What its orgasm? Whatever, it unfortunately will frighten and offend the puritans of the mind (do the two puritanisms share a common root?) even as it expands others and brings them joy[10].

The connecting ideal throughout, as even the foregoing evidence will suffice to indicate, is *non-coerciveness*. More specifically it is non-coercive *fun*; but still it is the element of non-coerciveness which is the fundamental one. The fatal flaw in all previous philosophy, it emerges, was a *moral* one (and the *same* moral flaw, I need hardly add, as that of American policy in Vietnam): its coerciveness. The necessary revolution in philosophy – and this book pretends to inaugurate nothing less – is that philosophy shall become non-coercive. 'Coercive philosophy' aims to produce *proofs*. It therefore involves *arguing*, hence 'raised voices, anger, negative emotion'.[11] 'A philosophical argument is an attempt to get someone to believe something, whether he wants to believe it or not.'[12] Now, Nozick asks, 'Is that a nice way to behave toward someone?' Just to make sure that we do not misunderstand this question, or give the wrong answer, Nozick answers himself: no, that is 'not . . . a nice way to behave toward someone'.[13]

Although I will not be easily believed when I say so, this objction is in fact all, or almost all, that Nozick has to urge against previous philosophy. Around 1933 my grandmother, by then a very old woman, used to try to calm the storms among her daughter's children by saying, 'Is that a nice way to treat your sister?', 'Little birds in the nest should agree', and the like. She had later, as she had not at the time, my sympathy. But it was not until much later still, namely the post-Vietnam period, that I learnt that the voice of philosophy itself is the voice of an old woman.

Whereas the old coercive sort of philosophy aimed to produce proofs, the new and better sort aims, rather, to produce *explanations*.

> There is a second mode of philosophy, not directed to arguments and proofs: it seeks explanations. Various philosophical things need to be explained: a philosophical theory is introduced to explain them, to render them coherent and better understood.
>
> Many philosophical problems are ones of understanding how something is or can be possible. How is it possible for us to have free will, supposing that all actions are causally determined? Randomness, also, seems no more congenial; so, how is free will (even) possible? How is it possible that we know anything, given the facts the skeptic enumerates, for example, that it is logically possible we are dreaming or floating in a tank with our brain being stimulated to give us exactly our current experiences and even all our past ones? How is it possible for something to be the same thing from one time to another, through change? How is it possible for subjective experiences to fit into an objective physical world? How can there be stable meanings (Plato asked), given that everything in the world is changing? How is it possible for us to have synthetic necessary knowledge? (This last question, Kant's shows, if none did earlier, that the question's presupposition that the item *is* possible may be controversial or even false, in which

case the question would be withdrawn.) The theological problem of evil also takes this form: how is evil possible, supposing the existence of an omnipotent omniscient good God? One central question of twentieth-century philosophy has been: how is language possible? And let us not omit from our list: how is philosophy possible?

The form of these questions is: how is one thing possible, given (or supposing) certain other things? Some statements $r_i$, . . . , $r_n$ are assumed or accepted or taken for granted, and there is a tension between these statements and another statement $p$; they appear to exclude $p$'s holding true. Let us term the $r_i$ *apparent excluders* (of $p$). Since the statment $p$ also is accepted, we face the question of how $p$ is possible, given its apparent excluders.[14]

. . .

The task of explaining how $p$ is possible is not exhausted by the rearguard action of meeting arguments from its apparent excluders. There remains the question of what facts or principles might give rise to $p$. Here the philosopher searches for deeper explanatory principles, preferably with some independent plausibility, not excluded by current knowledge. To show that these principles, if true, would explain $p$ involves deducing $p$ from them – at least so holds the deductive-nomological view according to which each explanation deduces the fact to be explained from general laws and initial conditions. Yet still, this is no attempt to prove $p$; and the explanatory hypotheses used in the explanation need not be known to be true, or be believed on grounds independent of $p$ itself.[15]

This philosophy of philosophy is as insubstantial intellectually as it is over-charged emotionally: in fact it is like nothing so much as a paper kite driven by a fifty-horsepower motor.

Between proofs or attempts at proof, and inconsiderateness, there is no special connection, and neither is there between explanations or attempts at explanation, and consideration for others. An explanation can be advanced and defended with any degree of overbearingness that one cares to imagine; and a proof can be advanced and defended apologetically enough to satisfy even a post-Vietnam American philosopher.

Then, take any train of thought in a philosopher's mind, or any discussion between two philosophers, which might be started by the question, 'How is it possible that p, given (the potential excluder) q?' Could not the very same train of thought, or the very same discussion, have equally well been started by the question, '*Is* p possible given q?', or by the question 'Isn't q a proof of the falsity of p?' If so, then the consideration of 'how-is-it-possible' questions is in no way an *alternative* to the consideration of putative proofs, and Nozick's claim to be setting philosophy on a new path is altogether hollow.

Nozick tried, then, to marry off explanation to considerateness, and philosophy to 'how-is-it-possible', questions, and both of these seem to be attempts doomed to failure. It is no better with his attempt to marry off explanation to the answering of 'how-is-it-possible' questions.

Suppose a philosopher asks, 'How is p possible given q?', and manages to give a true answer to this question. Is this answer an *explanation* of anything? Take Nozick's first example, 'How is it possible for us to have free will, supposing all actions are causally determined?' Here p is evidently 'We have free will', and q is 'All actions are causally determined.' Now if it is asked how this p is possible given this q, then the answer which many philosophers would give is this: 'An action's being an exercise of free will *is* its being causally determined in a certain way.' Suppose that this is a proper answer to the question, and suppose, even, that it is true. Still, why call it an explanation? What might it explain?

It can hardly explain p itself, that is, that we have free will. For that is, I take it, a contingent proposition (that is, one which is true or false, depending just on the way things happen to be); whereas our answer to the question, how this p is possible given this q, is evidently a *conceptual remark*. If it is true, as we are supposing it is, it is a necessary truth. But a necessary truth cannot explain a contingent proposition, and cannot even be an essential part of an explanation of a contingent proposition.

But then, what else is there that our answer to the question might be supposed to explain? Could it be, that p *is possible*? Or, that the conjunction of p with q *is possible*? That is, that it is possible we have free will; or that the conjunction of free will with universal causation is possible.

Hardly. These propositions, unlike the contingent propositions p and q from which we began, are attributions of a certain *modal* status (such as possibility or necessity) *to* those propositions from which we began. As such, they are either necessarily true or necessarily false. If they are necesssarily false, they cannot be explained: only truths can be explained. But equally, if they are necessarily true then they cannot be explained. To explain something is to explain why things are not otherwise. But there can be no explaining why something is not otherwise, which could not *be* otherwise.

Even apart from that, if what is *explained*, by an answer to the question how p is possible given q, is that the conjunction of p with q is possible, whatever can it be, distinct from that, that *explains* it? Nozick allows, as Kant did before him, that the answer to one of these 'how-possible' questions may be 'No how: p is *not* possible given q.' But where that is not so, in other words where the conjunction of p with q *is* possible, what information, more than that, is contained in a true answer to the question, 'How is p possible given q?' If there is *no* more, then a true answer to that question certainly cannot explain that the conjunction of p with q is possible, for the simple reason that no proposition explains itself. Still, I now begin to perceive where I may have gone wrong. I have written so far as though the word 'how' were a mere rhetorical flourish; as though, that is, there were no important difference between the questions '*Is* p possible?' and '*How* is p possible?', or between the questions 'Is p possible given q?' and 'How is p possible given q?' But perhaps this is an historical *faux pas*.

There is nothing at all puzzling about the questions 'is p possible? and 'Is p possible given q?' These are straightforward questions of logic, about the modal status of p or about the relation between p and q. We may not be able to answer the questions easily, or at all, in a given case, but we have no difficulty whatever in understanding what they mean. In fact questions of this sort are so lamentably lacking in depth that even 'pre-Critical' philosophers could and did understand them. But it is otherwise with the 'Kantian questions', 'How is p possible?' and 'How is p possible given q?' Some people simply adore these questions: Nozick is so much an enthusiast for them that he would have philosophers ask (near enough) no other kind. But such questions have one disadvantage: it is not at all clear what they mean. When a philosopher asks, not 'Is p possible given q?', but '*How* is p possible given q?', what does he mean?

In some cases we know what he means only too well, and to our shame. He means: 'Well, of course, p is *not* possible given q, but you surely don't expect me to give up either p or q on that account! Far from that, I am going to keep on insinuating, in public, that p *is* possible given q, by publishing countless pages about what I call the *problem* of reconciling p with q.'

An example from theology: let p be 'Christ was divine', and let q be 'Christ was a man.' Propound the question 'How is p possible given q?', and you have what is called in Christology 'the problem of the union of the two natures'. How *can* you go wrong? It's been a steady earner for two thousand years, hasn't it? An example from Popperite philosophy: let p be 'A statement is scientific only if it is falsifiable', and let q be 'No open statistical generalizations are falsifiable, though some of them are scientific.' Propound the question, 'How is p possible given q?', and you have what Popper called 'the problem of decidability'[16] of open statistical generalizations. Again, you can hardly go wrong: this 'problem' is only fifty years old, and is bound to have many more miles left in it yet.

This form of industrial pollution, by which real inconsistencies are turned into imaginary problems, is not only ancient but economically important. It accounts, I would say, for perhaps as much as 5 per cent of the GPIP, or Gross Published Intellectual Product, of the human race so far. Hume complained of it. 'Nothing can be more absurd,' he wrote, 'than this custom of calling a *difficulty* what pretends to be a *demonstration*, and endeavouring by that means to elude its force and evidence.'[17] Still, at that time the industry had hardly begun. Hume died before the Romantics discovered that problems are positively a good thing: so much more *fun* than solutions. What is not unrelated, he died before Immanuel Kant released on a grateful world a flood of 'how-is-so-and-so-possible' questions which left philosophy on the continent of Europe permanently waterlogged. Lucky David Hume!

Kant is always saying, with evident pride, that no one before him had ever so much as asked the questions which he asks. This is true, though whether it is a proper object of pride is another question. But that question, too, history has resoundingly answered in Kant's favour. His 'how-possible' questions have been object of universal admiration. Literally no one, as far as I know, has ever protested that these questions are unintelligible. Yet I find them so. When a philosopher asks '*Is* p possible?', or '*Is* p possible given q?', then (as I have said) I have no difficulty in understanding the questions, and neither does anyone else. The ones that beat me are when a philosoper aks '*How* is p possible?', or '*How* is p possible given q?' It is worse still when Kant asks, as he constantly does ask, 'how-is-so-and-so-possible' questions, in which the 'so-and-so' is not a proposition but a substantive noun. 'How is space possible?', 'How is cognition possible? – he just cannot stop asking these things. Undoubtedly Kant's greatest achievement in this vein, however, is the question 'How is Nature itself possible?'[18]

Nozick prefers those philosophical questions which 'make us tremble'.[19] Well, he should love this one: which of us will not tremble before so mortal a question as 'How is nature itself possible?' Kant has asked it, but will even he be able to answer it? If *he* cannot explain how nature is possible, there is little chance that anyone else will be able to do so. It may therefore even turn out that this is one of those cases in which the answer is 'No how', and that nature is *not* possible after all. Wretched luck for nature if so.

Kant's idea, of course, is that it is experience, and even (whatever he may say) human experience, that '*constitutes*' nature. If this is not madness, and more specifically the self-importance of the human species run mad, it will do until the real thing comes along. Kant had the 'how-is-so-and-so-possible' construction absolutely on the brain. It was his way of expressing, day in and day out, that 'wonder' in which philosophy really does begin: namely, *pretending* to wonder – that is, asking what appear to be questions but are not so. And the beauty of this Kantian tactic is that it is *always* available: you can ask 'How is p possible?' whatever p may be, and whatver the context. In this way you not only never have to stop talking, but can always be sure of sounding like an uncommonly deep thinker.

Kant has a good paragraph on pseudo-questions:

To know what questions may reasonably be asked is already a great and necessary proof of sagacity and insight. For if a question is absurd in itself and calls for an answer where none is required, it not only brings shame on the propounder of the question, but may betray an incautious listener into absurd answers, thus presenting, as the ancients said, the ludicrous spectacle of one man milking a he-goat and the other holding a sieve underneath.[20]

But no one ever needed this warning more, or heeded it less, than Kant himself. And then, what incomparable irony there is, given Kant's fame, in his saying that pseudo-questions bring shame on their propounders!

Nozick's appetite for incomprehensibility does not falter even at these non-propositional Kantian questions. Indeed, as we saw above, he even has some of his own invention: 'How is language possible?', and 'How is philosophy possible?' Nor will anyone suppose that the propounding of these questions has brought any shame on Nozick. Far from costing him any admirers, it almost certainly gained him some. And yet there is something a little mysterious in the distribution of fame and shame, because you or I could hardly add to our reputations by asking 'How are poached eggs possible?', or 'How is excruciating philosophical pretentiousness possible?', although it would take a sharp man to say why these questions are any worse than Nozick's.

Kant is not always as bad as his worst, and sometimes even his non-propositional 'how-possible' questions can at least be unpacked so as to yield a two-placed propositional question, 'How is p possible given q?' This is true of the central one, the famous question 'How are synthetic judgements *a priori* possible?' Kant believed that certain physical generalizations, such as that the quantity of matter always remains unchanged, are synthetic propositions, and yet are necessarily true and knowable *a priori*; and what he intended to ask was, for example, the question: 'How is it possible that 'the quantity of matter always remains unchanged' is necessarily true and knowable *a priori*, given that it is a synthetic proposition?'

That, then, is Kant's question; and *my* question is, as before, what did he mean, *how*? Without this word, that is, if his question had been instead, '*Is* it possible [etc., as above]?', then his question would have been perfectly intelligible. But as it is, what does it mean? Kant's questions are so strange and arresting that no one who has once heard them ever forgets them. It is just the reverse with his answers to them: no one can ever remember what these are! And there is a simple reason for this: the questions never get answered at all. Once they have served as an excuse for the darkening of a sufficient acreage of wood-pulp, they just get lost.

Kant's question was, 'How are synthetic judgements *a priori* possible?' And his answer, what was that? Well, it occupies a great many pages, but a sufficiently accurate summary of it is as follows: 'There is a certain process in the understanding, not of course an empirical process, and indeed not even a temporal one, which . . . or perhaps "structure" would be a better word than "process". Of course I don't mean a physical structure; still, it is an *actual* structure, not just a logical one, that I am talking about. Its name, by the way, is "the transcendental unity of apperception"; or else it is not that, but something else equally helpful. Well, this process, or structure, is very important, in fact experience would be impossible without it, because what it is, or at any rate what it does, is – well – it makes it possible for us to know, *a priori*, certain truths which are synthetic as well as necessary.'

In short, Kant's answer to 'How are synthetic judgements *a priori* possible?' is 'They *are* possible.' Now I cannot emphasize too strongly that this would have been a *perfectly* proper answer, if the question had been '*Are* synthetic judgements *a priori* possible?': a proper answer, not necessarily a true one. But the question was not whether, but *how*, such judgements are possible. And to this non-question, Kant returned a non-answer.

Even philosophers who are not otherwise easily imposed upon are apt to suffer the same mortifying fate, when once they allow themselves to ask Kantian questions. Take for example the question, without which the great 'problem of universals' could perhaps never even be propounded, and which is certainly, at any rate, the starting-point of David Armstrong's book *Universals and Scientific Realism*.[21] 'The same property can belong to different things. The same relation can relate different things. Apparently, there can be something identical in things which are not identical.

Things are one at the same time as they are many. How is this possible?'[22] 'How can two different things both be white or both be on a table?'[23]

That was Armstrong's Kantian question. His answer, almost a hundred pages later, is this: they can. 'We simply have to accept the fact that different particulars may have the same property or be related by the same relation.'[24] '[W]e must just stick with this proposition: different particulars may have the same property. Different particulars may be (wholly or partially) identical in nature. Such identity in nature is literally inexplicable, in the sense that it cannot be further explained.'[25] This is true, I think. But it is obviously no answer at all to the question which Armstrong had begun by asking.

In *Philosophical Explanations*, despite all the drum-beating for Kantian questions in the Introduction, Nozick does not in fact answer a single one of these questions. Indeed, once the Introduction is left behind, he largely forgets even to ask them. The 'how-possible' construction hardly occurs in the body of the book beyond half-way, and even before that occurs with low and ever-decreasing frequency. Where it does occur, it is evident that Nozick means nothing in particular by it. For example, the section entitled 'How are laws possible?'[26] could just as well have been called 'What is a law?', or 'How are laws related to their instances?', or just 'Laws'. What Nozick *really* likes, it is clear, about Kantian questions, and the ideal of explanation, is just that they make philosophers sound nicer: that is, '*gentler, softer, more considerate of others, respecters of their rights, and so forth*'.[27]

Is there in fact, in the entire history of philosophy, a single instance in which a Kantian question has been answered? I know of none. Yet in everyday life, in history, and in science, questions of the same form are constantly asked, are always intelligible, and are often answered. 'What can she possibly see in him?' 'How *can* he be poor? His family are an extremely clannish lot and have all been rich for generations.' Or, the question which was pressed on the early Copernicans: 'Given that the earth is in annual motion round the sun, how can it be that there is no detectable stellar parallax?'

In such cases it is clear enough what is meant by 'How is p possible given q?' It means the following, or something very like it: 'q is true and so is p, but p is very improbable in relation to q, and also in relation to q-and-r, for any r that I know. Now, is there some s which is true but not yet known to me, such that p is very probable in relation to q-and-s?' This is a perfectly intelligible question. And an answer, in the form of just such an s as is here enquired for, is often forthcoming. For example, the Copernicans' answer was: 'The stars are much too distant for their parallax to be detectable by our·telescopes.' In the case of 'How can he be poor?', the answer might be the following s: 'He is idle, spendthrift, and so generally vicious that even the most clannish family would draw the line at him.'

Why is it, then, that the 'how-possible' questions which *philosophers* ask are unintelligible and never answered? The conditions stated a moment ago perhaps supply the clue. Those conditions can be satisified only if p and s are both contingent; the reason being that only a contingent proposition can have a non-extreme probability, and that only contingent additional evidence can ever change a probability. Now philosophers not only have no expertise or interest which equips them better than other people to hit on true contingents s that probabilify other contingents p which are improbable in the absence of s; in fact the special expertise and interests which philosophers do have all direct them the opposite way, to the non-contingent. Consequently if *they* ask how p is possible, or how p is possible given q, the question stands a fair chance of being a fiasco, through the p not being contingent to begin with.

More specifically, there is *certain* to be a fiasco, *if p itself contains* (as with philosophers it is very likely to contain) *a reference to possibility or some other modality*. This is surely what happened in Kant's case. His question was: 'how is it possible that "the quantity of matter always remains unchanged" *is necessarily true and knowable a priori*, given that it is a synthetic proposition?' So that here Kant's p, in 'How is p possible given q?', was not 'The quantity of matter always remains unchanged', or any other proposition of that sort. It was an attribution of a certain modal status *to* that proposition. But whether or not a given proposition is itself contingent, the attribution to it of a particular modal status is never contingent. Here then is a condition, satisfied in all the cases (as far as I know) in which 'How is p possible given q?' is an intelligible question, which was not satisfied in Kant's case.

Something very similar happened, I believe, in the Armstrong case. The p, concerning which he asked how it is possible, itself contains an essential reference to possibility. His p was not (for example) that two different things are white. It was that two different things *can* be white. (I suppose it would have seemed too much like begging the question in favour of realism, to ask how it is possible that two different things *are* white; but whatever the reason was, it seems clear from the text that Armstrong's p *was* modalized.) Therefore when he asked, 'How is it possible that two different things can both be white?', he was asking how it is possible that it is possible that two different things are white.

Now who cannot see that, if that really was the question, then there were *bound* to be tears before bedtime? If that question is a proper one, and one which the realist is bound to answer, then so is the question, how it is possible that it is possible that it is possible that two different things are white; and so on, for ever. *Of course* there is no answering all those questions, or even the first of them. In the end the realist will just *have* to retire saying, sulkily, 'Well, it just *is* possible.' Quite right too, only it is not an answer to the question which he himself had asked: he should have contented himself with saying this from the start, rather than undertaking to answer a pseudo-question which he would only have to confess in the end is unanswerable. This mortification of the realist is entirely self-inflicted: he sets himself what he calls a problem, 'the problem of one over many', the 'problem', forsooth, of how it is possible that there could be two white things. Now you might call that possibility a 'problem' or a 'difficulty' *for the nominalist*, indeed, if you do not mind engaging in that abuse of language of which Hume justly complained. But for anyone else there is not the faintest trace of a problem in it.

In short, Armstrong's p, that it is possible that two different things are white, is either necessarily true, or necessarily false. And either way, a condition is violated which is satisfied in all cases (as far as I know) in which 'How is p possible given q?' is an intelligible question. In those cases, if an answer of the required kind is forthcoming, it is genuinely explanatory. That the stars are too distant for their parallax to be detected by early-seventeenth century telescopes is not only true, but a perfectly good explanation of the absence up to that time of detectable stellar parallax. If it is a fact, though otherwise improbable, that a certain man is poor, the explanation of it might well be that he is idle, spendthrift, and so generally vicious that even the most clannish family would draw the line at him.

Such explanations as these do not require any uncommon intellectual capacity. Yet what explanations has *philosophy* ever produced which might be set alongside even these modest achievements? What has philosophy ever explained? Nozick would have philosophy aim at nothing *but* explanation, yet the fact is that no intellectual discipline is less explanatory than philosophy. Philosophy has its great achievements, indeed: it is just that there are no explanations among them. How could there be? Explanation is by generalizations which you learn later, of particular facts or subordinate generalizations which you have learnt earlier. The particular facts from which a philosopher's education begins are that 'All men are mortal and Socrates is a man' entails 'Socrates is mortal'; that 'All the observed ravens have been black' does not entail 'All ravens are black'; that 'The sun rises in the east' entails 'If the sun rises in the east then the sun rises in the east', but not conversely; and so on. Yet the greatest philosopher in the world cannot *explain* a single one of these particular facts, any more than the beginner can. He will know in many cases, as the beginner will not, general truths of which such particular facts are instances; but in philosophy such general truths never *explain* their instances, or anything else.

Even if explanation were a possible ideal for philosophy, it is not in the least a non-coercive one. If there is one idea which may be called intrinsically coercive, it is the idea of truth; since what is true is independent of what anyone wants or believes. But now the idea of explanation, just like the idea of proof, is up to its eyebrows in the idea of truth. Just as p proves q only if p and q are both true, p explains q only if p and q are both true. (Nozick concedes this both on p. 21 and on p. 652, in a footnote to the Introduction; yet on p. 11 he had called a certain admittedly false proposition an explanation.) Nozick remains enmeshed, therefore, in spite of himself, in a coercive ideal of philosophy. Some other post-Vietnam American philosophers have been in this respect more thoroughgoing.

I have already quoted Nozick as saying, with evident indignation, 'A philosophical argument is an attempt to get someone to believe something, whether he wants to believe it or not.' Why, so it is. And so is a geometrical argument. So is a chemical argument, or a biological one. These old coercive disciplines too, then, must be put behind us. We must learn to see in Euclid one of the most frightful scourges of the human race, and bracket Mendeleev and Darwin with Stalin, Hitler, and (I suppose) Lyndon Johnson. The educational implications of this have no doubt much to do with the catastrophe which the Vietnam war brought on Western universities. But they are too appallingly stupid to be paused over here.

No ideal could be more destructive of human life than the ideal of non-coerciveness. A new-born human is so helpless, much more helpless even than the half-inch blob which is a new-born kangaroo, that it would never survive for one day if hands which are *both coercive and loving* did not guide it to the nipple which it would never find on its own. This was an observation of T. H. Huxley, in response to Rousseauite vapour about people being 'born free'.[28] Such biological common sense, and in particular some acquaintance with the work of Konad Lorenz, might have suggested to Nozick that he, and post-Vietnam America, had got things *exactly* the wrong way round: that in *Homo sapiens*, as in any species, close bonds between individuals are never formed *except* where the possibility of coercion is a known and standing element of the situation.

Of course, in the future, genetic engineering *may* work wonders on *H. sapiens*. But that is a trivial logical truth, and here is another one: it may not. Taking things as they actually stand, however, the only way of producing a non-coercive human being is to produce an autistic one, equally unable to care for itself or for anyone else. But then, autism is really the conclusion to which Nozick's conception of philosophy tends, just as it is the conclusion to which American foreign policy in the same period has tended. Autism is your only non-stop guaranteed-non-coercive fun. At least, it is, if 'fun' is the right word.

## Notes

1 Robert Nozick, *Philosophical Explanations* (Clarendon Press, Oxford, 1981).
2 Robert Nozick, *Anarchy, State, and Utopia* (Basil Blackwell, Oxford, 1974).
3 Nozick, *Philosophical Explanations*, p. 5.
4 Ibid., pp. 2, 474.
5 Ibid., p. 325.
6 Ibid., p. 628.
7 Ibid., p. 19.
8 Ibid., p. 474.
9 Ibid., p. 7.
10 Ibid., p. 24.
11 Ibid., p. 4.
12 Ibid., p. 4.
13 Ibid., pp. 5 (question), 13 (answer).
14 Ibid., pp. 8–9.
15 Ibid., p. 11.
16 K. R. Popper, *The Logic of Scientific Discovery* (Hutchinson, London, 1959), p. 196.
17 D. Hume, *A Treatise of Human Nature*, (1739; ed. L. A. Selby-Bigge, Oxford, Clarendon Press, 1888; re-ed. P. Nidditch, Oxford, Clarendon Press, 1978), bk I, pt II, sect. ii, p 31.
18 I. Kant, *Prolegomena to Any Future Metaphysics*, trans. and ed. P. Carus (Open Court, Chicago, 1902), p. 79.
19 Nozick, *Philosophical Explanations*, p. 1.
20 I. Kant, *Critique of Pure Reason*, trans. N. Kemp Smith (Macmillan, London, 1950), p. 97.
21 D. M. Armstrong, *Universals and Scientific Realism* (Cambridge University Press, 1978).
22 Ibid., p. 11.
23 Ibid., p. 12.
24 Ibid., p. 109.
25 Ibid., pp. 108–9.
26 Nozick, *Philosophical Explanations*, p. 143.
27 Ibid., p. 567.
28 T. H. Huxley, *Methods and Results* (Macmillan, London, 1898), p. 306.

# 4

## 'I only am escaped alone to tell thee': Epistemology and the Ishmael Effect

The narrator of *Moby Dick* introduces himself in the wonderful first sentence of that book: 'Call me Ishmael.' Melville named him, of course, after the biblical solitary, and by the end of the book he is solitary indeed. For by then everyone else who had been on board the *Pequod* has either drowned or been killed by the whale. But Ishmael clings to a floating coffin for almost one whole day and night, and at last is picked up by another ship. He quotes the Book of Job: 'I only am escaped alone to tell thee.'

But suppose a man told us that he had been one of those on board a certain ship, and that, in an encounter with a whale, *everyone* on board the ship had perished. Then his statment would suffer from a severe defect, of a peculiar kind, which I call (by a slight licence) the Ishmael effect: for if his statement were true, he could not have made it. It would be somewhat as if a man were to say to us in a bellow, 'I can't speak above a whisper'; or as if someone were to say, 'I don't know any words at all.'

In cases like those, the Ishmael effect could hardly escape detection, even by the stupidest person. Yet it often does go undetected. In newspaper advertisements, systems of betting on horse-races, guaranteed to make money for anyone who adheres to them, are always being offered for sale at a moderate price. It is therefore to be presumed that there are people silly enough to give some credence to such offers. Sensible people, however, decline to enter into the details of any offers of this kind, but reject all of them, out of hand, as fraudulent. They reason that if the advertisers did know of an infallible system for winning money on horse-races, they would not tell other people about it; but they do tell, *ergo*, etc.

Of course that is only a mild grade of the Ishmael effect. The severe grade, and the only one of philosophical importance, is that in which a statement is made which not only would not be made, but could not be made, if it were true. But even this grade of the Ishmael effect often escapes detection, where intelligence is depressed by strong wishes or by some other cause. The death of Moses is reported in one of the books of the Bible which Christians believed, for about 1500 years, to have been written by Moses. At *seances*, 'revenants' often report their own death. But let us draw a veil over these nether regions.

Closer to philosophy, a rich harvest of Ishmael effects is to be found in those marxizing sects which have suddenly swarmed in the last twenty years, like the plagues of Egypt, or like the gnosticizing sects of the early Christian era. These are the self-styled 'sociologists of knowledge', and the like. They are people who have so far succeeded in transcending the cognitive limitations of their own 'class-situation' as to be in a position to inform the rest of us that no one can ever transcend the cognitive limitations of his class-situation. They will tell you for a fact that there is no such thing as a fact. And so on. Some of these writers are conscious, of course, of the Ishmael effect which fatally dogs their statements, and they bravely try to smile it through. But the only result is what Tom Wolfe called, in another context, 'shit-eating grins'. Again, both for pity and for shame, let us look elsewhere.

Yet that kind of thing does have some affinity with philosophy. For it belongs, and some philosophy belongs too, to the class of what might be called veil-doctrines. I mean, doctrines to the effect that a certain impenetrable veil cuts us off from knowledge of the actual universe; or that we are prevented by some insuperable obstacle from climbing to the one vantage-point from which the cosmos can be seen rightly. Veil-doctrines, since they say what is on the other side, or at least that there is another side, of a veil which they also say no human mind can penetrate, are all mortally afflicted with the Ishmael effect. (At least, they are so, except in a certain degenerate case to be mentioned in a moment).

Outside philosophy, this veil or obstacle is apt to be identified with our *having a body* (as in gnosticism), or with our *having a 'class-situation'* (as in Marxism), or with something else equally anticlimactic. In philosophy the veil is conceived of more intelligently than that, at least. Indeed, it is not always obvious, in philosophy, when one *is* dealing with a veil-doctrine. More generally, it is not always obvious when a philosopher's statements are afflicted with the Ishmael effect. My object in this essay is to point out that effect in some central places in philosophy, where previously it has been only half-detected, or at least has never had a suitably strong and steady light thrown upon it.

Veil-doctrines stagger and humiliate the human mind. For that reason, they are apt to be ascribed, where they are embraced by the vulgar, to a *divine* author. Among the learned, for the same reason, they appeal especially to persons who are strongly disposed to self-abasement. That is why 'sociology of knowledge' and the like made its appeal to Western intellectuals after, not before, the defeat of America in Vietnam.

There is this much to be said for ascribing a veil-doctrine to a divine author: that if it did come from God, it would at least not suffer from the Ishmael effect. There would be a peculiar kind of pointlessness, indeed, in God's announcing to mankind the total cognitive depravity of mankind: since if his announcement were true, we could not believe it. This would be a case of what I call the *inverse*-Ishmael effect. (Somewhat similarly, the devil in certain medieval plays advises the audience not to take his advice.) But at any rate there would be no Ishmael effect. If God said to us, 'No human being is capable of believing anything true', he would not be exposed to the same fatal question as any human being would be who told us the same thing: how he alone had escaped this general doom, sufficiently to allow him to tell the rest of us of it.

In philosophy, Kant's metaphysics is a well known example of a veil-doctrine, or at least of the Ishmael effect. Kant brings us news, not much, admittedly, but still some news, of another world, which he says is inaccessible to the human mind: the world of noumena. Well! This news might have been credible (as I have just implied) if the bringer of it had been more than human; otherwise not. But Kant was in fact only an eighteenth-century German professor. Moreover, this fact was extremely well known even at the time. The Ishmael effect which plagued his doctrine was therefore so conspicuous as to arouse, from the very first, a good deal of vulgar, though alas only too well founded, derision. Equally inevitably, this derision raised up in its despite a new interpretation of Kant, according to which he had never been guilty, in all his life, of knowing anything about noumena. No doubt there is much to be said for both views.

A similar example, and of course a related one, is the representative theory of perception. This theory has been generally recognized as a victim of the Ishmael effect, at least since Berkeley criticized Locke's version of it. At Berkeley's hands, Locke is like a man apprehended by the police in possession of a large sum of money which he cannot innocently account for his having. Locke is in possession of a large fund of information about external objects, which information he cannot account for his having, consistently with his own theory of perception.

At least, that was the accepted criticism for more than 200 years. Recently, however, some good philosophers have defended the Representative theory against this long-standing reproach. They say that that theory only does what many a respectable scientific theory does: it postulates some unobservable entities, in order to explain certain observable phenomena. On this interpretation, the Representative theory might even be the *best* scientific theory for the job of explaining the phenomena of perception. It actually is so, according to one of these philosophers: Frank Jackson, in his book *Perception*.[1]

Michael Devitt's book *Realism and Truth*[2] is conceived in exactly the same spirit. 'Realism' means here, of course, not realism about universals, and not even realism about perception, but realism about the external world; and according to Devitt, the existence of an external world is 'an *inductive hypothesis*'. That is a phrase, all the better for its aggressively old-fashioned air, which Devitt takes from the most eloquent defender which this point of view has ever had: the late D. C. Williams. The conception of realism as a scientific theory was defended by Williams[3] against idealists of every shade; against the philosophers who think that the existence of an external world is a necessary truth; against the philosophers who think it is just a pragmatically unavoidable belief; and against all the philistines, lay or sophisticated, who repudiate the whole question of the existence of an external world as just too silly for words. These opponents, however, clearly add up to a majority, and the Williams-Devitt position is heterodox in the same way as Jackson's is: namely, an unpopular philosophical theory is embraced as being the best available *scientific* theory.

I like this recent tendency in philosophy. First, because it is realistic: anything else has about it a sickening smell, which no power on earth can disguise, of insincerity or insanity. Second, because it enables realism to be defended in the same way as a scientific theory can be defended: that is, soberly and modestly. If you are a realist, but think that realism is not a scientific theory, any defence you make of it is bound to be, by comparison, frivolous or dogmatic, and is almost certain to be both. For these two reasons, this whole movement of thought has a wholesome smell about it, and I believe it is no accident that Australian philosophers are prominent in it.

But I cannot agree with it. I cannot bring myself to believe that realism about the external world is a scientific theory. I doubt that 'An external word exists' is even a contingent statement, let alone a scientific one. Of course I too yearn for the respectability of science; only I am persuaded that philosophy can never achieve it. There is something radically wrong with even the best epistemology, and it can never be 'naturalized'. Once you have asked 'Is there an external world?', or 'What reason have we to believe an external world exists?', or 'Could it be that there is nothing at all except my experiences?': once you have allowed yourself to ask such questions as these, I say, irreversible damage has been done, whichever way you answer them. There is already something dreadfully wrong with what you say, whether you say realist or anti-realist things. Far better to say realist than anti-realist things; but in that you say anything at all on these questions, you are already one of the damned.

This essay is a defence of the necessity of realism. Better put, it is a defence of the inevitability of realism; though, as will emerge, I am far from thinking that this inevitability is only pragmatic. I hope to show, first, that denial, or even doubt, of the existence of an external world, is a helpless victim of the Ishmael effect. (There is nothing essentially new in this idea; but it has never been pressed home hard enough for its full force to be felt.) Second, I will try to show that 'An external world exists' is not a scientific theory or even an inductive hypothesis, and, almost certainly, is not even a contingent statement.

This sort of defence of realism, as I have already implied, can hardly avoid being both frivolous and dogmatic. Even so, my defence of the inevitability of realism can scarcely be worse than the defences of it which have been made by some men of genius. Wittgenstein did it by arguments which are so subtle that the non-elect can never even grasp what they are, and which, by a natural consequence, defeat their own purpose. Hume tried to do it not subtly, but rather by brute force, as follows. 'We may well ask, *What causes induce us to believe in the existence of body?*, but 'tis in vain to ask, *whether there be body or not?* That is a point which we must take for granted in all our reasonings.'[4]

This passage has been much admired by Kemp Smithian and Wittgensteinian commentators on Hume. But it is tripe for all that. It is just obviously false that we must take the existence of 'body' for granted in all our *mathematical* reasonings, for example; or in all our cosmological, or in all our theological reasonings. And if Berkeley, for example, in his reasonings intended to show that there is no matter, took for granted that there is, why did Hume not just point out a *contradiction* in Berkeley's philosophy? That would have been the honourable, as well as the easy and sufficient, thing to do. In fact, of course, as every philosopher knows, there is *no* contradiction in Berkeley's philosophy, and Hume was just bluffing. Identifiable contradictions are vanishingly rare in philosophy, and are something of a badge of honour when they do occur. What is really wrong with Berkeley's philosophy, and what is wrong with most philosophy, are things which are at once more trivial, and more disgraceful, than contradictions.

If Ishmael says that no one from the *Pequod* survived, his statement is fatally afflicted with the Ishmael effect. But the effect would evidently be very little different if, instead of making that statement, Ishmael were to ask the question, 'Did anyone from the *Pequod* survive?' For he could not ask this question, any more than he could make that statement, unless someone from the *Pequod* had survived. So there are Ishmael-questions, as well as Ishmael-statements. An Ishmael-question is one which the questioner could not ask unless the answer to it were a certain way, 'yes' or 'no'. Ordinary yes-no questions are, of course, not like that: they can perfectly well be asked, whichever way the answer to them is. 'Is today the 5th?' can be asked whether today is the 5th or not; 'Was Napoleon short?' can be asked whether the answer to it is 'yes' or 'no'; and so on.

Whether a statement is an Ishmael-statement depends, in some cases, on who makes it. That no one from the *Pequod* survived, is an Ishmael-statement if Ishmael makes it; made by someone else, it obviously need not be so. But there are other statements which would be Ishmael-statements whoever they were made by. For example, 'No one can ever make a statement.'

It is just the same with Ishmael-questions. 'Did anyone from the *Pequod* survive?' is an Ishmael-question if it is asked by Ishmael; asked by someone else, it need not be so. But there are other questions which would be Ishmael-questions whoever asked them. For example, 'Do I know any words?'; or 'Can a human being ever ask a question?' (At least, the latter would always be an Ishmael-question if it were asked by a human being).

If Ishmael says *to himself* that no one from the *Pequod* survived, then that is an Ishmael-statement, just as much as if he says it to someone else. For it is still true in that case that he could not have said this if it were true. And if Ishmael asks himself, 'Did anyone from the *Pequod* survive?', that is an Ishmael-question, just as much as if he asks it of someone else. For it is still true in that case that he could not have asked this question unless someone from the *Pequod* had survived. Similarly, 'No one can ever make a statement' is evidently an Ishmael-statement, not only whoever makes it, but even if one says it only to oneself. Again, 'Can a human being ever ask a question?' is evidently an Ishmael-question, not only whoever asks it, but even if someone asks it only in the privacy of his own thoughts.

It would be quite wrong, then, to think that the Ishmael effect can occur only where there is *public utterance*: only where a statement is made to, or a question is asked of, someone else. In some cases, the effect *does* depend on public utterance. It does so in the mild case of the advertisements for betting-systems, and in the severe case of a man bellowing that he can't speak above a whisper. But the Ishmael effect does *not* in general depend on public, or on any, utterance. We have just seen this, in the case

of Ishmael saying to himself that no one from the *Pequod* survived, or asking himself whether anyone did. And the effect does
not depend on utterance, either, in the philosophically important
case with which I am concerned: the case of the question, 'Does
an external world exist?' This is an Ishmael-question, we will
find, not only whoever asks it, but even if someone asks it only
inwardly.

Ishmael could not ask whether anyone from the *Pequod* survived unless the answer to this question were 'yes'. But not only
must the answer to it *be* 'yes': Ishmael must *know* that the answer
is 'yes', unless he is suffering from loss of memory, or some other
severe mental defect. If his mind is not thus impaired, his question
can only be an insincere one, in the sense that it is not really
intended to elicit the information which it appears intended to
elicit. The same holds for most, perhaps all, Ishmael-questions.
Certainly no one could sincerely ask, for example, 'Do I know
any words?', or 'Can a human being ever ask a question?', unless
something were seriously wrong with his mind.

I say that this holds for *perhaps* all Ishmael-questions, because
I think that there could be Ishmael-questions so long and complicated that it could easily happen to a normal human being that
he should ask them without realizing that he already knew the
answer. But even if there are such cases, they are of no importance
for my purposes. For they do not include the *philosophically*
interesting cases, which are all of them very short and simple
questions. They are questions like 'Is there an external world?',
or 'Does anything exist except myself?' Questions like *these*,
beyond any doubt, can only be asked either insincerely, or by
someone seriously disordered in his mind.

Both of those possibilities are painfully real. Mental disorder
is interwoven very intimately, and on a large scale, with the history
of philosophy, and especially with the history of phenomenalist or
solipsist epistemology. We have generally managed to keep this
fact dark, even from ourselves. Only a stunning recent article by
Hiram Caton[5] has begun to let the air into this matter. But
affectation or insincerity, especially in the form of pretending not
to know the answers to questions when in fact one does know
the answers to them perfectly well, is a failing even more characteristic of our profession. This, indeed, unlike our propensity to

insanity, is notorious. In fact insincerity of this sort is often used by the public as a test, and really is quite a good test, of whether a given person *is* a philosopher or not. That philosophy begins in wonder is a stupid remark which has been repeated for 2500 years, although anyone might easily have observed at any time that philosophers are often the most incurious of men. No, philosophy typically begins in *pseudo*-wonder, expressed by asking 'questions' which are really no questions at all.

Here is another example of an Ishmael-question: 'Is there at least one human being?' At least, this is always an Ishmael-question if it is asked by a human being. Asked by an ignorant minor deity, or by a Martian, or by a talking horse, it obviously need not be so. Nor is it necessary, in order for this to be an Ishmael-question, that it be asked *of* a human being. It might be asked of a God or a Martian, of another human being, or of oneself, but as long as it is asked *by* a human being, it is an Ishmael-question. For in that case the questioner could not ask the question unless the answer to it were 'yes'. And, as is usual with such questions, this one could not be asked by a human being unless he were either insincere or disordered in his mind.

The question whether at least one human being exists is, then, an Ishmael-question, at least if it is asked by a human being. And I venture to affirm (in defiance of all Plato-worshippers and the like) that at any rate up till now, all philosophers have been human beings. It follows that this question is an Ishmael-question if it is asked by any philosopher, past or present. Not, of course, because it is a necessary truth that at least one human being exists: on the contrary, the statement, 'At least one human being exists', is evidently contingent. But it *is* necessary that at least one human being exists, in the sense that, unless this statement *were* true, none of *us* could so much as ask ourselves, or others, whether it is true.

This example probably appears pointless, because in fact no philosopher ever has asked, 'Is there at least one human being?' Still, many philosophers have asked, and have dwelt at length on, a question which must be, on any metric, a very close neighbour of that one: namely, 'Are there at least two human beings?' This question was surely a large part, at least, of what was at stake in those thousands of pages which we have all read, headed 'Self and Others', 'Our Knowledge of Other Minds', and the like. The Ishmael-question, whether at least one human being exists, is thus a very close neighbour of a very close neighbour of those staple philosophical topics. So, by the short-transitivity of 'very close neighbour of', it probably is a question of philosophical importance after all.

And indeed it is. For when we have shown, as I have now easily shown, that it is an Ishmael-question whether at least one human being exists, then we have shown the same thing concerning that great question which has so much exercised philosophers' minds: whether an external world exists. But why this is so, needs a little explaining.

'Realism', as I am using the word, is just the statement that an external world exists. Now some philosophers keep the name 'realism' for a statement which says more than that. Michael Devitt is one who does so.[6] Frank Jackson, I think it is clear, is another. For he writes, admittedly not about realism as such, but about the realistic component in his own representative-realism, as follows: it 'is *not* that there is a square table in that room, a red tomato on that mantelpiece, and so on; it is not, that is, a set of *particular* hypotheses. It is, rather, a *general* hypothesis to the effect that there are external objects existing independently of us whose properties bear a systematic relationship to those of our sense-data.'[7]

I do not think that Jackson can possibly have meant that realism, in this strong sense of his, or even realism in my weak sense, is logically *independent* of all 'particular hypotheses'. Because at that rate someone could deny the existence of an external world, say, without having to give up any of the particular hypotheses, about tomatoes and so on, which the rest of us believe. For example, a would-be solipsist could say: 'Oh, there's a tomato on that mantelpiece all right, also a table in the next room, and there is all the rest of the cosmos too, but now the question to be decided is whether an external world exists.' But that is just nonsense.

I take it Jackson only meant that it is not logically *necessary*, for realism to be true, that a particular tomato or table should exist. And this is perfectly true, not only for realism in his strong sense, but for realism in my weak sense. Indeed, even for realism in my sense, it is not even logically necessary that there be any tomatoes or tables at all. If there are no ghosts, but only hallucinations of or false beliefs in ghosts, it does not follow that there is no external world; and likewise, it does not follow that there is no external world, if there are in fact no tomatoes or tables, but only hallucinations of or false beliefs in them. An external world could perfectly well exist without being so varied or so big as we think it is: it does not have to contain tomatoes *and* tables *and* cabbages *and* kings. It is not even necessary that it contain even one tomato or table or cabbage or king.

But though the existence of a particular tomato or table, or of any tomato or table, is not logically necessary for, still it *is* logically *sufficient* for the existence of an external world. If there *is* a tomato on that mantelpiece and a table in the next room, then for sure (and Jackson no doubt would agree) an external world exists all right; and similarly if there is a tomato or table at all. So, then, while the falsity of 'An external world exists' does not follow from 'There is no cabbage or king', the truth of 'An external world exists' does follow from 'There is at least one cabbage or king.' A commoner would do as well as a king, of course, for this purpose. In fact any human being would do.

That is to say: 'An external world exists' follows from 'At least one human being exists', just as it follows from, say, 'At least one cabbage exists.' Now, necessarily, no human being could ask, even inwardly, whether an external world exists, unless at least one human being exists. And necessarily, if at least one human being exists then an external world exists. Therefore, necessarily, no human being could ask whether an external world exists, unless an external world does exist. The question whether an external world exists is therefore an Ishmael-question, and of the severest grade. It is *logically* impossible that a human being should ask this question, even inwardly, without the answer to it being 'yes'. Not only must the answer to it be 'yes': anyone not under some terrible mental infirmity must know that the answer to it is 'yes'. If a person's mind is unimpaired, and he asks whether an external world exists, his question can only be insincere, in the sense that it is not really intended to elicit the information which it appears intended to elicit.

The question of the existence of an external world is, then, an

Ishmael-question. This was the first thing I set out to show. It is also a pseudo-question, I mean an insincere one, if it does not stem from some serious mental defect. And I venture to think that, with the help of the idea of the Ishmael effect, I have actually explained two things. One is, exactly what that 'self-refutingness' is which philosophers have often detected in denials or doubts of the existence of an external world. The other is, the odour of insincerity or insanity which is inseparable from such denials and doubts.

Since 'An external world exists' follows from 'At least one cabbage exists', it follows *a fortiori* from the observation-statement, 'There is a cabbage on that table.' Indeed, it follows from every, or just about every, observation-statement. But no scientific theory, and not even any 'inductive hypothesis', follows from any observation-statement. Still less does any scientific theory, or even any inductive hypothesis, follow from every, or just about every, observation-statement. So 'An external world exists' is not a scientific theory, or even an inductive hypothesis.

Of course it does not follow that realism is not a contingent statement. It is only the most brutal perverters of language in our profession who call *every* contingent statement 'a theory', or 'a scientific theory'. Nor does it follow that 'An external world exists' is not contingent, from the fact that it is an Ishmael-question whether an external world exists. For as we saw earlier, it is an Ishmael-question whether at least one human being exists, although the statement, 'At least one human being exists', is perfectly contingent.

What reason is there, then, for thinking that realism is not contingent? This reason: that it seems to have no contingent contrary, whereas almost any contingent statement has a virtual infinity of contingent contraries. If p is contingent, then for every contingent q which is logically independent of p, the conjunction of q with not-p is a contingent contrary of p. That is an illustration of just how easy it is, as a general rule, to form contingent contraries of a contingent statement. But 'An external world exists' seems to have no contingent contrary whatever. In other words, there seems to be no alternative to it which is possible.

But a statement is a *necessary* truth, if there is no possible alternative to it.

Idealism of the kind which is called objective is no alternative to realism. Objective idealism says, 'An external world exists, and is of a mental or spiritual constitution.' This conjunction might be contingent, if its second conjunct makes sense; as perhaps it does, although the conception of a spiritually constituted cabbage is one which not all of us can rise to. But contingent or not, this conjunction is not a contrary of realism, since its first conjunct *is* realism.

In fact it is only *solipsism* which seems to offer any possible alternative to realism. Solipsism certainly denies the existence of an external world. The only question is, therefore, whether solipsism is logically possible. Presumably most philosophers think it is, since solipsism is a permanent item on their agenda. And certainly many philosophers have *said* that solipsism is logically possible. Yet you will be inclined to the opposite conclusion, if you examine the versions of solipsism which they actually produce. For these always turn out, at least in my experience, to be either necessarily false, or else not expressions of solipsism at all. In particular, they all seem to be utterly defeated, one way or another, by what I call the pronoun-problem.

All of us have noticed something of this problem, as far as one pronoun goes: 'others'. We have all laughed at Bertrand Russell's story, that he 'once received a letter from an eminent logician, Mrs Christine Ladd Franklin, saying that she was a solipsist, and was surprised that there were no others'. Russell's next sentence is, 'Coming from a logician, this surprise suprised me.'[8]

Mrs Franklin's folly certainly deserved to be laughed at; and yet the fault has not been all on her side. For we tend to think, as Russell's comment makes clear that he thought, that her folly lay only or mainly in her being *surprised*; but it did not. Suppose that Mrs Franklin had instead said to Russell that she was a solipsist and was therefore *not* surprised at the non-existence of other solipsists, or of non-solipsists either. Then her logic would have been better, but her folly would have been no less. For that lay in her saying in the first place, to Russell or anyone else, that she was a solipsist. And the folly in *that* lies, of course, in its inverse-Ishmael effect. She tells another person something which entails that they don't exist. She therefore tells them something which, if it were true, could not possibly be believed by them.

But was Russell surprised by Mrs Franklin's telling him she was a solipsist? Oh no! *That* he would have thought unworthy of a philosopher. In philosophy in our century, the governing principle is, 'It's an outrageous proposal but we'll certainly consider it'. And part of the heavy price we pay is this: that we become so 'callused by doing philosophy' that we hardly even notice a thing like the Ishmael effect, or else we easily excuse it, unless it has, as it happened to have in this case, an additional spice of illogicality laid on top of it.

Russell's calluses were thicker than most. Some people may have been entitled to make fun of Mrs Franklin, but he was not. If she deserved to be laughed at over the pronoun 'others', what did he deserve, for some of his uses of the pronoun 'we' in the following passages?

> In this chapter we have to ask ourselves whether, in any sense at all, there is such a thing as matter. Is there a table which has a certain intrinsic nature, and continues to exist when I am not looking, or is the table merely a product of my imagination, a dream-table in a very prolonged dream? This question is of the greatest importance. For if we cannot be sure of the independent existence of objects, we cannot be sure of the independent existence of other people's bodies, and therefore still less of other people's minds, since we have no grounds for believing in their minds except such as are derived from observing their bodies. Thus if we cannot be sure of the independent existence of objects, *we shall be left alone in a desert* – it may be that the whole outer world is nothing but a dream, and that *we alone exist*. This is an uncomfortable possibility; but although it cannot be strictly *proved* to be false, there is not the slightest reason to suppose that it is true. In this chapter we have to see why this is the case.
>
> . . .
>
> There is no logical impossibility in the supposition that the whole of life is a dream, in which *we ourselves create all the objects that come before us.*[9]

'*We alone* exist', and '*we* shall be left *alone in a desert*': *this* is solipsism, according to Russell, and solipsism is said here to be logically possible! You are not supposed to laugh at Russell, or at his use of English, yet these desert solitaries of his would have to belong to the same breed as the cowboys in the old Stephen Leacock story. A small valley is empty of human life until, at dawn one day, a solitary cowboy rides over the ridge and makes his camp in the valley. An hour later another solitary cowboy does the same. This goes on all day. By nightfall the valley is full of solitary cowboys.

To be brief: the pronoun 'we' means 'each of us'. Therefore 'We alone exist' means 'Each of us is the only thing that exists.' Now that is *not* logically possible. And I am surprised that this 'eminent logician' said it is: or to be truthful, I am not surprised.

Dreams are not now so popular with philosophers as they were in 1912, when Russell first published what I have just quoted. But hallucinations are more than ever the rage. Many philosophers now seem to think that solipsism is logically possible, and that the question whether it is true is the question whether 'we are not always hallucinating'. I take this phrase from Frank Jackson[10], and he certainly appears, from chapter 6 of his book, to be one of these philosophers.

Well, it is true, and also contingent, that some of us sometimes hallucinate. But it does not follow from that, (even if Descartes thought it did), that it is logically possible that all of us are always hallucinating. Some children in a school-class may happen to be below the average level of ability of children in that class, but it is not logically possible that all of them are. Neither is it logically possible that *we* are all always hallucinating. For we – that is, all human beings – are perceived by (unless indeed we are hallucinations of) at least one human being: ourselves if no other. Whence, on the supposition that we – that is, all human beings – are *always* hallucinating, it follows that all human beings are hallucinations of at least one human being. And that is not logically possible.

'We alone exist', then, and 'We are always hallucinating', are both necessarily false. Of course it does not follow that *every* version of solipsism which contains a plural personal pronoun is necessarily false. Still, that is the conclusion which common sense strongly suggests, and in what follows I will take it for granted. A version of solipsism which is contingent, therefore, will contain either no personal pronoun, or only singular ones. You might think it need not contain any pronoun at all, but you would be wrong. Solipsism denies the existence of an external world, and here, of course, 'external' means 'external *to us*', or else it means 'external *to me*'. Indeed, as every philosopher knows, it is only by a bit of professional shorthand that we ever leave the pronoun out. But as we have just seen, the solipsist had better *not* mean, by 'external', 'external to us'. In a contingent solipsism, then, the pronoun must be singular.

The same goes for the word 'independent', and all its family. No one is contending for or against a world which is 'external' *sans phrase*, and neither is anyone contending for or against a world which 'exists independently' *sans phrase*. All parties to these disputes understand that 'existing independently' is here just short for 'existing independently of us' or else for 'existing independently of myself'. And again, it will need to be the latter that it is short for, if solipsism is ever to achieve a contingent expression.

Nothing is to be gained by taking a refuge in the pseudo-singular pronoun, 'one'. I would have thought this too obvious to need saying, yet some philosophers, anxious to leave open the logical possibility of solipsism, but uneasily aware of its pronoun-problem, have actually had recourse to titles like 'One's Knowledge of the External World'. Was there ever a more pitiful device? Intended to elude the pronoun-problem, it only succeeds in drawing attention to it. As a pronoun, 'one' is of course not really singular at all, but plural: 'one's knowledge of the external world' means 'our knowledge of the external world', and so on. It will therefore not appear in a contingent version of solipsism.

There is a second kind of pseudo-singular personal pronoun which a contingent solipsism wil need to avoid. I do not think grammarians know of this one, so I will christen it myself: it is the first-or-second-person singular-*philosophical*. Examples: 'Why should I be moral?'; 'Do I have privileged access to myself?'; 'What reason have you to expect the future to be like the past?' Every philosopher understands that these pronouns are not the genuine 'you' or 'I' of conversation or biography. It is only your dentist, or someone like that, who mistakes the question, 'What reason have you to expect the future to be like the past?', for an invitation to launch into the story of his life. In fact, of course, these philosophical pronouns are really plurals: this kind of 'I' or 'you' means 'we' or 'one'. Among philosophers, and in most contexts, this device is perfectly harmless. But it would evidently be fatal to allow it into a version of solipsism, where plurals breed necessary falsity. (Philosophers have presumably been misled into their absurd plural versions of solipsism, such as Russell's 'We alone exist', by precisely this pseudo-singular 'I'.)

Descartes, of course, pretended that his philosopical 'I', 'me', and so on, *were* the genuine autobiographical article. This was a degree of affectation uncommon even by the standards of our profession. You or I might perhaps be excused if we sometimes toyed with solipsism, especially when we reflect on the utter failure of our writings to produce the smallest effect in the alleged external world. But René Descartes, knowing that Mersenne is at his door, poised to launch a campaign of saturation-advertising, and knowing, therefore, that what he writes will be read, almost before the ink is dry, by every single person of learning in Europe – *this* man writes that perhaps he alone exists, and pretends he means it! This spectacle is as contemptible as it is ridiculous, to my mind, and like Mrs Franklin in another case, I am surprised that no others seem to be of the same opinion.

If there is to be a contingent version of solipsism, then, the pronoun in it must be the genuine first-person singular article. The statement must be 'Only *I* exist', or 'Nothing exists except *myself.*'

With 'plural solipsism' the trouble, as we saw, is necessary falsity. 'We alone exist' says so much that it cannot possibly be true. With 'singular solipsism', as we now have it, the trouble, we will soon see, is of an opposite kind. it says so little that, whether it is contingent or not, it is not solipsism.

What must a statement affirm or deny in order to be solipsism? Well, it must at least deny the existence of something which non-solipsists believe in the existence of: it must express, I shall say, 'a *reduced* ontology'. This much is obvious. Otherwise there need not be any disagreement, as of course there must be, between the solipsist and non-solipsists, as to what exists, or how much. Of course solipsism must not *say* anything about non-solipsists or their beliefs. But if a given statement does not deny the existence of something which non-solipsists *in fact* believe in the existence of, then it is not solipsism, whatever else it may be.

But now, the statement 'Nothing exists except myself' does not satisfy this necessary condition of solipsism. It does not express a reduced ontology. In fact it does not deny the existence of anything at all. That probably sounds badly wrong. Yet I think I can convince you of it.

It sounds wrong, because the very *form* of the statement, 'Nothing exists except . . . ', appears at first to guarantee that the existence of *something* would be denied, however the gap were to be filled. *Every* instance of that schema, it seems, first denies the existence of something, and then asserts the existence of something, namely the exception that it goes on to refer to.

It is not so, though. Some instances of this schema do indeed deny the existence of something; and some of them deny the existence not only of something, but of much, that non-solipsists believe in the existence of. For example, 'Nothing exists except Christine Ladd Franklin.' That expresses a reduced ontology all right, and *a fortiori* denies the existence of something. But other instances of the schema do not. For example 'Nothing exists except the cosmos', or 'Nothing exists except everything that does exist.' This statement does not deny the existence of anything. Or, if a counter-example is wanted in which the exception referred to is a little less cosmic: 'Nothing exists except the cosmos *as it will be described by science in the year 2000.*' This statement does not deny the existence of anything. For example, it does not even deny the existence of witches. It says that there are no witches *if* there are no witches in the scientific cosmology of the year 2000; but that is as close as it comes to denying the existence of witches.

These counter-examples are, admittedly, statements of extremely low information-content. Still, they are not degenerate, that is, tautological instances of the schema 'Nothing exists except . . . '. For they all at least entail the statement, 'Something exists.' Yet they do not deny the existence of anything. They therefore suffice to show that there are (non-degenerate) instances of 'Nothing exists except . . .' which do not deny existence. They also serve to remind us, more generally, that the information-content of an instance of this schema – how much, if anything, it asserts the existence of, and how much, if anything, it denies the existence of – depends *entirely* on what, and how big, the exception is which it goes on to refer to. Well, of course: that should have been obvious! Yet it was not obvious. For our first thought was the contrary one, that the schema *itself* guarantees that any instance of it will deny the existence of something.

Here is another counter-example to that thought: 'Nothing exists except this.' On the side of assertion of existence, the information-content is again nearly zero here; though again not quite, because even this statement entails 'Something exists.' But on the side of denial of existence, the information-content is again absolute zero. This statement does not deny the existence of anything.

What prevents 'Nothing exists except this' from containing any but trivial information is, of course, the fact that it does nothing to identify the exception it refers to: it says nothing as to what, or how big, that exception is. This failure is due, in turn, to the fact that there is no limit to what a pronoun like 'this' can be used to refer to. The statement 'Nothing exists except this' might be made by someone (perhaps Mrs Franklin) pointing to Mrs Franklin. But it *might* be made by someone gesturing at the entire cosmos. (That gesture is one which philosophers, at least, are rather often reduced to making.) Or the 'this' might be being used, again, to refer to something less than the cosmos, but more than Mrs Franklin. If the maker of the statement was pointing to Mrs Franklin, the statement was intended to express a reduced ontology. If the maker of the statement was gesturing at everything that exists, then the statement was not intended to express a reduced ontology. But neither of those intentions, nor any other specific intention, and in particular no intention to deny existence, actually finds expression in the statement 'Nothing exists except this.'

The case is no different if we substitute for 'this' another 'indexical' pronoun, 'myself'. What prevents 'Nothing exists except myself' from containing any but trivial information is, of course, that it says nothing as to what, or how big, the exception is to which it refers. This failure is due, in turn, to the fact that there is no limit to what a pronoun like 'myself' can be used to refer to. The information-deficiency in this case is exactly the homely one which would meet us in a telephone message which just said, 'This message is from no one except myself.' The 'myself' in this message, or in 'Nothing exists except myself', may of course be Mrs Franklin. But it *may* be a talking horse; or one of those extra-terrestrials whose conversation NASA is always trying to attract; or the World-Soul; or God; or the entire cosmos. If the maker of the statement was Mrs Franklin, the statement was intended to express a reduced ontology. If the maker of it was everything that exists, then the statement was not intended to express a reduced ontology. But neither of those intentions, nor any other specific intention, and in particular no intention to deny existence, actually finds expression in the statement itself. So 'Nothing exists except myself' does not deny the existence of anything. So it does not express a reduced ontology. So it is not solipsism.

Scientists may one day arrive at the fundamental individuals, whatever they are – particles, or space-time singularities, or sub-spatio-temporal monads – which make up the cosmos. They may then find that each of these encodes in some way or other a certain message. If scientists crack the codes, they may find that every single fundamental particle (or whatever) carries the following message: 'Nothing exists except me, God or Nature, with all my infinite attributes and all their individual modes, exactly as described by my favourite author-mode, B. Spinoza.' This, then, is a possible message from the cosmos. But though the statement begins with 'Nothing exists except me', there is evidently nothing in the least solipsistic about it. If anything, it goes further in ontology than most of us non-solipsists do. At any rate, it certainly does not go less far.

'Nothing exists except myself' differs in no important respect from a message which just says, 'Nothing exists except the source of this message.' Neither of these statements is solipsism, because neither of them denies the existence of anything. In order to become solipsistic, they must be supplemented by some 'station-identification', as they say in radio. Some identification must be made of the exception, that is, of the source of the message, that is, of 'myself'; and this identification must be such as to exclude the possibility that the source of the message is in fact the entire cosmos.

Supplemented in that way, these statements may become solipsistic. But then they will also become, at the very same moment, necessarily false. For they will then become: 'Nothing exists except the source of this message, which is not everything that exists'; and 'Nothing exists except myself, and I am something less than everything that exists.' And these statements are plainly self-contradictory.

Of course I have not *proved* that there is no contingent version of solipsism; though I think I have given some reason to believe this. Nor did I prove that solipsism is the only possibly-contingent contrary of realism. Even if both of those things were proved, it would still not be proved that realism is not itself contingent. For perhaps there can be a contingent statement which has *no* contingent contrary. 'Something exists' may be an example of that.

This statement, 'Something exists', if it is indeed contingent, furnishes a reason for thinking that I am wrong, and that realism is contingent after all. For 'An external world exists' entails 'Something exists'; contingents are entailed only by contingents or necessary falsities. and it is definitely not a necessary falsity that an external world exists.

'Something exists' is the weakest of all contingent statements (supposing it to be contingent); and it is of interest to consider what its logical relation is to 'An external world exists.' The latter obviously entails the former; but how could even the converse entailment fail? Only by there being *something*, and yet *nothing external*: that is, nothing except myself. In other words, if (as I have tried to show) solipsism is not logically possible, then these two statements are actually logically equivalent. So if I am right about solipsism, then realism is either not contingent (as I suspect), or it is contingent, but equivalent to that contingent statement which is the least open to doubt of all contingent statements.

But suppose I am wrong in the second half of this essay: suppose that solipsism is logically possible, and realism is contingent. That will not take anything away from a result of the first half: that the question whether realism is *true* – whether an external world exists – is a question which no human being who is mentally in working order can so much as ask without insincerity.

## Notes

1  Frank Jackson, *Perception: a Representative Theory* (Cambridge University Press, 1977).
2  Michael Devitt, *Realism and Truth* (Princeton University Press, 1984).
3  See especially the article 'Realism as an inductive hypothesis' in D. C. Williams, *Principle of Empirical Realism* (Charles C. Thomas, Springfield, Illinois, 1966).
4  D. Hume *A Treatise of Human Nature* (1739; ed. L. A. Selby-Bigge, Oxford, Clarendon Press, 1888; re-ed. P. Nidditch, Oxford, Clarendon Press, 1978).
5  Hiram Caton, 'Pascal's syndrome', *Zygon: Journal of Religion and Science*, XXI, 3 (September 1986), pp. 319–51.
6  See Devitt, *Realism and Truth*, ch. 2.
7  Jackson, *Perception*, p. 146. Italics in text.
8  Bertrand Russell, *Human Knowledge: its Scope and Limits* (George Allen and Unwin, London, 1948), p. 196.
9  These paragraphs are from pp. 17 and 22 respectively of Bertrand Russell, *The Problems of Philosophy*, (reprinted Home University Library, Oxford University Press, 1951). Italics not in text.
10  Jackson, *Perception*, p. 150.

# 5

## Idealism: A Victorian Horror-Story
## (Part One)

### I

Cortés and his men were sometimes mistaken for gods when they first arrived in Mexico. As the Mexicans had known nothing until then of men clothed in metal, or of horses, or guns, their mistake was not only natural but reasonable. They did not take long to correct it, even so. And it goes without saying that they knew perfectly well who had been the most intelligent and powerful beings in Mexico *before* the Spaniards came: themselves.

Well, of course: that indeed goes without saying. How could people *not* know at least that much about themselves and their surroundings? Almost everyone, at any time, knows of someone in his environment who is more intelligent and capable than himself: someone human, that is. But no one knows of any such *non*-human being; or rather, everyone positively knows that there *is* no such thing in his environment. Yet, while everyone knows this, and must always have known it, almost everyone has always believed the opposite as well: that there *are* beings, more intelligent and powerful than any human, at work in their environment. In short, men have always believed that there are gods around them, though they knew there were none.

Hegel held that animals have no religion, but as against that, Darwin (and others before him) said that, to a dog, its master is a god. If this is true, it is to the credit of canine intelligence, since the evidence for this theism is obvious and overwhelming. But where is the evidence for *our* belief that *we* are somebody's cattle? What is there that could even have rationally first suggested this belief to our minds? Of course we might *be* somebody's cattle *and* have no evidence that we are: but that is only a trivial truth of logic. The question is, what on earth, or in the sky, or in the sea, could have given the cleverest species of animals on earth reason to believe that it is not the cleverest? That it ranks only third, or tenth (or whatever subordinate degree your religion assigns us to), in the order of intelligent beings? I have never met with a satisfactory answer to this question, or even with a promising answer.

In that sense, religious belief is unintelligible to me. But in another sense, religious beliefs are perfectly intelligible, to me as to everyone else. A religious man will tell me, say, that there is someone who lives in the sea, Poseidon by name, who is more intelligent and powerful than any human and is able, for example, to raise storms at sea by his mere command. Now there is nothing in this, or in any other typical religious belief, which defies understanding. It defies rational *belief*, indeed, since just as my informant and I both know that there are no storm-compelling men about, so we both know that there are no men-compelling supermen about. And then, the only 'evidence' which my religious informant can offer for his beliefs is of the usual pitiful kind: stories, one about a vessel which sank in a dead calm after its captain had neglected to sacrifice, another about a ship saved from disaster only by the prayers of a pious passenger; and so on. But it is *only* rational belief which is set at defiance by this man's propositions about the existence and powers of Poseidon. There is nothing at all in those propositions which defies *understanding*.

The emotion which is the fuel for religious beliefs is also easily understandable. Religion is a *deprivation*-effect: people have religious beliefs partly *because* they know that those beliefs are false. But to explain.

Our sensory apparatus, if it is deprived of its normal volume of external information, 'cuts in' at a certain point, and proceeds to make up some of the deficiency with artifacts of its own. In extreme darkness, for example, one's eyes play a certain trick, which I first noticed as a child when fishing from deserted beaches on very dark nights. In those circumstances the sky and the sea are uniformly black, but the beach, stretching away indefinitely on either side, is faintly light. Your eyes search constantly for any singularity which this uniform field might afford, and if they find any such interesting object – a piece of driftwood, say, twenty yards away up the slope of the beach – then it quickly becomes even more interesting. For as you look steadily at it, it appears to sprout limbs, and to move, in a vaguely alarming way, though without ever changing its position. Similarly, if you camp at night beside a noisy mountain creek, the monotony and loudness of the noise sooner or later furnish to your ear a cock's crow, or a human voice, as coming from perhaps a hundred yards away; although you know that there is no cock or human there, and that you could not hear them if there were. These are obviously deprivation-effects. Our information-absorbing system is in operation, and indeed is on 'high alert', but it is being underfed: information is not coming in at anything like the accustomed volume. So the system takes to fabricating some materials of its own.

While our information-absorbing system is thus occasionally underfed, our *care*-absorbing system is underfed absolutely always, and extremely. It is simply imposible for us ever to have enough interest taken in us. Pascal was chilled by the void of space, and so are we all, for as long as we let our attention fasten on it. If you lie face-up in the open air on a clear night, you are suddenly reminded that, in a line drawn from your face outwards, there is nothing, however near or far, which takes or even could take the smallest interest in you. This reminder is extremely disagreeable while it lasts, and it is therefore fortunate that any optical barrier – clouds, a roof, even closing your eyes – is sufficient to interrupt it. And even the best of human environments is far more like the void of space than we can bring ourselves to realize. How many people are there who feel, or could feel, any interest in you? A few kindred, a few friends; perhaps if you are a writer, a few readers. How many non-people? Well, you may have a dog or two. That is as far as it goes at the very best. How little way it goes at the worst, and how common the worst is: these are among the many things which should not be told to those, such as the young, who are fortunate enough not to know them. Such are the facts, and we all know them; but we are so constituted as to be unable to take them in. This is why, incidentally, when we suffer some grave wrong at the hands of our fellows, we are subject to an almost irresistible delusion that this wrong cannot go indefinitely unrighted. (The Whig interpretation of history thus has a certain basis in human biology; even though only in a biologically rooted error.)

This is the emotional source of religious belief. We populate the world with superior non-humans who can take an interest in us, precisely because we know that there aren't any, and wish there were. Why this should be so – why *Homo sapiens* should be burdened with a demand for care which is grotesquely dispro-portioned to any empirically possible supply of care – may be hard for evolutionary theories to explain. But then, those theories are beset by any number of such problems of grotesque or 'gratu-itous' formations: the eight-feet spread of the antlers of certain species of deer, the peacock's tail, etc., etc.

Whatever may be the explanation, the fact is as I have stated. Indeed, so imperfectly adapted are we to the indifference of the universe, that we not only cannot take it in: we cannot even express it properly. For, as the least reflection suffices to show, the word 'indifference' is not really right: indifference is a certain state of *feeling*. Thus the phrase, 'the indifference of the universe' itself incorporates the very delusion which we try to dispel by insisting upon it. There is, indeed, no way, which is both accurate and short, of expressing what we intend to express by using that phrase; and this fact in turn speaks volumes for the strength of the emotion which we are then contending against.

Of course gods are not *just* projections of our wishes: otherwise they would all be conceived in the image of ideal parents, which notoriously is not the case. Religious beliefs are, quite naturally, subject to some broad empirical constraints, including ones sup-plied by hostile or dangerous elements of our environment. Besides, what humans want from superhuman intelligent agents is not necessarily love, or protection, or sustenance: it *is*, necessarily, *attention*. Even hostile attention is better, beyond all comparison, than no attention at all. A version of the vulgarism, 'There is no such thing as bad publicity', is engraved on the human heart.

Religious beliefs are discreditable, and about equally discredi-table to our heads and to our hearts: the beliefs are irrational, and the emotion from which they spring is bad. The irrationality of the beliefs consists in their being groundless, and inconsistent with other beliefs which we know to be true. The bad emotion behind religion is, nearly enough, that 'restless appetite for applause'[1] which, as Hume said, Christianity ascribes to the deity; although it ought really to be ascribed only to ourselves.

But of course there are worse things than either of these. Indeed, even stemming from the very same emotion as religion stems from, there is a kind of belief which is more irrational, in fact very much more irrational, than ordinary religious beliefs are. I mean what in philosophy is called idealism.

# II

That idealism *is* a child of religion, needs no argument: it is obvious. An idealist is a person of a philosophical turn of mind, who can no longer stomach either the raw barbarisms of the popular religion (divine births, marriages, adulteries, wars, deaths, etc.), or the metaphysical cooking which may suffice, at an intermediate stage, to disguise the pungency of those primitive materials; but a person in whom, nevertheless, the religious determination to have the universe congenial is still sovereign. This is as much the description of Plotinus as it is of Berkeley, of Bradley as it is of Kant, of McTaggart as it is of Norris, of Green as it is of Hegel. *All* idealists are engaged, above everything else, in satisfying the religious demand for the universe to be reassuring or consoling, or at the very least, *kindred*. Nor is there anything tendentious in saying this. Idealists themselves, by and large, have always known well enough that this is what they were doing; and some of them have said so quite explicitly.[2]

Nineteenth-century idealism, accordingly, provided an important holding-station or decompression chamber, for that century's vast flood of intellectual refugees from Christianity;[3] or at any rate, for the more philosophically inclined among them. The situation of these people was truly pitiful. The burden of their biblical embarrassments had become intolerable. In attempting to ward off biological, geological, and logical criticisms of the Book of Genesis, they had exhausted their interpretative ingenuity – in vain. An Anglican Bishop of Natal had suffered the ultimate mortification, of having arithmetical and other impossibilities in the Book of Exodus drawn to his attention by some of the very Africans with whose conversion to Christianity he was charged. When T. H. Huxley wrote that, in the matter of the Gadarene swine, Jesus had set a bad social example by wilfully destroying other people's property, and no less a person than Mr Gladstone, resenting this 'accusation against our Lord', rushed into print to point out triumphantly that the Jew who owned those pigs was thereby in breach of the Mosaic law,[4] it was painfully clear to very many people that the defence of biblical Christianity could only result in uncontrollable farce.

And then, how could you seriously offer, to the unfortunate refugees from this sort of thing, the J. H. Newman solution? This solution was that certain bishops of the city of Alexandria, around AD 330, had got the relation between the first and second persons of the Trinity exactly right, and that, with this point settled, every serious intellectual obstacle to the acceptance of Christianity had been removed. This solution was in fact offered to the refugees, of course: but the offer was generally, and rightly, considered to be not only ludicrous but unfeeling.

The problem was how to part with the absurdities of Christianity, while keeping cosmic consolation: no one dreamt of parting with the latter as well (it should hardly be necessary to say), or at any rate no philosopher did. There were plenty of solutions available, of course, for people who were either deficient in religious emotion, or lacking in the philosophical bent: unitarianism, Comte's 'religion of humanity', 'the wisdom of the East', psychical research, and so forth. But for those who combined a powerful religious impulse with the philosophical turn of mind, there was only one possible solution: idealism. That is, something like Berkeley's pan-spiritualism, as long as it could be freed from its embarrassing implication of universal hallucination. If Berkeley's too gaseous world could be solidified (so to speak), or at least 'jellied', by being passed through a strong field of Kant-Hegel radiation: *that* would be the very thing. Let the refugees from Christianity be told, on the highest possible philosophical authority, that Nature *is* Thought, that the Universe *is* Spirit, that the Absolute is experience, that the dualism of matter and mind, like the related dualism of fact and value, is a superficial one, and 'ultimately' (as the Hegelians loved to say) even a self-contradictory one. That should buck them up, as nothing else could.

Of course no two philosophers, even if both idealists, can ever have been of *exactly* the same opinions or attitudes with regard to religion. In the nineteenth century, idealism not only evolved intellectually, but embodied different attitudes towards Christianity at different times and places. In Germany the alliance between idealism and Christianity was neither as close nor as long-lasting as it was in Britain, while at its beginning, in Kant and Hegel, idealism even retained some faint tincture of the century in which those men were born. These two oracles, at any rate in their off-duty hours, did not always handle the Christian religion with all the reverence which, as being the principal historical expression of Spirit, it was entitled to receive, especially from professors of idealism. In their philosophical lectures and books, on the other hand, they laboured mightily and with faces unerringly straight, to disclose the deep and unique truths of metaphysics or of ethics, which Christianity had merely adapted to common understandings in the doctrine of the Incarnation, or of the Kingdom of God, or whatever it might happen to be.

The German idealism which first Coleridge, and later Stirling, brought back to Britain, was represented by those importers as being remarkably, or rather, providentially, adapted for the defence of the Church of England against both foreign Jacobinism and domestic Non-conformity. But that particular graft never 'took': *Anglican*-Hegelianism is one of the few wings which Hegelianism never grew. On the contrary, when the professional philosophers, beginning with Green, took over the idealist enterprise in Britain, idealism acquired a low-Church tone which it never subsequently lost. The revival, earlier in the century, of a Bible-based and evangelical Christianity had swept away every vestige of sympathy with the eighteenth century. Green passed his formative years in a domestic atmosphere of extreme evangelical piety. Later, of course, the exodus from Christianity engulfed him too, and for him the 'parting with the Christian mythology [was] the rendering asunder of bones and marrow'.[5] (These powerful words are ones that Green used to Mrs Humphry Ward, who duly put him into her novel, *Robert Elsmere*, one of the many popular novels of the time about adorable young Englishmen who have lost their faith.[6]) Anyone who should suppose that Green's 'parting with the Christian mythology' prevented him from taking Anglican orders, or made him any the less ardent in giving addresses on New Testament topics. or any the less diligent in ensuring the attendance of his Balliol undergraduate charges at their religious observances, must understand very little of the Church of England, and even less of nineteenth century idealism. Newman, after all (to say nothing of a thousand lesser men), had found it possible to assent to the Thirty-nine Articles by understanding them (as the memorable phrase was) 'in a non-natural sense'. Idealism must have been a poor horse indeed, and Kant and Hegel must have laboured to very little purpose, if a disciple of theirs could not effortlessly clear so trifling a hurdle as those Articles, which countless other men had easily surmounted without the help of any philosophy at all.

What Green began was continued and developed by Edward Caird, John Caird, Bosanquet, R. B. Haldane, Andrew Seth, and many scores of others. The Caird brothers, by their eminence in Scottish university and Church life, were especially effective in providing cosmic consolation for ex-Presbyterians in particular. But all the idealist philosophers were doing essentially the same work, and for the same class of people. The low-Church tone, as I have said, adhered to British idealism until its death around 1940. For example, as late as 1927, Hume's essay on miracles still aroused the same fury in the idealist A. E. Taylor[7] as it had in such people as the Baptist minister John Foster more than a hundred years before.[8] This instance is all the more remarkable because, of course, the idea of miracles was absolute anathema to idealists in general: they regarded it as a typical relic of exploded dualistic metaphysics.

Bradley alone is an exception to what I have just said, for he made little concession to any specifically Christian ideas at all. But this was to be expected. By his time, idealism had triumphed so completely in British philosophy that it could easily afford to indulge in a little plain speaking, at any rate *da capo*. If you are, as Bradley was, the undisputed leader of philosophy in the English-speaking world, and you have already proved in print, to the satisfaction of all competent persons, that 'the reality is *experience*',[9] then you have fully satisfied the basic demand of religion: the universe is indeed our kindred. That point being established, no one could reasonably object too much if you went on to unburden yourself of a few harsh words about the personality of God, or immortality, or some other extravagance of official Christianity.

It was not enough, though, that the refugees from Christianity should be supplied with still reassuring, even if somewhat elusive, objects of *belief*. Their deepest *feelings* had been so ploughed up, and their numbers were so great, that they constituted a whole class of people for whom some practical reorientation of life simply had to be found.

A few, to be sure, could still be sent off to Caird Bros, investment experts, specialists in designing belief-portfolios which were Christian enough to qualify their holders for Church employment, yet not so Christian as to attract adverse biological or geological notice. (The Cairds certainly should have been experts: it was their own livelihood.) But this line of work could at best suit only a few, for it called for exceptional intelligence, or else exceptional stupidity. Even apart from that, the number of professional religious positions available was constantly shrinking, while most of the refugees in question had contracted an unconquerable aversion to clerical life in any form.

Green knew better. He looked forward, not back, and, almost unaided, he opened the way to a new perspective on life for any number of bewildered ex-Christians. When he lost all his Christian beliefs (except that minimum which idealism preserves, plus a half-belief he retained in immortality), he lost none of the flaming evangelical zeal which had at first accompanied those beliefs. His life remained devoted to preparing for the consummation of that 'Rule of the Saints' in Britain, which had been so tragically interrupted in 1660. Cromwell, Ireton, Lambert, Milton, and the like, were his boyhood heroes, and they remained his heroes to the end. But even those he ranked below that nonpareil, Sir Henry Vane the younger.

Vane was one of the leaders in the seditions leading up to the Civil War, in the parliamentary side of that war, and in the Commonwealth. He was also the author of innumerable tracts, on religion and on government, which are generally agreed to have no consistent or even intelligible meaning, except that nothing has ever been got right or even half-right, in religion or politics, but that Harry Vane has got everything right this time: he did not deny that even he had got something wrong in his previous pamphlet. Very early in his life, Vane had earned the enmity of the bishops and the court, and by the end he had even managed to arouse the sluggish animosity of the restored king, and was executed. But in between he had worn out the comprehension, the patience, and the trust, of all his successive allies and intimates: Presbyterians, Arminians, Independents, Republicans, Fifth Monarchy Men, Anabaptists, Levellers, Marrow Men, Brownists, Muggletonians. When he tried to resist the termination by force of the Long Parliament, Vane even exhausted the patience of Cromwell himself, in whose counsels he had been as deep and as long as any man. The Lord Protector himself sued for protection, crying out in a loud voice, 'Oh Sir Henry Vane, Sir Henry Vane; the Lord deliver me from Sir Henry Vane'.[10] His fall from power, a contemporary wrote, gave universal satisfaction: "he being unhappy in lying under the most catholic prejudice of any man I ever knew."

Yet one was found at last, though only two hundred years later, to love and even venerate this restless scourge of his fellow men: the idealist philosopher Mr T. H. Green of Oxford. If only we had followed Vane, Green says, 'Two centuries of government by borough-mongering and corruption, of church-statesmanship and state-churchmanship would have been saved'.[11] The following are some other samples of Green on Vane.

The higher enthusiasm which breathed in Cromwell and Vane, was not puritanic or English merely. It belonged to the universal spiritual force which as ecstasy, mysticism, quietism, philosophy, is in permanent collision with the carnal interests of the world, and which, if it conquers them for a moment, yet again sinks under them, that it may transmute them more thoroughly to its service.[12]

'The people of England [Vane said on the scaffold] have been long asleep. I doubt they will be hungry when they awake'. They have slept, we may say, another two hundred years. If they should wake and be hungry, they will find their food in the ideas which, with much blindness and weakness, he vainly offered them, cleared and ripened by a philosophy of which he did not dream.[13]

In the days when, not in fancy but in sober seriousness, Vane built his splendid political theories, and Cromwell seemed about to embody them in act, when even the common people saw the dominion of the saints at hand, Milton might well 'see in his mind's eye a noble and puissant nation rousing itself, like a strong man after sleep', and even rise in thought from the perfection of earthly politics to the city of the heavenly host. But it is hard for men who are versed in political theories which have all been found wanting and whose eyes are dimmed with the dust that rises from the hubbub of modern life, to see the history of mankind 'orbing itself to a perfect end'.[14]

For Green, then, as much as for his hero, a total revolution in human life was at hand, a triumph over all 'carnal interests'; though it was to be based, not on the Bible, but on 'a philosophy of which [Vane] did not dream'. (I think we can guess which philosophy is meant.) And this revolution is to be effected, not 'hereafter', and in another world – for that idea is one more instance of the dualism which an objective idealist most detests – but now, in the actual world, which is, after all, the one true spiritual substance; and effected, first of all, 'in England's green and pleasant land'. Green was, in short, a revolutionary socialist of the visionary English kind, a Victorian William Blake with brains. He began the Balliol tradition, which continues (I am told) to this day, of releasing upon the world a stream of graduates charged with a political mission like his own. How far the world ought to feel gratitude, or the opposite, towards Balliol for this gift, it might be unsympathetic to enquire. But it is curious to reflect that, through the Reverend Green's idealism, a causal connection exists between George Berkeley, Anglican Bishop of Cloyne, and those Anglican clergy of the present day whose main pastoral work is collecting money for the distribution, to the needy of Africa and elsewhere, of Kalashnikov rifles.

With Bosanquet, too, idealism led to socialism, and thus to permanent and fruitful redirection of the energies of thousands of ex-Christians: see, for example, *The Philosophical Theory of the State*.[15] Hobhouse and others accused this book of maintaining that the state can do no wrong, which it does not maintain.

But it is certainly true that the worship of gods has here been superseded by worship of the state. Nothing could have been less congenial to Bosanquet's emollient mind, however, than the military-religious zealots who were Green's idols. Bosanquet is a socialist only for the most general and least inflammatory of reasons: in broad terms, that just as objective idealism is the right answer to 'individualism' in metaphysics and epistemology, so it is the right answer, too, to individualism in morals, politics, and economics. His political affinities were therefore rather with the Fabian socialists than with the revolutionary sort: as may be seen, for example, at many places in his *Civilisation of Christendom.*[16]

Bosanquet even had, pending the arrival of socialism, interim chapels, of a kind, for ex-Christians to join. For he was one of the leading lights of those Ethical Societies – what volumes the very name speaks! – which sprang up late in the century, first in London and then beyond, in a natural response to the crying needs of the refugees. These societies met to hear and discuss addresses on subjects of general intellectual and moral importance – evolution, for example, or industrialism, or eugenics – but they also discussed practical aspects of 'the social problem': what amendments the Poor Law needed, the future of Sunday observance, etc., etc. Nothing could have been less specifically Christian than meetings of the Ethical Societies: even so notorious an agnostic as Leslie Stephen often addressed them. But nothing could have been more specifically ex-Christian, either, or more specifically proto-socialist.

Thus the idealist philosophers, from about the middle of the nineteenth century, tempered the wind to the shorn lambs: providing ex-Christians not only with fundamental intellectual support, but with appropriate redirection of their lives. Among the lambs, accordingly, gratitude was for a long time the prevailing emotion. But in the end the leading idealists rather overplayed their hand, and provoked a certain reaction among their flock.

The exchange had been, after all, really a very unequal one. The ex-Christians had got from the philosophers, indeed, satisfaction of their *basic* demand: a congenial universe. But beyond that bare minimum, they had got nothing at all, at any rate from any idealist later than Green. A personal God, a unique historical revelation, miracles, immortality, efficacy of prayer, a divinely inspired ethics, even a guarantee against Darwinism – all these things were blankly refused them, even rudely refused them by Bradley, and only more politely refused them by Bosanquet. The Absolute of those two philosophers was a fine garbage-disposal unit for matter and space, but alas, it shredded and emulsified minds as well as bodies, values as well as facts, religion as well as science, all with the same sublime indifference.

For certain ex-Christian idealists, things had gone too far. Late in the nineteenth century therefore, and early in the twentieth, some of them attempted to frame an idealism less insatiably monistic, and combined it with a more recognizable Christianity than the Absolute would allow. Andrew Seth, W. R. Sorley, James Ward and A. E. Taylor were among these. They have left little mark on the history of philosophy, partly of course because they were busily buying back many of the very intellectual troubles which had brought about the exodus from Christianity in the first place. But they deserve some credit, both for the comparative sanity of their philosophy, and for the comparative honesty of their religion.

For idealists in general, however, actual restoration of Christian beliefs or institutions was never either desirable or possible. The idealists after Kant were all, indeed, to the very end, still bobbing up and down on the waves that *la guillotine* had set rolling around 1793; but they were not philosophical counterparts of a Montalembert or a Newman. They were not so much friends of the gods, as convinced that Prometheus needed a restraining hand, and a few good lectures on dualism. To restore the sacred mysteries was no part of their object: to check the arrogance of secular intelligence, was. Probably every idealist has always in his heart believed, with St Augustine, that 'Melior est fidelis ignorantia, quam temeraria scientia',[17] and Kant once actually said in print, as everyone knows, that he had 'had to abolish knowledge to leave room for faith'.[18] (I suspect he thought we might not notice this if he did not tell us himself.) Still, while idealism has always satisfied the *minimum* demand of religion, it has seldom done more than that.

That minimum is not, of course, the existence of God, but the congeniality of the universe. It is perfectly consistent, though indeed very unusual, to be an idealist and yet deny the existence of God: all it means is that the required amount of congeniality has then to be made up in other ways. McTaggart was such an atheist-idealist, and he, to be sure, laid on the congeniality with a sufficiently free hand, or rather, with a steam-shovel. Nothing exists except spirits like ourselves, but these spirits, though finite, are immortal, and will eventually swim in an ocean of love – according to this poor demented man.

For idealist philosophy to be a major movement of thought, as distinct from an individual crotchet, it must be in symbiosis with a popular religion which is losing its hold on intelligent people. If the religion loses too much of its hold, and is not replaced by another, then idealism will simply die, like a tree severed at its tap-root. This is, of course, what happened to British idealism as the twentieth century went on. By somewhere around 1940 there were simply not enough intelligent people, needing a substitute for Christianity, to keep the business going. Where the grand-parents had been refugees from Christianity, the grandchildren had virtually forgotten Christianity, or had never taken it seriously to begin with. Likewise, for idealism ever to return as a major force in philosophy, there would first have to be a major revival of religion. There is at present no sign of the latter, at least in the West, and therefore no prospect of the former.

It is true that there are various 'idealisms' of a sort, current in that underworld of thought which nowadays largely constitutes arts faculties in Western universities. There is Goodman's non-sense about 'worldmaking' (see Essay 2 above). There is a sort of linguistic idealism, according to which each language 'makes its own world'. Neo-Marxist hysterics affirm 'the social construc-tion of reality'. From Kuhn and Feyerabend (see Essay 1 above), innocent undergraduates learn that the observable world depends on 'theory'. And so on. I have said something in Essay 3 about the historical events which have recently made faculties of arts into forcing-houses for every known kind of intellectual pathogen. But in this essay I am concerned only with serious idealist philos-ophers.

# III

*In 1887 almost every philosopher in the English-speaking countries was an idealist.* A hundred years later in the same countries, almost all philosophers have forgotten this fact; and when, as occasionally happens, they are reminded of it, they find it almost impossible to believe. But it ought never to be forgotten. For it shows what the opinions, even the virtually unanimous opinions, of philosophers are worth, when they conflict with common sense.

Not only were nearly all English-speaking philosophers idealists a hundred years ago: absolutely all of the best ones were. The philosophers of the preceding generation – Hamilton, Mill, Lewes, and Spencer, for example – had retained some traces of realism, or of materialism, or at least of dualism, and they were made mincemeat of by their idealist critics. Those critics were Hegelian more than they were any other kind of idealist, and it is true that Hegelian idealism is a perfect hide-out for intellectual frauds. But among the British idealists there is, as far as I know, only one intellectual fraud: William Wallace, who succeeded Green as Whyte's Professor of Moral Philosophy at Oxford, and who translated and expounded Hegel's writings on logic. In general, the British idealists were not only not frauds, but were *good philosophers*. Green, Bosanquet, Bradley, and Andrew Seth, in particular, were *very good philosphers indeed*. These facts need all the emphasis I can give them, because most philosophers nowadays either never knew or have forgotten them, and indeed, with a partial exception in favour of Bradley, they cannot really believe them. They *are* facts, nevertheless, and facts which ought never to be forgotten. For they show what the opinions even, or rather, especially, of *good* philosophers are worth, when they conflict with common sense. (They therefore also throw some light on the peculiar logic of the concept 'good philosopher': an important but neglected subject.)

Now I, like most philosophers in the English-speaking countries nowadays, am one of those naturalists or realists or 'materialists, atheists, etc.', whom Berkeley was always claiming to have refuted, and who must indeed be wildly wrong if Berkeley is right, or if any form of idealism is right. But all those labels are merely an encumbrance here: none of them stands, in my case at least, for anything at all technical. On the contrary, *my* materialism (etc., etc.) could be epitomized, adequately for most purposes, as follows: human beings are a race of land-mammals, the most intelligent things known to exist, but things which are born, develop, and die like all other mammals.

'But everyone knows *that!*' Of course they do. Only, almost everyone also believes other things which are inconsistent with it: for example, that people don't really die, or that there is in the sky, or sea, or somewhere, some being more intelligent and capable than any of the human kind.

'Oh, be fair – that's *religion*! Surely no *philosopher*, idealist or any other, has ever denied the obvious truth you mentioned a moment ago?'

*That* is something which it is not at all easy to be rationally sure of. Berkeley practised, as well as preached, 'speaking with the vulgar while thinking with the learned': and who cannot see that this policy, in such a case as his, *must* create some uncertainty as to what he denies, and what he does not? Few idealists, it is true, would *say* they denied that humans are terrestrial mammals: but you cannot afford to take a philosopher's word for it, what his philosophy denies and what it does not. This is not because philosophers are dishonest: they scarcely ever are. It is because they are too clever by half, and have a constitutional weakness for leading an intellectual double life. But idealism, let us remember, runs on the same emotional fuel as religion does. Perhaps, then, idealist philosophers are just mentally divided in the same tiresome way as religious people are: they know that man is a terrestrial mammal, but they just happen to believe the opposite as well. Anyway, I will try, later on, to find out what idealism *does* deny, and what it does not.

Nowadays many philosophers say that they are materialists only because of the pressure of scientific evidence. They say, for example, that a Cartesian-dualistic view of man is not only logically possible, but not even absolutely excluded by any empirical evidence so far available.[19] Or they say that their materialism is a *scientific* theory, recommended, like any other scientific theory, only by its explanatory success in general, or in specific recent developments, for example in molecular biology, or 'artificial intelligence', or whatever. I could not truthfully say anything like these things. That man is one terrestrial mammal among others, though distinguished by superior intelligence, is not a *theory*, scientific or other. It is not something to be open-minded about. It is not only something which everyone knows *now*, like the roundness of the earth: everyone always did know it. My sort of materialism, then, owes nothing whatever to modern science, biological or other.

Nor is my sort of materialism open to revision, in the light of future scientific developments; any more than it is open to revision in the light of future scientific developments, for example, that kangaroos are land-mammals, or that the English oak is a broad-leafed deciduous tree. If philosophy or religion prompts a person to deny or doubt that humans, or that kangaroos, are land-mammals, the only rational thing to do is to ignore him; and the same holds for science, too, whether past, present, or future.

I may be reminded that some respected physicists have said in recent years that something like Berkeleian idealism is actually a logical consequence of their best fundamental theories. (One of them wrote, for example: 'We now know that the moon is demonstrably not there when nobody looks'.[20]) It would be irrational to believe this logical claim, but if it is true then it would be irrational to believe these physicists' best theories. Fundamental physical theories never say anything about a particular macroscopic physical object, such as the moon; but if they did say something about the moon, then they would say the same thing about all macroscopic physical objects, hence about all land-mammals, and hence about the particular land-mammal, Professor N. D. Mermin, who wrote the sentence I have just quoted. Now it may perhaps be true that Professor Mermin depends for his ease of mind on being an object of attention. This would not even be especially surprising, in view of the powerful emotional root which idealism has in common with religion. But that he depends for his very existence on being an object of attention, is entirely out of the question: it is much more likely (to say the least) that one or more of his scientific theories is wrong. Mammals are very complex, of course, and depend for their existence on a great many things; but somebody's looking at them is not among those things, and everyone knows this.

'It seems to me that you refuse to take idealism seriously. Yet surely, if there was, as you say, almost-universal acceptance of idealism by good philosophers in Britain a hundred years ago, then there must have been good, or at least persuasive, arguments in its favour'.

A remark like that betrays a most serious misconception of the part which is played in philosophy by argument. Argument has been overwhelmingly important, it is true, in post-idealist English-speaking philosophy; a fact connected, incidentally, with the acknowledged inability of that philosophy to influence common life. So it has been at some other times and places too. But this state of affairs is not typical.

Some of the best philosophers never argue at all, or even pretend to. Santayana, for example. He simply tells you how he thinks the world is, and delicately makes fun of some other philosophers, almost always unnamed, who think there is more to the world, or less, than he does. Bentham is another philosopher who is entirely innocent of arguments, as distinct from satire, against his opponents. Other philosophers, it is true, *are* almost always arguing: Leibniz, for example. Others, again, are always pretending to argue, but never do: Spinoza is such a one. By nature he was a pure world-portraitist, like Santayana, but current intellectual fashion had unluckily afflicted him with Euclidean ambitions. The result is that, though on the surface his philosophy swarms with arguments, these arguments are all of the form, rigorously valid indeed but otherwise without merit, 'p, so p'. It is not to be simply *assumed*, then, that the currency of an opinion among philosophers owes *anything* to argument in its favour.

Then, a philosopher's standard of argument, and the need he feels for argument at all, decline, of course, in proportion to the degree to which his *heart* has laid down his conclusion in advance. Think, for example, of the arguments in Plato's *Phaedo*, for the immortality of the soul. These arguments have commanded respect, and even in some cases (if tradition is to be believed) assent, for no fewer than 2400 years. Yet, although elsewhere in Plato there are some good arguments, these are so contemptible that, on their own merits, they could hardly ever have imposed upon a child of eight. But of course, they never *have* had to make their way on their own merits: they have always had a powerful wish in their sails.

The case is similar with idealism (and the two matters even have, of course, some connection). The part played by argument in making a man an idealist is little more, in most cases, than the part played by argument in making a man a Hindu, a Christian, or a Moslem. In idealism, as in religion, the heart has laid down the conclusion (and basically the same conclusion) in advance, and it is this conclusion alone which matters. If the head can find arguments for it afterwards, that is well: if not, well again. To suppose that arguments for idealism were ever of the essence with Berkeley, or Kant, or Hegel, or Green, is to suppose that counter-arguments *against* idealism, if these had been pressed upon them, might have quite overcome their wish for a congenial universe, and changed their minds. Only someone colossally ignorant of the psychology of modern philosophy could believe that.

In the whole history of modern idealism, there was in fact only one point, and that an early one, at which argument played a decisive part. The story is easily told.

Modern philosophy began from Descartes' world-view. That world-view is so awkwardly disjoint, and especially as to what it says of man, is so palpably a tightrope act, that it fairly begged to be abbreviated at one end or the other. In various ways it got what it begged for. According to both Leibniz and Spinoza, two kinds of substances, the spatial and the spiritual, are one more than enough; according to Spinoza, indeed, even more than one *particular* substance is more than enough. They made their respective economies accordingly. A little later, some French materialists, who were not interested in the metaphysics of the thing, made a different economy. They just closed with the physical half of Descartes' offer, and wrote off the spiritual half as a bad debt.

But the most obvious way to abbreviate the Cartesian world-view, and easily the most inviting way if spiritual interests are uppermost in your mind, is along the faultline between the spiritual and the spatial worlds, and at the expense of the latter. If you cut *there*, and do no more, the result is, of course, a Berkeleian kind of idealism. Malebranche, naturally, saw this possibility at once, and saw its attractions as a 'short way' with materialists, etc.; though he thought that one needed to do more than just cut the Cartesian world in half. Even John Norris could see the possibility. Arthur Collier saw it. In fact, by about 1710, the very dogs must have been barking for an idealist amputation to be carried out on the Cartesian world-view. From a Cartesian starting-point, 'the external world' is certainly a gratuitous hypothesis, perhaps a senseless one; and if a Collier and a Norris could see this, then a philosopher as good as Berkeley must have seen it (as cricketers say) as big as a watermelon.

Berkeley is one of those philosophers who are always arguing, and he gave a number of arguments for abridging the Cartesian world-view to the exclusive benefit of its mental half. Once he had done it, everyone could see, even if they had not seen before, that Cartesianism *had* begged for an idealist abridgement, *and* that it had got it from Berkeley.

There was only one catch; but it was a rather serious one. This was that no one could believe the world-view to which those arguments of Berkeley led. Or rather, no one could even mention what this world-view was, without smiling: much as Cicero says that no two augurs could meet without smiling. It was all very well to have the 'materialists, atheists, etc.', driven from the field by force of argument: philosophers were in favour of *that*, almost to a man. But not at *this* ridiculous price!

What was to be done? No one thought seriously, at the times of which I am speaking, of going right back *beyond* the Cartesian starting-points, of dualism in metaphysics, and representationism in epistemology. The future of philosophy was therefore fixed: it *had* to be idealistic. Reid, and then Hamilton, tried indeed to stem the idealist tide, but their attempt was half-hearted, and in any case it came too late: idealism has so powerful a *wish* behind it that, once you have conquered your common sense and actually tried the stuff, it is almost impossible to break the habit.

Of course idealism did not at once sweep the field clear of all rivals. The history of thought is never neat, and there are always stragglers. Hence the amputative surgery, which Berkeley had performed on Descartes (via Locke), had often to be done over again, even in the middle of the nineteenth century, on stray autodidacts such as Herbert Spencer, when they ignorantly wandered on to the field of battle. But for the professional philosophers the great desideratum, after Berkeley, was simply this: a version of idealism which was not, like his, a proper object of general derision.

It was precisely this which Kant appeared, at least, to supply, and the philosophical profession, almost as one man, and with inexpressible relief, closed with his offer. This was the unique service which Kant rendered to modern idealism: he seemed to prove, in his own person, that you could be an idealist without looking a complete fool. That is what entitles Kant to Nietzsche's superb description of him, as 'this catastrophic spider'.[21] Berkeley's web had caught no one; but Kant's web, promising idealism-without-subjectivity, proved irresistibly attractive, and for the next 150 years almost no philosopher escaped it.

This 'objective' idealism was not reached by argument: argument had nothing to do with it. It was reached by the biggest, though also the simplest, bluff ever tried. Kant simply said, in effect, 'Let us say that the physical universe is objective *as well as* ideal: *that* should satisfy *all* parties (or at least stagger them)'. It did, too. You can easily, as the poet sang, 'vanquish *Berkeley* by a grin', and every person of sense does so. Besides, Berkeley's ghostly vocation had always left a suspicion of interestedness hanging over his ghostly philosophy. But an eighteenth-century German professor, with no clerical axe to grind, and with many apparent and some real marks of intellectual authority, who informs you that space is *empirically real* (even if it is also transcendentally ideal), is certainly no laughing matter. *He* couldn't be joking, could he? (Or equivocating? He couldn't possibly mean, by 'objective' and 'empirically real', just 'non-idiosyncratic' or 'believed in by *everyone*', could he? *Surely* he couldn't, could he?)

Even when Kant wrote, then, the time had passed when arguments for idealism were felt to be needed. Some later idealists who, for one reason or another, lie outside the main nineteenth-century stream – Ferrier, Royce, and McTaggart, for example – *did* invent arguments of their own, for the conclusion which everyone was embracing anyway. But those arguments remained their own. The philosophers of the main stream, by contrast, hardly ever troubled themselves at all with arguments for their idealism. At the most they might echo one of Berkeley's arguments, or hazard a variation on it; but even this was unusual. These philosophers simply *started from* two assumptions: first, that the physical half of Descartes' world had been knocked out by Berkeley's arguments; and second, that Berkeley's own 'subjective' idealism is too bizarre to be taken seriously. If you had gone against the first assumption, they would have reproached you with reviving Locke's 'material substances' or Kant's 'things-in-themselves'. If you had gone against the second, they would have reproached you for thinking that the mighty fabric of the world can be reduced to a little scatter of ideas in human minds.

It was entirely needless, therefore, for these philosophers to try to furnish arguments for their objective idealism. *All the necessary work had been done.* Refuting materialism, naturalism, etc., would have been, even by Kant's time, slaying the slain. Bosanquet explained in a letter why, in one of his writings, he had not argued against naturalism, or even bothered to mention it. 'I don't think it important,' he says, 'the universe is *so obviously* experience'.[22] *That* is the authentic voice of mainstream nineteenth-century idealism.

Berkeley, then, played two parts in the drama of modern idealism. He was the hero, as being the victorious leader in the great anti-materialist war, and he had done the argumentative work which made all subsequent effort, in the way of argument for idealism, unnecessary. But he was also the villain, because his own form of idealism depleted the actual universe so absurdly that, left as it stood, it made idealism a byword for learned folly.

His ungrateful heirs soon forgot the former immeasurable service which he had done them, and concentrated instead on the latter, the offence which he had given them.[23] If they had been Bolsheviks, they would undoubtedly have accused Berkeley of being actually in the pay of 'foreign materialism', and of having the secret aim of bringing idealism into ridicule and contempt. But they did their best to discredit him. In every idealist manual after Kant, the first lesson is the same: *kick Berkeley.* This is sure to start things off on the best possible footing, by engaging your readers' common sense on your side. This way, you cut off their retreat, and you can then torment them at your leisure, about how, although the universe is *of course* thought, it is not, indeed, *your* thought, or my thought, or even everybody's thought. It is objective, or public, or Absolute, Thought.

This was easy enough work, once you had been shown it. But for the pathfinder, Kant himself, it was a Herculean, and a lifelong, work. What he had to do, after all, was nothing less than this: simultaneously take Berkeley on board, as being the rightful captain of the ship, *and* drop him over the side, as a wrecker of it. This was always going to be no mean feat. It called for the use of literary and linguistic muscles which no one before even knew existed, and it placed a fearful strain on them. Kant tried all his life to distance himself from Berkeleian idealism, but with as little success as though it had been his shadow. Between 1755 and 1783 he published no fewer than five 'refutations of idealism', as he hopefully entitled them: all in vain. No one was deceived for a moment. Everyone could easily see that, even after all his long and violent contortions, Kant was himself an idealist still, and near-enough Berkeleian. All that those contortions really accomplished was to inflict on the German language, as an instrument of philosophizing, injuries such as it had never received before, and from which it has never recovered since.

Kant's heirs, Schelling and Hegel, were no more deceived than anyone else, and were rather less disposed than most to give him the benefit of any doubt. They could see perfectly well that Kant's idealism was still fatally 'subjective', far too akin to Berkeley's. An hallucination does not become 'objective', or 'empirically real', just because *all humans* happen to be subject to it. What had Kant done, after all, then, except to give to what were, by his own account, just some widespread hallucinations, certain *rather dignified names*: names like 'forms of sense', and 'categories of the understanding'? Idealism, if it was in earnest about dissociating itself from Berkeley, would not continue to subordinate itself in this way to mere accidents of the human condition. Those 'forms' and 'categories' ought to be ascribed, not to a contingent unanimity among private, finite, and fallible human minds, but to a necessary, public, objective, and infinite Mind: a mind which could no more be in error than space, according to materialists, could be in error.

There never were, then, any arguments for idealism that mattered, except those which Berkeley gave or suggested. Kant and all the later mainstream idealists argued, when they argued at all, *from* idealism, as a starting-point: you will search their pages in vain for their own arguments *to* idealism. To Kant or Hegel, to have argued for idealism would have seemed as absurd as trying to launch a ship that is already in mid-ocean.

After Kant, indeed, argument of *any* kind largely disappears from German idealism. This was partly owing to the particular turn of mind of his successors: Schelling and Hegel were philosophers of the kind who would quickly starve to death if their food supply depended on their ability to argue. But it must also have been owing in part to the damage which Kant had done to the German language as an instrument of philosophical argument. As an instrument of mystification, of course, he left it far better than he found it.

Although Kant and Hegel dominated the scene in nineteenth-century Western philosophy, it is a mistake to think of nineteenth-century idealism as *principally* a German phenomenon: it is principally a British one. In Germany, idealism did not last so long, nor did it ever achieve so complete an ascendancy, as it did in the Britain of Queen Victoria and beyond. In particular, idealism prevailed, with scarcely an exception, among British *academic* philosophers, at a time when the race of non-academic philosophers, such as Mill, was approaching extinction.

This is not to say that *accusations* of materialism (etc.), against philosophers, were not common enough in Britain at this time: quite the contrary. Just as, where almost everyone is a democrat, you can expect people to be frequently accused of being anti-democratic, so, when almost every philosopher is an idealist, philosophers will be especially anxious to deny one another that title. It should almost go without saying, for example, that Green was accused of materialism,[24] or that he in turn denied Berkeley's right to be called an idealist.[25]

Some philosophers, though, really did lie under a reasonable suspicion of being materialists: namely those, such as Huxley, Clifford, Karl Pearson, and Mach, who were distinguished scientists as well. Yet so complete was the triumph of idealism late in the century, that these four men were all able to protest passionately, and with perfect truth, that in fact they were good idealists, just like everyone else. Their idealism, it is true, was of a distinctly old-fashioned or 'subjective' kind: the reason being, that they had got it directly from their own reading of Berkeley and Hume. They owed nothing to Kant, Hegel, or the intervening incomprehensibles. The idealism of the professional philosophers, on the other hand, while ultimately, indeed, it too stemmed from Berkeley, was, in almost every case, of the post-Kantian German fashion.

If a Marcus Aurelius had wished to renew, in Britain in 1890, his endowment of all the main rival schools of philosophy, he would have found his purpose frustrated: idealists would have got all the money. Things got to such a point, in fact, that Britain's nearest approach to a philosophic emperor, the sometime prime minister Mr A. J. Balfour, was reduced to the necessity of taking the field *himself*, almost alone, against the massed legions of idealism. His attacks[26] were not without merit, either, as Seth, for one, acknowledged;[27] but of course they had little effect. In any case even Balfour, for all his remarkable power and independence of mind, seems later to have decided to 'get with the strength' (as the saying is); for in 1911 he writes that he 'can heartily rejoice' in the triumph of idealism.[28]

# IV

Berkeley's idealism, what was that? It was the seminal and stock example of 'subjective idealism'; but what is that?

There is a popular mistake about this, which needs to be got out of the way first. This is, that Berkeley held (as the physicist I quoted in section III of this essay does hold) that 'the moon is not there when nobody looks', is there when somebody does look, and is there at those times *because* someone is looking.

This might be called the Tolstoy mistake. When he was a young man, Tolstoy read philosophy so intensively at one stage that he became alarmed for his sanity; nor was his alarm groundless. Sometimes when alone, for example, he would turn around, and then turn back again as quickly as he could, in an attempt to see whether the things he had just turned his back on were indeed fading out of existence.[29] Of course many other people have done the same, especially during their adolescence, and even without the stimulus of reading idealist philosophers. But Berkeley in particular has very often been misunderstood as sanctioning this particular kind of lapse from sanity: a misunderstanding, it must be admitted, which was encouraged by certain things that he himself said. People think, that is, that Berkeley maintained a *causal* dependence of physical objects on perception: that things go in and out of existence, depending on whether or not we are perceiving them; or maintained that if they do not, it is because God is perceiving them, even when no finite spirit is on the job.

This may be good clean fun; and then again, it may be no fun, and bad, and unclean. In any case it is certainly not Berkeley. His world-view is a far simpler one than this, and far more insane. If Tolstoy had really understood it, there is no telling what it might have done to him, and, through him, to millions of people.

Berkeley's world contains one infinite spirit, and many finite spirits. The former is God, the latter are supposed to be us. (Dogs and the like miss out again here, even more completely than they did with Descartes.) Finite spirits, or at least some of their actions and passions, are in time; but spirits are not spatial, or *in* space in any sense: not even in the sense in which geometrical points are in space. They are unextended unlocated intelligent substances. Berkeley holds that there is no causation except volition, and hence nothing can be caused, in his world, except by some act of some will. At any time there are occurring, in finite spirits (though never in the infinite spirit), certain perceptions or affections or ideas (as it might be, of colour, shape, hardness, and so on). These are caused in every case, *ex hypothesi*, by some act of will, and in fact are caused in almost every case by an act of the Divine Will. The benevolence and steadiness of the Divine Will, and nothing else, ensure that the ideas produced in the various finite spirits are, on the whole, in harmony with one another.

That is the *whole* story: I have now told you all there is in Berkeley's world. There is no question, then, of physical objects being, for Berkeley, causally dependent on perception or ideas. Since perception is not volition, *nothing*, according to Berkeley, can possibly be causally dependent on perception. Besides, there are no physical objects in Berkeley's world, to *be* causally dependent, on perception or on anything else. The dependence which he contended for, then, of physical objects on perception or ideas, is not causal: it is logical. It is not like the dependence of oysters on salt-water, or of human consciousness on a supply of oxygen to the brain. It is like the dependence of redness on colour, or (more exactly) like that of fatherhood on being a male parent. Talk about fatherhood is talk about being a male parent. And Berkeley's claim is that, similarly, talk about physical objects, *rightly understood*, is talk about certain groups of ideas which the Divine Will impresses from time to time on finite spirits.

It would seem to follow that no common man has ever rightly understood a single remark about a physical object; or else that common men have always understood such remarks in Berkeley's way. Berkeley agrees, and coolly embraces the latter alternative. When Jeremy Collier, almost at the same time, published a world-view almost the same as Berkeley's, he had the minimal decency to admit that he was in the most violent possible collision with common sense. Berkeley had the unparalleled indecency to claim that his world-view is substantially identical with that of common sense, and is inconsistent only with certain fabrications of the learned.

What should one think of this philosophy? I will say what I think, even though it is certain to be seriously offensive to many people. I think that it is so perverse a use of our common, innocent, and priceless gift of language, that it should never have been allowed to be published: and that, since it was published, it has done so much damage to sanity that, if syphilis had been introduced into Europe deliberately by one man, that man would have done less harm than Berkeley, who deliberately and almost single-handed introduced idealism into modern philosophy.

It is no good saying that Berkeley's idealism was sufficiently punished by the ridicule which it excited: no good, because not true. The vulgar, indeed, laughed at what they heard of it, and the learned, apart from the philosophers, also shrugged it aside. But the *philosophers* scorned the vulgar scorn, and neglected the learned neglect, of Berkeley. Even they could not for a moment *accept* his world-view; but they did regard it as an essential, though imperfect, first step towards a true metaphysics, and, for the 150 years which begin with Kant, they devoted themselves to improving it.

But if Berkeley should never have published his philosophy in the first place, is it any more excusable that I or anyone else should discuss whether that philosophy is true, or canvass the merits of his arguments for it? To do so *in earnest*, you would have to be at least half-mad. To do so not in earnest – what possible excuse could there be for that? And you cannot do it at all, in earnest or not, without causing *some* erosion of the sanity of yourself and others; because Berkeley's philosophy, like some blood-borne virus which attacks *every* part of the body, attacks *all* sane use of language.

You cannot expose yourself to even a short course of Berkeley's philosophy, without contracting at least some tendency to think, as he wants you to think, that to speak of (say) kangaroos is, *rightly understood*, to speak of ideas of kangaroos, or of kangaroo-perceptions, or 'phenomenal kangaroos'. But on the contrary, all sane use of language requires that we never relax our grip on the tautology that when we speak of kangaroos, it is kangaroos of which we speak. Berkeley would persuade us that we lose nothing, and avoid metaphysical error, if we give up kangaroos in favour of phenomenal kangaroos: in fact we would lose everything. Phenomenal kangaroos are an even poorer substitute for kangaroos than suspected murderers are for murderers. At least a suspected murderer *may* happen to be also a murderer; but a phenomenal kangaroo is a certain kind of experience, and there is no way it might happen to be also a kangaroo.

I will not, here or elsewhere, discuss in earnest whether Berkeley's philosophy is true, because I am not even half-mad: and there could be no excuse for discussing, not in earnest, whether it is true. I *will*, later, discuss his *arguments for* his idealism, but not, I hasten to say, in order to determine whether any of them is good. Having the conclusion that they do, it is impossible that any of them should be *good*. (They might of course be valid, or ingenious, or some such.) My only object in discussing them will be to determine the particular way or ways in which they are bad.

Whether it is justified to attempt even that, may reasonably be doubted. But it is on Berkeley's arguments (as I said in Section III) that all later idealism depends, so far as it depends on arguments at all, and I will hardly, by discussing them, add to the immense damage they have caused; while I also have some hopes of repairing some of that damage. These hopes may well be groundless, but anyway they constitute *some* justification for discussing Berkeley's arguments. I do not think that there could be any other.

In the preceding section I said that it is not at all easy to be rationally sure of what it is that idealist philosophers deny. But if the summary which I gave earlier in the present section, of what there is in Berkeley's world, is correct and (as I claimed) complete, then much, at least, of what *his* idealism denies, is clear enough. For example, it clearly denies the existence of human beings. Indeed, there are no land-mammals at all in Berkeley's world. In fact there is not even any land.

Yet Berkeley was a land-mammal himself, of course, and must have known this, as we all do. So it will be easily agreed, concerning *this* form of idealism at least, that (as I said at the end of section I) it is incomparably more irrational than any ordinary religious belief. The common people of Cloyne no doubt believed a great many impossible or groundless things, about the loaves and fishes, virgin birth, and what not. But if you set these beliefs beside the world-view of the Bishop of Cloyne, then those people clearly emerge from the comparison as models of rationality.

# V

We have just seen what Berkeley's subjective idealism is. But what is objective idealism?

This is a far less easy question. With Berkeley, you know where you are. What he thinks there is, and what he thinks there is not, you can find out by reading him; even if what he *says* he thinks there is, is occasionally rather misleading. But what is the world-view which is shared by (for example) Hegel, Edward Caird, and Bradley? A daunting question, that.

It is quite hard enough to answer this question even for any *one* of the objective idealists, or for one of their books. Take, for example, Bosanquet's most elaborate metaphysical utterance: his Gifford lectures for 1911, published as *The Principle of Individuality and Value*.[30] Can we learn from this book what *his* worldview was?

You might expect so. Yet it does not seem very profitable to ask a man what he thinks there is, and what he thinks there is not, if almost the first thing he tells you is that there are *degrees* of reality. When he further tells you that the degree of reality which something has, is the same thing as its degree of logical value; and the same thing too, *ultimately*, as its degree of ethical value; and the same thing, again, as its degree of individuality, or spirit – well, the question you began by asking has by now a very naive and threadbare sound. You realize that you are dealing with a *philosopher* this time all right, and with a ripened idealism; not with just a clever young priest like Berkeley, who saw 'the Church in danger' (as the cry was at the time), and knocked together an amateur idealism almost overnight.

The case may well appear hopeless. A man who tells you that there are degrees of reality could easily tell you next that those degrees themselves are of different degrees of reality: at which point, if not before, we should presumably all give up. Still, we ought not to despair at once. Even if we do not know straight-off what the objective idealist world-view is, we do know two things which it was certainly *intended* to be.

First, we know that all the objective idealists were *determined to restore the objective and public world*. They could not accept, any more than anyone else could, Berkeley's dissolution of the public world into a number of private ones, mere 'subjects' without objects, dependent for the mutual adaptation of their 'ideas' entirely and directly on God's will. Second, we know that, for these philosophers, this restored common world could not possibly be just the plain old common world of common sense, naturalism, and science. The objective idealists were *idealists* after all, and were certainly not about to hand back the universe, on a platter and free of charge, to the 'materialists, atheists, etc.'. No *sir*, not on your transcendental or Christian Scientific life! (From about 1875 onwards, all idealists were dogged by a common and cruel parody, though a fitting one: Mrs Mary Baker Eddy.)

Yet how could these two intentions be carried out together? By dethroning Berkeley, you would only restore a status quo which had not been idealist at all, unless there is some *difference* between the public world which objective idealism restores, and the public world which subjective idealism had abolished. What *is* this difference? This was the problem of 'product-differentiation' (as you might say), which always beset objective idealism. It is also *the* problem for us, when we try to understand what objective idealism is.

This problem became pressing only gradually; because, of course, subjective idealism did not suffer from it, and there was no sudden change, by which subjective idealism gave way to the objective kind. The transition was long and slow, and Kant's idealism was only the first phase of it.

To 'place' a given philosopher in the history of modern idealism, there are two useful rules of thumb. One is that, the harder he finds it to swallow the idea of a stage in the earth's history when there was no conscious life either on it or focused on it, the earlier he is. The other is, that the more definite and affirmative he is about immortality, the earlier he is. Of course these rules are only rough guides. A writer can easily be ahead of his school on a particular issue, or behind it, or again, on different issues, both ahead of and behind it. The application of these rules is also complicated by the fact that Green at first owed much more to Kant than to Hegel, so that, with him, and in Britain, idealism to some extent hiccuped and began all over again. Still, they *are* two useful rules, and are, indeed, no more than might have been inferred, from the progress during the nineteenth century of geology and biology.

So, for example, Berkeley believed that immortality was put on a sure footing for the first time by his philosophy; and it is certainly true that in Berkeley's world there is no wear and tear on people. And his idealism was so far from leaving room for a pre-conscious stage of earth-history, that he had to talk very fast indeed to satisfy his brother-bishops that it even left room for the biblical Creation. (Between ourselves, it did not.) This is stage one, subjective idealism. In the middle stage, of earlier objective idealism, Green, for example, like Kant and Hegel, retains only a version of immortality so half-hearted and metaphysical, that no ordinary Christian could even have recognized it, let alone have been satisfied with it. But on the other hand Green is positively truculent against there ever having been a stage of earth-history devoid of consciousness.[31] This pitiful bluff-posture against science and common sense, like a frog inflating itself against a man, was still being adopted by some idealists, for example Haldane, as late as 1883.[32] But in the final stage, of full-blooded objective idealism, you find Bradley, for example, treating the idea of immortality with the contempt it deserves;[33] while to suppose that he, or someone of the comprehensive intellectual culture of Bosanquet, did not fully accept the best geology and evolutionary biology of their time, would be simply ludicrous. Bradley and Bosanquet could as easily have been flat-earthers, or stationary-bloodists, as quarrel – or at least quarrel *openly* – with anything in the science of Lyell or Darwin, or dignify the contemporary *seance* industry by giving it the least encouragement.

But of course, exactly in proportion as idealism grew more sensible about things like earth-history and immortality, its own product-differentiation problem grew more pressing. Berkeley had had no such problem and Green not much. But what did *full-blooded* objective idealism affirm, that commonsense materialism denies, or deny, that that affirms? How *does* the 'new improved' public world of objective idealism differ from the plain old public world?

Well, how might it differ? What ways are there in which the universe might be at once objective *and* 'ideal'? None too many, when you come right down to it. The way which Kant offered was not a serious candidate, hardly more so than Berkeley's way: far too much ideality, thank you professor, not nearly enough objectivity. There *is*, of course, the ancient idea that the physical universe is the body of which God is the mind. But even apart from its other drawbacks, this is dualism-writ-large, whereas objective idealism is the deadly enemy of dualism in any form. Pantheism is not a solution at all, at least on its own: the world-god could be quite devoid of ideality, or, as with Spinoza, have it only as one among infinitely many attributes. What is wanted is (as Oersted said) 'the soul *in* nature', and somehow filling it. That is easy to say, but what does it mean? Would it mean, for example, that once upon a time, Objective Mind 'posited itself as' *stars*? Or that the earth's successive rock-strata are successive Absolute Thoughts? Some objective idealists *did* try saying things like that, especially in Germany around 1800. But it is not the sort of thing which even philosophers, except the most incorrigible, can keep saying for long. For one thing, it is likely to get you mistaken for an ordinary lunatic, and treated as a public-health problem. For another, there is always some philistine who thinks he is funny, and will ask you, for example, what the difference would be between sandstone-thought-by-the-Absolute and sandstone not so blessed. A question like this was the product-differentiation problem in a nutshell, of course, and more easily asked than answered.

Most of the objective idealists were distinctly evasive when confronted with this problem, but Bosanquet never was. He faced it repeatedly, and he consistently solved it in a surprising way. His answer was that there is *no* difference in the objective idealist product. Extremes meet, he said: 'a consistent materialist and a thorough idealist hold positions which are distinguishable only in name.'[34] He disliked the word 'idealism' as a name for the prevailing philosophy, and proposed replacing it with some other name less misleading; because, he wrote, as long as the name 'idealism' is retained, 'the muddle with mentalism is so recurrent.'[35] He is always complaining about people who imagine that, according to idealism, mind 'volatilizes'[36] nature: somehow transmutes it into some finer stuff, rather as bubbles of carbon dioxide turn certain still white wines into champagne.

This bold solution to the problem of product-differentiation was well calculated, of course, to take the wind out of the sails of 'materialists, atheists, etc.'. But equally, it had the effect of mystifying and infuriating many of Bosanquet's own idealist allies. McTaggart, for example, who was a sort of neo-Berkeleian, wanted to have Bosanquet's idealist-licence revoked;[37] and many a rank-and-file idealist must have wondered what sort of runaway train he had boarded, when he gave up Christianity.

But a philosopher needed to get up very early indeed to be ahead of Bosanquet. He *also* insisted (as we have seen), that 'the

universe is so obviously experience'; and when McTaggart said
in print that 'nothing exists except Spirit', he calmly went out of
his way to express his emphatic agreement.[38] And do you think
that I have just now caught Bosanquet in the act of embracing
*inconsistent* opinions? Then you are either no logician, or else
your eyes are poorly adjusted to the twilight world of objective
idealism.

But even if the objective idealism of Bosanquet and Bradley is
not inconsistent, it is certainly extremely elusive. Suppose that, in
an attempt to reach an understanding of it, we *give* these philosophers their darling Absolute. Concede to them everything else
that they say about the Absolute: still why do they *also* keep
saying that it is *experience*? What does *that* add? What do they
mean? Or take Green's carefully worded summing-up of *his* objective idealism: that the actual universe is that 'which is eternal,
self-determined, and *thinks*'.[39] The jolt which he gave to grammar
here, by using a verb where the reader expects another adjective,
was of course perfectly deliberate. But it is only too successful.
'Thinks', in this context, defeats understanding just as much as
'shrinks', or 'blinks', would have done. What can he possibly
*mean*?

This question is not an effusion of Logical Positivist malice. It
is an inevitable expression of a bewilderment which any rational
person, reading the writers in question, will feel. The question is
a perfectly fair one: what are they *selling*, these people who call
themselves objective idealists, that a commonsense *materialist*
could not consistently buy? But we have not found the answer.

You cannot find the answer to this question by reading the
objective idealists themselves. You cannot find it by reading what
historians of philosophy have written about objective idealism. Is
it to be supposed, then, that *I* am about to tell you what the
answer is? That would be a most unreasonable fancy. There is
*no* answer to the question, what differentiates the objective idealist
product. There *is* no difference.

*Of course* Bosanquet was right, and the extremes of idealism
and materialism meet. Any objective idealist who did not see this,
or saw it only dimly, must have been sleeping on the job. A
moment ago I imagined objective idealists embarrassed by the
question, what the difference is between sandstone on the one

hand, and sandstone-thought-by-the-Absolute, or sandstone filled with mind, on the other. But in fact the question is quite misdirected, and whether or not it ever did, it never should have embarrassed any objective idealist. It would have been *obviously* silly, and unfair, to ask an objective idealist to *point out a specimen* of each of the two kinds of sandstone; since his doctrine is, of course, that there *is* only the mind-filled kind of sandstone. And it would have been silly and unfair even to have asked him what the difference *would* be, if there *were* the two kinds of sandstone: for his doctrine is, after all, that there *could* not be any kind of sandstone, except the kind that has thought in it.

It has been well said of Matthew Arnold that he brought thousands over to the side of reasonableness about religion, by quietly letting it be understood 'that Atheism is the religion of the Church of England'.[40] The objective idealists were engaged in something very similar. They were not out to take anything *away* from the world of common sense and science: quite the contrary, as I have said, half of their object was to put guts back into the world which Berkeley had eviscerated. But they were not out to *add* anything to that world either. They left *that* sort of thing to vulgar 'mediums', to those clergymen who still believed in eternal torments, and to the few dualists then surviving in metaphysics, epistemology, or ethics. Neither adding nor taking away, they quietly let it be understood that it is commonsense materialism which is the world-view of objective idealism.

When, therefore, Bradley says that the Absolute is experience, or Bosanquet says that nothing exists except spirit, they do not mean, despite all appearances, anything which a commonsense materialist denies. When *Berkeley* implied that nothing exists except spirit, he *did*, of course, mean something inconsistent with commonsense materialism. Subjective idealism portrays the universe as being quite literally congenial: its *doctrine* is that there is nothing except what is like us in our mental capacities. But objective idealism portrays the world rightly, and as everyone knows it to be, with congeniality confined within the very narrow limits which everyone knows it to have. Only, it breathes an *atmosphere* of congeniality over the whole, and through every part. The world of objective idealism is simply the actual world *spoken of in pulpit tones*, or more exactly, in the tones of a

lecturer to the London Ethical Society around 1885. Whereas
Berkeley was openly and artlessly anthropocentric, Bosanquet is
an emphatic and effective critic of anthropocentrism. He leaves
you with a strong *impression*, of course, that human beings are
much dearer to the universe's heart than rocks, grasses, or lob-
sters, and he does so deliberately and systematically. But that is
not part of his *doctrine*.

It is all done by rhetorical means, some of which are obvious
enough. One is an unfailingly unctuous and buoyant tone.
Another is constant appeal to the authority of Hegel, or Kant, or
Plato, or Aristotle, it being constantly suggested that everything
the objective idealist contends for was proved by these demigods
long ago, and that you would know this if you were not so
amazingly ignorant of the history of philosophy. There is also a
steady cannonade of violent solecisms: saying or implying that
some common English word, such as 'reality', or 'thought', means
– something staggeringly remote from what it does in fact mean.
Most important of all, of course, there is a deliberate and systematic running-together of evaluative and non-evaluative language:
of ethics with metaphysics, ethics with logic, ethics with everything. Often, however, the means by which the objective idealists
conveyed cosmic reassurances are too complex for me, at least,
to analyse. For example, like some other philosophers, they are
monists, and hold that all finite existence is self-contradictory, or
'goes beyond itself'; but only *they* would have chosen to express
this by saying, for example, that '*self-sacrifice* is the fundamental
logical structure of Reality', and thrown in for good measure a
reference to the Atonement![41] Who will disentangle for us this
disgusting mixture of metaphysics, ethics, and logic, with Christian barbarism about a god who died to pay a debt?

The cosmic reassurance which objective idealism offered, then,
was rhetorical rather than substantive, or ethical rather than
metaphysical. Of course it was not left for me to point this out.
Indeed, and as usual, it was pointed out by some of the idealists
themselves. In *Man's Place in the Cosmos*, Andrew Seth said that
'every idealistic theory of the world has for its ultimate premises
a logically unsupported judgement of value'.[42] You must of course
understand that Seth was not *complaining* when he said this. He
was not *against* you letting a preference control your philosophy,

and did not mean that anthropocentrism is a fault in his fellow-idealists. Quite the contrary, he held that, as against the 'natural-istic tendency, philosophy must be unflinchingly *humanistic*, anthropocentric.'[43] This was, to be sure, deliberately more pro-vocative than orthodox; Seth was in partial revolt (as I said in section II) against the full-blooded objective idealism of Bradley and Bosanquet. *Their* anthropocentrism was the reverse of unflinching; in fact you could call it flinching: you can feel it everywhere in their writings, but you can pin it on them nowhere. Once, though only once, Bosanquet *seemed* to have been caught red-handed, and to be gone for all money. This was when he seemed to say, in his *Logic*, that European civilization is *logically* safe from earthquakes and every other kind of catastrophe.[44] But he took it back so promptly in a footnote, that they had to let him go.

It does not require any originality, then, to point out that the cosmic reassurance which objective idealism afforded was entirely extraneous to its world-view. But this reassurance also had a certain intrinsic *logical* defect, which has never, perhaps, been pointed out as distinctly as it might be.

It was observed in section I above that belief in ordinary religious propositions has an unusual, and illogical, origin: such propositions are believed partly because they are known to be false. People would not think that there are interested higher powers around them, but for the fact that they know there aren't, and wish there were. Now, objective idealism is so remote and refined a descendant of popular religion, that one would not expect it to inherit a trait so grossly illogical as this one, or anything like it. Yet it does, and in fact an even worse form of it.

The message of objective idealism, put briefly but not unfairly, is this: '*All* sandstone is of the better, or mind-filled, kind; in fact, everything is; indeed, the better or mind-filled kind of reality is the only possible kind of reality.' Now, you could not be reassured or consoled by this message, unless you understood it. To under-stand it, you have to know what is meant by calling something 'better'. A person does not understand what is meant by calling something 'better', unless he knows that, if something is better, then it is at least possible for something else to be worse or inferior. But if a person does know that, then he knows that the third of the above clauses is logically false. So, much as popular religion can be believed only by someone who knows that it is false, objective idealism can reassure or console only someone who knows that it is impossible.

We philosophers of the Jazz Age cannot read the objective idealists without experiencing that *horror victorianorum* of which I spoke in Essay I, and when we read them a lot, that feeling reaches the point of nausea. We have a strong though indistinct suspicion that we are being offered a kind of cosmic consolation which is even more nauseous than the ordinary religious consolation of Victorian times: more nauseous, because it even manages to be *logically* absurd, which the ordinary religious kind never is. We can scarcely escape the conviction that the objective idealists *must* have been hypocrites. I think I have shown, in the preceding paragraph, that our suspicion, and our nausea, are justified; and shown, too, that like subjective idealism, objective idealism really is far more irrational than ordinary religious belief.

But the objective idealists were *not* hypocrites. They were just, like many philosophers, divided in their minds. They were like some stage-performer who said, in order to ingratiate himself with his audience, 'You are all wonderful people', but unluckily felt constrained to add (perhaps because he was a Christian Scientist), 'All audiences, *necessarily*, are all wonderful people.'

The trouble does not lie, as it has sometimes been supposed to do, in the mere fact that some predicate, normally applied to some things but not others, is given *universal* application. Objective idealism does of course universalize the application of certain descriptive predicates, such as 'experience' or 'thought'. But it is not this which generates the logical falsity that I am speaking of. The objective idealists' trouble, like the stage-performer's, is that they give *necessarily*-universal application to a predicate, such as 'higher' or 'better', which is favourably *evaluative*. The absurdity is most conspicuous when *comparative* predicates, such as those are employed, but even that is not necessary: 'good' would be enough to produce the logical falsity. And you do not even need a *purely* evaluative predicate. The all-time-favourite predicate with objective idealists is 'spiritual', and it, of course, *combines* evaluative with descriptive elements: it gives you 'better', and 'mind-filled', at once. But it is only the evaluative element here, not the descriptive one, which generates the logical falsity I am speaking of when the universe is said to be necessarily spiritual. The cleft stick that the objective idealists were in, what divided their minds, was this. Without some favourably evaluative predicate or other, their philosophy could not have conveyed any reassurance at all: which, as I have said all along, it is the basic purpose of all idealism to do. And without the *necessary*-universalization of that predicate, any reassurance which they could have conveyed would have been at best contingent, and not *philosophical* at all. A reassurance which was only contingent could sink further, into a reassurance which was only finite, and even merely local, or temporary, or ambiguous. And *that* would be no different from the reassurance which is afforded by belief in finite, and even local, or capricious, or warring, gods. If you are determined, as the objective idealists were, to be *both* reassuring *and* philosophical-as-distinct-from-religious, then you are locked into the absurdity of *everything* being necessarily better or higher.

Bosanquet easily fended off Seth's implied criticism,[45] and for similar reasons no competent objective idealist would have been troubled by the criticism I have just made. The distinction, for example, between judgements of value and other judgements, or between evaluative and descriptive predicates, is one of those 'dualisms' which objective idealists regarded as merely superficial, and which they criticized so persuasively. The distinction, again, between wishes and thoughts, would have been smeared up equally effectively by any competent objective idealist. In any case, my criticism, as I said, touches only the rhetorical exterior of objective idealism.

Still, this was a case in which it was the husk of a philosophy, not its kernel, that was historically all-important. It was the consolatory *sound* of objective idealism, not its prosaic substance, which principally recommended it. And this held good not only for the readers of it, but for the writers as well. Philosophers are hardly ever cynical manipulators of their readers' minds. They do not produce delusions in others, without first being subject to them themselves; and the present case was a typical one in this respect.

# VI

Objective idealism, then, falls into logical falsity by giving necess-arily-universal application to some evaluative predicate; though this criticism, as I admitted, affects only the rhetorical exterior of that philosophy. But objective idealism does also give universal application to certain *descriptive* predicates, such as 'experience', or 'thought', and this too has always aroused the deepest suspicion among non-idealists. The suspicion is well founded. In fact this line of criticism will take us much nearer to the heart of objective idealism than the one I have just been discussing. It also affects idealism of every sort, not just objective idealism.

Many philosophers, for example A. N. Whitehead and Samuel Butler, have thought that consciousness, or thought, or experi-ence, is present in some degree throughout all nature: that even billiard balls, rocks, atoms, electrons, all possess some faint rudi-ments, at least, of mentality. Leibniz, of course, believed some-thing very similar. Now, suppose this were true.

In that case, congeniality would certainly be spread far more widely in the world, and mind would count for more in nature, causally speaking, than common sense and science now suppose. Yet here is a curious thing: this theory is not at all an *idealist* one. Every philosopher can tell, straight off, that this theory does *not* belong to the same breed as Berkeley's, or Kant's, or Hegel's, or any kind of idealism. If this theory were true, it would be the most amazing turn-up in physics and biology. But that is all it would be. We would not have changed our *philosophy*, and become idealists, if we accepted it.

Now, *why* is this theory not a form of idealism? What is the difference between it and every kind of idealism? What *would* make idealism true, if universal mentality is not enough to make it true? The answer to this question will take us into the very heartland of our subject.

Surely the answer is the following: that while, on this theory, thought, or something thought-like, is given more 'seats' in reality (so to speak), and a bigger causal *role*, than common sense or science allows it, still, thought is not here credited with *constituting* reality, whereas *that* is what idealism claims for it. Ordinary religious belief, after all, also gives thought more seats in reality, and exaggerates its causal *role*, sometimes even crediting it with a creative power; but there is nothing idealistic about ordinary religion. Philosophical idealism demands something quite different: the *identity* of reality with thought or with something thought-like. It is not enough for idealism that a billiard ball, and everything else, 'be thought', in a *predicative* sense: I mean that the billiard ball, while being (for example) round and hard and shiny, be thought as well – supposing we could understand even that. Still less is it enough for idealism that a billiard ball, and everything else, 'be thought' in a *relational* sense: I mean, that it be thought *of*, by someone or something. What idealism requires is that billiard balls, and everything else, *be* thoughts (or experiences, or ideas, etc.), in the sense of 'be identical with'. Idealism is an identity-claim, or it is nothing: nothing but some variety or other of dualism.

It seems to be essential to thoughts that they are had by, or thought by, someone or something; but an objective idealist will deny this. In the case of the *Absolute's* thoughts, he says, there is no distinction between the thought and its thinker; and perhaps he will be able to beat us down on this point. There is one point about thoughts, though, which no one could possibly beat us down on. Even if thoughts do not have to be *by* anything, they do need to be *of* something. An object of thought does not need to be a real object, of course: we can think of Pegasus, for instance. But a thought without any object of thought at all, is just not on. And with *this*, we find to our relief, even idealists all agree. (As far as I know, everyone does: even those philosophers of the present day who are so desperate as to deny the existence of thoughts, do not deny, I think, that if there were a thought it would be a thought of something.)

According to idealism, then, a physical object, such as a red billiard ball, is a thought. According to everyone, a thought has to be a thought of something. So according to idealism, a red billiard ball is a thought of something.

Let us ask an idealist, then, what it is that a red billiard ball is a thought of. As soon as we frame this question, a nightmarish possibility crosses our minds. Perhaps the idealist is going to reply that a red billiard ball is a thought of a white billiard ball, or a thought of a red rose, or of money, or Monteverdi, or muchness. If he did, it would be knock-off time for all concerned; but in fact, of course, the idealist is not going to give any answer like those. There is method in his madness, and even a rather admirable sort of simplicity. His answer is, that the thought which a red billiard ball is, is a thought of a red billiard ball. Well, 'for this relief, much thanks': it could have been so much worse.

Here, then, is an epitome, brief but not at all unfair, of all idealism: 'A red billiard ball is a thought of a red billiard ball.' According to Hegel and Bosanquet, a red billiard ball is *the Absolute's* thought of a red billiard ball. According to Malebranche, a red billiard ball is *God's* thought of a red billiard ball. According to Berkeley, if we suppose for a moment that I am the *only* finite spirit, a red billiard ball is *my* thought of a red billiard ball. According to Kant, if we re-name all his 'forms', 'categories', and other bureaucracy, simply 'the bureaucracy', then a red billiard ball is *the bureaucracy's* thought of a red billiard ball.

But now idealism, in any form, is exposed to two criticisms, both of which were to some extent foreshadowed in my discussion of objective idealism. One is, that it produces a meeting of extremes which makes idealism pointless. The second is, that it requires anyone who believes it to fulfil a peculiar condition: he must know that it is impossible.

Idealism is an assertion of identity: that a red billiard ball *is* a thought of a red billiard ball. Suppose, then, that idealism is true, and a red billiard ball is a thought of a red billiard ball. In that case, it is also true that a thought of a red billiard ball is a red billiard ball.

Was there ever a more desolating anticlimax? The spiritual or ideal red billiard ball, when you finally reach it, turns out to be nothing but a common red billiard ball! What sort of a reward is this, I want to know, for all the effort which idealists had put into cosmic reassurance, for all those decades, and long after the cowardly *priests* had given up? After all their heavy breathing, as they laboured to infuse a little spirituality into things, do they get a better class of red billiard ball, a red billiard ball redeemed by Spirit? Not in the least: just an ordinary red billiard ball, which anyone could have had for the asking from the outset.

But we must not let our indignation obscure the fact that the idealists, like many other unfortunates, had only got what they wanted most. They *would* attempt to spiritualize the physical world, and nothing less than identity would satisfy them. But the symmetry of identity is not one of its more *recherché* properties, after all. So they can scarcely complain when they find that, if they do succeed in spiritualizing the physical world, they physicalize the spiritual world at the same time.

The meeting of extremes, then, which Bosanquet to his credit always insisted upon, is by no means a peculiarity of objective idealism. Idealism of any kind cannot afford to settle for anything short of the identity of thought with thing; and then the mere symmetry of identity does the rest. Even in Berkeley, you can see in the distance this chicken flying home to roost, in the fact that he could never make up his mind whether '*esse est percipi*', his identity-claim about 'sensible objects', is a grand truth, or a triviality: the most astounding and consoling discovery of all time, which utterly abolishes billiard balls, or something quite banal and non-consoling, which everyone had always known, and which leaves billiard balls just as they were.

There is, of course, a way out of this problem of the meeting of extremes: in fact not just a way, but a way which has been worn smooth by the usage of a million travellers. I mean directed, or *one-way*, identity. For years now, Malcolm Muggeridge has been collecting examples, from the most various authors, of one-way identity and one-way resemblance: a hobby which can be guaranteed to afford hours of fun and profit. Perhaps even Muggeridge's own writings might be found to furnish a specimen or two. It is hard, for example, for a believer in the Trinity not to feel that Mary's boy-child must be, at any rate, *more* identical with the Father, than the Father can possibly be with Mary's boy-child. A certain hankering for one-way identity can be detected even in the contemporary advocates of the identity of mental states with states of the brain (according to a suggestion of my colleague Mr Lloyd Reinhardt). Whether or not this particular suggestion is true, there is certainly a lot of it about. But for idealists, of whatever kind, one-way identity is not merely a temptation, or an optional extra. If you are an idealist, and do not want to be equally a materialist, then you simply cannot afford to be without it.

The home-coming of this first chicken, the meeting of extremes, does not make the idealist roost uninhabitable, of course: it just makes it pointless to inhabit it. The home-coming of the second chicken is more disruptive.

I asked, why are Whitehead and Butler and Leibniz not idealists, and again, what *would* suffice to make idealism true, since universal mentality would not? But the answer I gave implied that there is *no* possible way that the world might be, which would make idealism true. To confirm this, take a theory like Whitehead's, and exaggerate it. Let the universe, down to its last electron, be of as high a grade of intelligence as you please. Suppose even (since there is no point in stinting ourselves here) that it is bung-full of love too. It is still perfectly clear that there is nothing at all idealist about this theory. If the world is that way, then that is the way the world is, and *thought's* only concern in the matter is to acknowledge that there *is* this much thought, love, and so on around. Our physics and biology would then be miles away from where they are now. But our *philosophy* would not be one inch nearer to being idealism.

The spirituality, or thought, or ideality, then, which idealism ascribes to the world, is not any sort of possible way the world might be, or any sort of contents it might have. No amount of intelligent electrons, affectionate air, etc., will ever suffice to make idealism true. To make idealism true, what is needed is that electrons, if they are intelligent, be identical with thoughts of intelligent electrons; and that electrons, if they are not intelligent, be identical with thoughts of non-intelligent electrons; and so on, for red billiard balls, and everything else.

Yet that is what can never be, and even the idealist knows it can never be. For you cannot believe that a red billiard ball is a

thought of a red billiard ball, unless you understand it. To understand it, you have to know what is meant, respectively, by the
phrases, 'a red billiard ball', and 'a thought of a red billiard ball'.
But if you do know what those phrases mean, then you know
that a thought of a red billiard ball cannot possibly be the same
thing as a red billiard ball, just as a thought of a murder cannot
possibly be the same thing as a murder. Only someone who knows
that idealism is impossible, then, can believe it. The spirituality
which idealism ascribes to the world is therefore not only a 'light
that never was on land or sea', and never could be: it is a light
which the idealist himself, if he believes his philosophy, knows
there never could be.

To say this is not to accuse idealists of hypocrisy. They are
not hypocrites. They are merely divided in their minds, and
overwhelmed by a wish. With half of his mind an idealist knows,
quite as well as everyone else does, that a red billiard ball cannot
be a thought of a red billiard ball. But he also *must* have the
world congenial, saturated all through by thought, and nothing
short of the identity of thing with thought will make that congeniality intimate enough.

But while idealism is not hypocritical, it *is* hard to beat for
anthropocentricity. What are *we* best qualified for, what is the
strongest part of *our* game? Why, thought, of course: both in
general, as being members of the most intelligent species, and in
particular as being philosophers. Well then, thought must perforce
be the very constitution of reality. And if this is not possible, that
does not make it any the less imperative.

The only way to be *more* anthropocentric than ordinary idealism would be if some heterodox sect of idealists were to identify
reality, not with thought in general, but just with *false or senseless*
thought. For surely *that* is the *really* strongest part of our game:
that is where neither animals nor angels nor God can come near
us, and where we philosophers leave even our fellow-men for
dead. If a philosopher wants to make the universe *maximally*
congenial, he should identify reality with error, contradiction, and
absurdity. This would, after all, spread *real* ideality all round,
and stamp our distinctive trademark indelibly on all reality in a
way which mere *true* thought never could.

This *doubly* impossible kind of idealism, it is likely enough, actually was embraced by some philosophers in the third or fourth century AD: it certainly has a sort of neo-Platonist, or perhaps a Gnostic-Christian, ring to it. But even if no one ever has held it, it is nevertheless the very conclusion to which all idealism inevitably tends. This statement will probably seem outrageous or unserious, but I am convinced of its truth. The reason is that, just as ordinary religion is believed partly because it is known to be false, so idealism, whenever it has been believed, has been believed partly *because* it was known to be impossible: believed from an active *preference* for absurdity, and for more absurdity rather than less.

Almost any philosopher will sometimes take a certain pleasure in maintaining, for fun or in the hope of learning something, some logical impossibility which he does not at all believe, but cannot see his way to avoid. But this is taking an occasional, superficial, and innocent pleasure in impossibility. Idealist philosophers are very different: they take a pleasure in impossibility which is neither occasional, nor superficial, nor innocent.

In the case of the objective idealists, this fact is even obvious. Hegel and Bradley are always bringing bad news, of course, of the outbreak of 'contradictions' in even the most settled districts: but who cannot detect that they do so with *satisfaction*? They pretend to be only fire-spotters, but anyone can tell that they are actually firebugs. Some people's idea of paradise is to have flowers springing up around one's feet at every step: *theirs* is to have impossibilities doing the same.

The same thing is sufficiently obvious in Kant: recall this attitude to his famous four 'antinomies'. These things, precisely because they are supposed to impose impossibilities inescapably on us, are quite clearly very precious to him, like children to a doting parent; even though these ones are, to any non-parental eye, uncommonly feeble and ugly. But Kant would have killed to keep them, or at least would have had forty more if he could have come by them.

And even as to Berkeley, what do you think it was that made his philosophy so pleasing to his own mind, and so inexhaustibly attractive to other minds? Was it his celestial mechanics of spirits: the business about the infinite immaterial television-station and its flock of little television-receivers? Of course not: there is not even anything really *idealist* about *that*. If the world is 'will and idea' in that particular way, then that is the way the world is, and *thought* does not constitute it so. Whereas it is precisely that, of course – the most paradoxical, incredible, impossible thing of all – which is the priceless thing to Berkeley's mind: that perception or thought is the essence of physical things. Or in other words, that perceptions or thoughts *of ours*, to which *according to Berkeley himself, nothing corresponds or could correspond*, are the very constitution of physical reality.

What all idealism does, then, and the secret of its attraction, is this: it diffuses through all reality that falsity, or impossibility, or absurdity, which in fact *distinguishes*, and which we *know* distinguishes, human beings from all other things, and philosophers from all other human beings. It is by one touch of *erring* human nature that idealism makes the whole world kin. And this is why idealism inevitably gravitates towards its doubly impossible special case.

If this suggestion seems to you too fanciful, and the preference for impossibility which I impute to idealists too improbable to be true, then I think you must know little of the lengths that intelligence will go to, once deprived of popular religion, to hide from an indifferent universe. But I will also remind you that the nineteenth century was not only the century of objective idealism, but the century of romanticism. If I had said of certain *poets* of that time, that the only world that attracted *them* was not only not the actual world but not even a possible one, and that its impossibility was for them an essential part of its attraction, then I would have been thought to utter a commonplace of literary history, rather than a paradox. Yet is is only another case of this same preference for the *known*-to-be-impossible, that I ascribe to the philosophical contemporaries of those poets.

Neither of the two criticisms I have made in this section would disturb a competent objective idealist. He would deny, of course, that he knows his own philosophy to be impossible if he believes it. He would point out that, in my argument for that conclusion, I took for granted that if two things are different (such as a red billiard ball and a thought of a red billiard ball), then they are not identical. But this, he would rightly remark, is to embrace precisely that 'abstract' conception of identity, against which he has argued so long and so persuasively. All identity, he holds, is identity-*in*-difference, just as all difference is difference within some wider identity. As to my first criticism, about the extremes meeting, he would say that it is not only no criticism, but a truth on which he himself has insisted all along.

The possibility of these replies may be depressing. But then it would be merely foolish to hope to triumph by argument over someone who combines first-rate philosophical ability, an overpowering religious impulse, and an active preference for more rather than less impossibility. In fact this would be a signal instance of something I warned against in section III above: the overestimation of the importance of argument in philosophy.

But I regret to find that I have said nothing which would convince a reader, unfamiliar with the objective idealists, that the philosophical ability of the best of them *is* first-rate. So I will mention here that, if you want an exposition and defence of the commonsense-materialist view of the mind, the best I know of is in Bosanquet's *The Principle of Individuality and Value*, especially lecture V. Indeed, that book as a whole is as good as any philosophy book I ever read; and I am not forgetting Hume's *Dialogues*, or Frege's *Foundations of Arithmetic*. It is an independent question, of course, whether it is better, or not, that the book should ever have been published at all. If, on the other hand, the reader is still not convinced that Victorian idealism, even at its best, was a sickening evasion, forever restoring religious consolation while pretending to take it away, he should read chapter XXII of *Appearance and Reality*. This is entitled 'Nature', and it will enable anyone who reads it to form an accurate estimate of the great philosopher F. H. Bradley.

The reader, who perhaps thought that what I said earlier about sandstone was unfair to the idealists, will here find Bradley gravely asking, 'Is there in fact such a thing as inorganic Nature?'[46] Suitably to the difficulty of this question, his answer is long and complicated. But the upshot of his answer appears to be, 'Probably not': wretched luck for sandstone, but there it is. Here, too, the reader will find Bradley's characteristic way of getting around that old pitfall for idealism, the 'pre-organic time' in the history of the earth, which geology and biology imply.

Bradley does not, of course, quarrel *openly* with that implication. He falls back instead on his well known bag of tricks for discrediting science and common sense *in general*: the 'contradictions' which, he says, infest our ideas of space, of time, of things-and-their-relations, and so on. His conclusion is that 'Nature without sentience . . . is a mere construction for science, and it possesses a very partial reality.'[47] To find out what this last phrase means, you must, of course, read the later chapter entitled 'Degrees of truth and reality': and if you find *that* as clear as mud, this will only prove your philosophical incompetence. But Bradley's overall strategy, at least, is clear: for the sake of protecting his smelly 'spiritual' universe from the evolutionary part of science, he would persuade us that *all* science is only an *ad hoc*, and even a basically practical device. It is doubtful whether the entire literature of modern idealism furnishes any spectacle more disgusting than this one.

## Notes

1  D. Hume, *Dialogues concerning Natural Religion*, ed. N. Kemp Smith, (Oxford University Press, 1935), p. 280.
2  For unusually explicit acknowledgements of this fact, see, for example, B. Bosanquet, *The Civilisation of Christendom* (Swan Sonnenschein, London, 1899); J. M. E. McTaggart, *Studies in Hegelian Cosmology* (Cambridge University Press, 1901), p. 196; A. Seth, *Man's Place in the Cosmos* (Blackwood, Edinburgh and London, 1897), *passim*.
3  On this subject, see two classic works: J. M. Robertson, *A History of Freethought in the Nineteenth Century* (Rationalist Press Association, 1929; reprinted Dawsons of Pall Mall, London, 1969), and A. W. Benn, *A History of English Rationalism in the Nineteenth Century* (Longmans, Green, London, 1906).
4  Benn, *A History of English Rationalism* vol. II, p. 454.
5  Quoted by Robertson, *A History of Freethought*, vol. I, p. 223n.
6  Two other examples are J. A. Froude's *The Nemesis of Faith* (1849; reprinted Walter Scott Publishing Co., London and Newcastle-upon-Tyne, 1904) and Henry Rogers's *The Eclipse of Faith* (1852; 9th edn, Longman, Green, Longman & Roberts, London, 1860).

7    A. E. Taylor, *Philosophical Studies* (Macmillan, London, 1934), ch. IX.

8    John Foster, *Critical Essays contributed to the Eclectic Review* (Bell and Daldy, London, 1871), vol. I, pp. 95–110.

9    F. H. Bradley, *Appearance and Reality* (Clarendon Press, Oxford, 1893), p. 129. Italics not in text.

10   This quotation, and the next, are from the article on Vane in *The Dictionary of National Biography*.

11   *Works of T. H. Green*, ed. R. Nettleship (Longmans, Green, London; vol. I, 1885; vol. II, 1886; vol. III, 1889), vol. III, p. 346.

12   Ibid., vol. III, p. 364.

13   Ibid., vol. III, p. 364.

14   Ibid., vol. III, p. 17.

15   B. Bosanquet, *The Philosophical Theory of the State* (Macmillan, London, 1899).

16   B. Bosanquet, *The Civilisation of Christendom* (Swan Sonnenschein, London, 1899).

17   'An ignorant faith is better than an over-confident knowledge.' Quoted in Sir W. Hamilton, *Discussions on Philosophy and Literature, Education and University Reform* (Longman, Brown, Green and Longmans, London, 1853), p. 636.

18   I. Kant, *Critique of Pure Reason* trans. N. Kemp Smith (Macmillan, London, 1950), p. 29.

19   See, for example, D. M. Armstrong, *A Materialist Theory of the Mind* (Routledge and Kegan Paul, London, 1968), pp. 36–6.

20   N. D. Mermin, 'Quantum mysteries for anyone', *Journal of Philosophy*, LXXVIII, 7 (1981), pp. 397–408.

21   F. Nietzsche, *The Antichrist*, in *The Portable Nietzsche* trans. W. Kaufmann (Penguin Books, Harmondsworth, 1976), p. 578.

22   J. H. Muirhead (ed.), *Bernard Bosanquet and His Friends* (Allen and Unwin, London, 1935), p. 243.

23   This ingratitude is widely recognized: see, for example, A. C. Ewing, *Idealism: a critical survey* (Methuen, London, 1933), p. 384; F. C. S. Schiller, *Studies in Humanism* (Macmillan, London, 1907), p. 231.

24   See the memoir by Nettleship in his *Works of T. H. Green*, vol. III, p. xli.

25   J. A. Passmore, *A Hundred Years of Philosophy* (Penguin Books, Harmondsworth, 1968), p. 57.

26   In A. J. Balfour, *A Defence of Philosophic Doubt* (Macmillan, London, 1879), and again in A. J. Balfour, *The Foundations of Belief* (Longmans, Green, London, 1895).

27 In A. Seth, *Man's Place in the Cosmos* (Blackwood, Edinburgh and London, 1897).
28 A. J. Balfour, *Essays Speculative and Political* (Hodder and Stoughton, London, 1920), p. 111.
29 N. Tolstoy, *The Tolstoys* (Coronet Books, London, 1985), p. 279.
30 B. Bosanquet, *The Principle of Individuality and Value* (Macmillan, London, 1912).
31 E.g., Nettleship, *Works of T. H. Green*, vol. II, p. 76. But Green makes a nervous admission of the possibility of humans being descended from lower animals, in T. H. Green, *Prolegomena to Ethics* (2nd edn, Oxford University Press, 1884), pp. 88–9.
32 See A. Seth and R. B. Haldane (eds), *Essays in Philosophical Criticism* (reprint by Burt Franklin, New York, 1971, of 1st edn, 1883), pp. 57–8.
33 Bradley, *Appearance and Reality*, pp. 444–51.
34 B. Bosanquet, *Knowledge and Reality* (Kegan Paul, Trench, London, 1885), p. 7.
35 Muirhead, *Bernard Bosanquet and His Friends*, p. 152.
36 For example, Bosanquet, *The Principle of Individuality and Value*, p. 282.
37 See *Mind*, (XXI(NS), July 1912) 433.
38 B. Bosanquet, *The Meeting of Extremes in Contemporary Philosophy* (Macmillan, London, 1921), p. xii.
39 Nettleship, *Works of T. H. Green*, vol. I, p. 299.
40 Quoted in J. M. Robertson, *Modern Humanists Reconsidered* (Watts, London, 1927), p. 125.
41 Bosanquet, *The Principle of Individuality and Value*, pp. 243–4.
42 Seth, *Man's Place in the Cosmos*, p. vii.
43 Ibid. p. 40. Italics in text.
44 B. Bosanquet, *Logic* (2nd edn, Oxford University Press, 1911), vol. II, p. 220.
45 Bosanquet, *The Principle of Individuality and Value*, pp. 291ff.
46 Bradley, *Appearance and Reality*, p. 239.
47 Ibid., p. 245.

# 6

## Idealism: a Victorian Horror-story
## (Part Two)

### I

Francis Bacon made a collection of what he called 'idols of the tribe': falsities which every human being believes or has some tendency to believe. A useful collection could be made of idols of the *philosophical* tribe: falsities which are carefully handed down, as though they were precious truths, from each generation of philosophers to the next.

That philosophy begins in wonder, is one of these. Another is that philosophers never all agree, or that there is no opinion so absurd but that some philosopher has held it. This was repeated by Cicero after Varro, by Hobbes after Descartes, by Hamilton, and by a thousand others before and since. In fact this silly slander against philosophers has always been such a favourite with the victims of it, that it could almost serve as its own sufficient counter-example.

But straightforward counter-examples to it are not hard to find. Here is one: that whatever follows from a necessary truth is a necessary truth itself, or that necessary truths have no contingent consequences. The negation of this is an opinion so absurd that no philosopher has ever held it. Of course this truth, like any other, can be expressed in many different ways, and it has been so expressed. Hume, for example, never wrote, and never would have written, 'Necessary truths have no contingent consequences.' Still, that is quite certainly part (though only part) of what he meant when he wrote, as he repeatedly did write, that 'there can be no demonstrative arguments for a matter of fact and existence.'[1]

There is an important special case of the truth that necessary truths have only necessarily-true consequences: namely, that tautologies have only tautological consequences. This too has never been denied by any philosopher. Again, it can be, and has been, expressed in different ways.

But of course it is one thing to know a certain general principle, and another to recognize its application in every particular case. It is only too easy, as everyone knows, to fail to see the application, in a given case, of some general rule which we know perfectly well. This is most common, perhaps, where the rule is a moral one, and the case is a case of our own conduct; but the same thing is common enough where the general rule is one of fact, or logic, or whatever. A physicist may be satisfied of the truth that energy is conserved, but fail to see that his own pet theory or invention requires that it be not conserved. A logician may be guilty, in a particular case, of what in general terms he recognizes as a fallacy. And so on.

Just so, the fact that philosophers all know that necessary truths have only necessarily-true consequences, and tautologies only tautological ones, is no guarantee that they will always bring this knowledge to bear in cases where they should. It is still perfectly possible that they will mistake a particular argument, say, from a tautological premise to a contingent conclusion, for a valid one.

Not only is this possible: it is a temptation to which everyone, including philosophers, is constantly exposed. For we all want, as it is perfectly reasonable to want, our conclusions to be as interesting as possible, our premises to be as certain as possible, and our reasoning to be as conclusive as possible. And who cannot see that this threefold want, if it is not restrained by our own better knowledge, will sometimes lead us to imagine that these three desiderata have all been maximally satisfied at once: for example, that some non-tautological conclusion has been rigorously derived from a tautological premise?

It is in just that way that millions of people, some of them philosophers, *have* concluded that all human effort is ineffectual, from the premise that whatever will be, will be; have concluded that everyone is selfish, from the premise that a man's desires are necessarily *his* desires; have concluded, from the tautology that every effect has a cause, that every event has a cause. Shall I go on? Shall I remind you of Socrates, concluding, from the premise that whatever becomes F must have previously been not-F, that the soul has an interminable, though undulatory, history? Shall I mention the thousands who have thought that a naval battle tomorrow is either impossible or inevitable, because it is necessary that there will be one or not? Hegel, fixing the number of the planets, with no other premises than truths of logic? Bentham, whose only real argument for 'the principle of utility' was, that 'it is but a tautology to say, that the more consistently it is pursued, the better it must ever be for mankind'?[2]

Tedium forbids that this list be lengthened: we have all heard this complaint far too often. Ever since Francis Bacon, a hurricane of complaint has been blowing, to the effect that philosophers have tried to do '*a priori*', or 'deductively', or 'speculatively', what can be done only 'inductively' or '*a posteriori*', or 'naturalistically', if it can be done at all. In this way (so the criticism goes), philosophers have not only made no progress in their own enquiries, but have effectively prevented enquirers of another kind from making progress where progress was possible. This hurricane of complaint is blowing still. In many of its forms it is, and always has been, stupid, ignorant, vulgar, and destructive. But it is, and always has been, also essentially right.

It was and is wrong, indeed, if it implies that it is *only* philosophers who try to conjure contingent conclusions out of necessary truths. When Hegel pretended to fix the number of the planets from premises of logic, he met with some small part of the derision he deserved; but when a famous scientist, Sir Arthur Eddington, pretended to fix the number of electrons in the universe from premises of mere arithmetic, he met with nothing worse than polite silence. More importantly, it is *the people* who are most hopelessly addicted to inferring fatalism from 'Whatever will be, will be', and to inferring universal selfishness from the fact that no man can have interests or desires other than his own. Even if those contemptible arguments *originated with* philosophers, which they may or may not have done, it is philosophers alone who, to their credit, have laboured to expose them.

Yet it must be admitted that this temptation to produce non-tautological rabbits out of tautological hats is especially strong for philosophers. For consider. Rigorously valid reasoning is both part of philosophers' subject-matter, and one of their boasts; philosophers' conclusions are, characteristically, extremely general and interesting, not to say amazing; and yet, except *per accidens*, they have no more knowledge of any contingent matter, that could serve as the premises of their reasonings, than the next man has. Any special expertise which they possess is all confined to 'the realm of essence'. Clearly, therefore, it must be an *occupational* hazard for philosophers, to be tempted to milk interesting results out of tautologies; even though they are also the very people who best know that the thing cannot be done.

When interesting conclusions are drawn from tautological premises, it is sometimes quite obvious that that is what has been done. But it is much more common to meet with arguments which you cannot be certain are of that kind, though you have strong and rational suspicions that they are so. The usual reason for this uncertainty is that the premise is ambiguous, between one meaning which is tautological, and another which is not.

In these cases, it especially-often happens that the premise is ambiguous, between a tautological meaning from which the interesting conclusion does not follow, and another meaning from which the conclusion does indeed follow, but only because the conclusion is actually logically-equivalent to the premise. Where this is the case, you cannot, of course, say straight out that the argument is invalid. You have to content yourself with saying instead that it is *either* invalid, *or* it 'begs the question' in favour of the conclusion. Such a disjunctive verdict is very often the best one can do in philosophy.

A stock example is, and deserves to be, Locke's lamentable attempt at an *a priori* proof that every event has a cause. His premise was that 'Non-entity cannot produce any real being.'[3] Any person of common sense, who was not trying to bewilder people, would take this without hesitation to be just an outlandish way of saying that every event has a cause, and would accordingly say that Locke had simply begged the question. But Locke writes as though this premise were merely one of a number of necessary truths about the many inabilities which the unfortunate Non-entity labours under. Another one which he mentions is that

'Non-entity . . . cannot be equal to two right angles.' And who, indeed, *can* confidently say, concerning barbarisms so disgraceful as 'Non-entity cannot be equal to two right angles,' or 'Non-entity cannot produce any real being,' that they are *not* necessary truths? But we *can* confidently say, of the latter, that *if* it is a necessary truth, then 'Every event has a cause' does not follow it, because *that* is not a necessary truth; and that if it means the same as 'Every event has a cause,' then Locke's argument, though valid, is question-begging.

# II

One of Berkeley's arguments for idealism is an argument of the very kind I have been speaking about: from a tautological premise to an interesting conclusion. And it is one of the grosser, less disguised ones, too. It is not quite as gross as the argument from 'Whatever will be, will be', to 'All human effort is ineffectual'; but it is very little better.

The idealist conclusion is that the existence of trees or any other physical objects, 'without the mind', is self-contradictory, impossible, inconceivable: you cannot even *think of* such a thing. In short:

You cannot have trees-without-the-mind in mind.

Yet Berkeley's only premise for this interesting conclusion is:

You cannot have trees-without-the-mind in mind, without having them in mind.

Which nobody can deny.

Here is this argument in Berkeley's words, in Paragraph 23 of *The Principles of Human Knowledge.*

But, say you, surely there is nothing easier than for me to imagine trees, for instance, in a park, or books existing in a closet, and nobody by to perceive them. I answer, you may so, there is no difficulty in it. But what is all this, I beseech you, more than framing in your mind certain ideas which you call *books* and *trees*, and at the same time omitting to frame the idea of any one that may perceive them. But do not you yourself perceive or think of them all the while? This therefore is nothing to the purpose: it only shews you have the power of imagining, or forming ideas in your mind; but it does not shew that you can conceive it possible the objects of your thought may exist without the mind. To make out this, it is necessary that you conceive them existing un-conceived or unthought of; which is a manifest repugnancy. When we do our utmost to conceive the existence of external bodies, we are all the while only contemplating our own ideas. But the mind, taking no notice of itself, is deluded to think it can and does conceive bodies existing unthought of, or without the mind, though at the same time they are apprehended by, or exist in, itself. A little attention will discover to any one the truth and evidence of what is here said, and make it unnecessary to insist on any other proofs against the existence of *material substance*.

Berkeley also advances this argument in the *Three Dialogues*.[4]

Philosophers, I have noticed, unless they are Berkeley specialists or have lately re-read him, forget that he used this argument. When I remind them of it, they utter a groan. Well might they forget it, and groan at any reminder of it. Many of Berkeley's arguments are very good, but this one is so bad that it is hard to believe that it has ever deceived anyone. The alleged impossibility of having trees-without-the-mind in mind, or of having (in plain English) trees in mind, does not need, though it has received, the labours of earnest logicians to refute it. The feat is so far from being impossible, that every bird that alights on a tree manages it easily.

Berkeley himself does not give anything like the prominence to this argument which one would have expected him to do, if he had been really satisfied with it. The argument occurs only once in the *Principles* and only once in the *Three Dialogues*, and is not otherwise referred to: circumstances distinctly suspicious, to say the least, in a philosopher so little averse to repetition as Berkeley. For all the badness of this argument, I will need to refer to it again. It will therefore be convenient to have a short name for it. I will call it 'the Gem'.

Berkeley has a second argument for the conclusion that physical objects cannot exist 'without the mind'. Its premise is about what it *means* to say that a certain physical object exists or has a certain quality. So I will call this 'the meaning-argument'.

The premise (putting it in my own words) is this:

> When we say that a certain physical object exists or that it has a certain quality, we mean that this object or quality is perceived, or that it would be perceived under such-and-such circumstances.

The conclusion is:

> It either makes no sense or is self-contradictory, to say of a physical object or a quality of a physical object, that it is unperceived and would not be perceived whatever the circumstances were.

Here is one of Berkeley's versions of the meaning-argument.

> That neither our thoughts, nor passions, nor ideas formed by the imagination, exist without the mind is what everybody will allow. And to me it seems no less evident that the various sensations or ideas imprinted on the Sense, however blended or combined tog-ether (that is, whatever objects they compose), cannot exist other-wise than in a mind perceiving them. I think an intuitive knowledge may be obtained of this, by any one that shall attend to what is meant by the term *exist* when applied to sensible things. The table I write on I say exists; that is, I see and feel it: and if I were out of my study I should say it existed; meaning thereby that if I was in my study I might perceive it. There was an odour, that is, it was smelt; there was a sound, that is, it was heard; a colour or figure, and it was perceived by sight or touch. This is all that I can understand by these and the like expressions. For as to what is said of the *absolute* existence of unthinking things, without any relation to their being perceived, that is to me perfectly unintelli-gible. Their *esse* is *percipi*; nor is it possible they should have any existence out of the minds or thinking things which perceive them.

This is Paragraph 3 of the *Principles*. The same argument is advanced in Paragraph 24, and in the *Three Dialogues*.[5] But

Berkeley often alludes to this argument in other places; as he never does for the Gem.

This meaning-argument is of a very different kind from the arguments I have been speaking about so far. The trouble with all of those was that the premise is too true (so to speak) to sustain the interesting conclusion which is drawn from it; here the trouble is just the opposite. The premise entails the conclusion all right, but it is so astoundingly false that it defies criticism, at first, by the simple method of taking the reader's breath away. This was a method which the neo-Hegelian idealists later perfected: reasoning from a sudden and violent solecism. Say or imply, for example, that in English 'value' means the same as 'individuality'. You can be miles down the track of your argument before they get their breath back.

This method is not only physiologically but ethologically sound. Of course it should never be used *first*. You need first to earn the respect of your readers, by some good reasoning, penetrating observations, or the like: *then* apply the violent solecism. Tell them, for example, that when we say of something that it is a prime number, we mean that it was born out of wedlock. You *cannot* go wrong this way. Decent philosophers will be so disconcerted by this, that they will never do the one thing they should do: simply say, 'That is NOT what "prime number" means!' Instead, they will *always* begin to display feverish 'displacement activity' (in Lorenz's sense), casting about for an *excuse* for someone's saying what you said, or a half-excuse, or a one-eighth excuse; nor is there any danger that they will search in vain. And with this, not only is your philosophy of arithmetic launched, but you have already got other people working for you, free of charge, at its development. This is as much a fact about philosophers, as any fact in Lorenz or Tinbergen about dogs or seagulls.

But the only rational response to Berkeley's meaning-argument is simply to say that we do *not* mean that a physical object or quality is perceived, or would be perceived under such-and-such circumstances, when we say that it exists. And this is something which (to borrow a phrase from Berkeley) *'whoever understands English, cannot but know'*.[6]

I have never met with the meaning-argument in any later idealist. One is often reminded of it, it is true, as for example when

Green says: 'To say that it *really* is so, is to say that it is so for the *thinking* consciousness.'[7] This has the same breathtaking falsity as Berkeley's premise, since, of course, to say that something really is so is, precisely, to say that it is so whatever anyone or anything may think or not think. But, because Berkeley's conclusion here is interchangeable, near enough, with his premise, such a remark is no evidence that the writer of it endorses the meaning-*argument*: it only shows that he endorses its idealist conclusion.

Many later philosophers *have*, of course, endorsed Berkeley's statement, that if I am not in my study, and I say there is a table there, I 'mean thereby' that I would have tablish perceptions if I were there. A. J. Ayer, most notably, struggled for decades to make these two kinds of proposition come out logically-equivalent: the categorical ones about unperceived physical objects, and the conditional ones about the perceptions which would be had if things were different. A hopeful undertaking! It is perfectly obvious that there might be a table in my study and yet that I should have no tablish perceptions if I were there, for any one of a billion reasons: practical jokers, heart-attacks, divine intervention, etc., etc. For the same number of reasons, it is also possible that there should be no table in my study, and yet true that if I were there I would have any quantity of tablish perceptions that might be called for. That is the very kind of work we *pay* demons and super-scientists for in philosophy: to say nothing of more probable agencies.

Nor should we feel either sympathy or admiration for Ayer's fruitless labours. People who erect a metaphysics on the basis of saying that common English words mean something which everyone knows they do not mean, deserve all the neglect we can give them. This applies to Berkeley even more than to Ayer. For there can be few solecisms, even among the later idealists, more violent, or more contemptible, than his 'meaning thereby', and his three 'that is'-es, in Paragraph 3 of the *Principles*, quoted above. Take, for example, 'there was a sound, that is, it was heard.' It is always painful to think of a person drowning far from help, with his cries for help heard by no one but himself; but a peculiar painfulness attaches to the idea of a *deaf* person dying so, his cries unheard even by himself. It is therefore a comfort to learn, on the authority of a great philosopher, that no such thing has ever happened, or ever can happen, since it is logically impossible. No sound was heard: *that is*, there was no sound.

*Of course* all we philosophers are subject to the weakness of the professional flesh, and are sorely tempted to say: 'Oh, but Berkeley was getting at a real point all the same, you know. Physical objects or qualities which were perceivable in *no* circumstances would be . . . (etc., etc.).' But we will resist this temptation if we are rational. For that is precisely how people begin the making of excuses for the inexcusable premise of Berkeley's meaning-argument. And you will find, if you do once allow that process to begin, that there is no rational way in which you can stop it.

There is a third argument for idealism in Berkeley. It is the first part of the central stem of his philosophy, so I will call it 'the central argument'. What this central stem is, Berkeley makes perfectly clear, and repeats, in part or whole, many times over; for example in the *Principles*, Paragraphs 4 and 5, and in the *Three Dialogues*.[8] Scarcely departing at all from Berkeley's own words, it goes as follows:

1  We can immediately perceive the sensible qualities of physical objects.

2  We can immediately perceive nothing but our own ideas.

So,

3  The sensible qualities of physical objects are nothing but ideas.

4  Ideas can exist only in a mind.

So,

5  The sensible qualities of physical objects can exist only in a mind.

6  A physical object is nothing but its qualities.

So,

7  Physical objects can exist only in a mind.

The last step, which depends on the premise (6), need not concern us. Our business is with idealism, and idealism has no essential connection with the question whether a physical object is or is not just its qualities. An idealistic result has been arrived at in this argument with the very first step: with (3), which follows from (1) and (2).

Premise (1) is, of course, the thing which enabled Berkeley to play a game he adored: dressing up as a defender of common sense.

Premise (2) is a version of that fatal 'internalism' (as it might be called), which Descartes bequeathed to the next 250 years of philosophy. It is shared, accordingly, by both Berkeley and all his contemporary opponents. Descartes and Locke, though officially subscribing to internalism, forgot about it most of the time, and most philosophers for the next 250 years followed this comparatively sensible example. But Berkeley and Malebranche could never forget it, and as a result they raised the grotesque monuments to consistency which we still marvel at today. I should add that, although (2) is a premise in the above argument, it may be that Berkeley thought of (2) as also itself a conclusion: namely, as being the conclusion of the Gem argument. I do not think he did, and yet, of course, the conclusion of the Gem *is* a version of internalism. But whether or not he meant his first argument to 'feed into' his third one in this way, does not make any difference for my purposes.

The premises (1) and (2) suffice for (3), and with (3) (as I said) idealism, or enough idealism to go on with, has arrived. But necessary falsity has arrived with it.

Premise (3) is an assertion of identity: 'are nothing but' means 'are identical with'. Now Berkeley always puts the words 'our own', or 'our', before 'ideas', when he is asserting premise (2); but when he passes to (3), he always omits those words (as I have done above), and concludes only that the sensible qualities of physical objects are *ideas*. Obviously, though, those words do not *have* to be omitted. Instead of (3) we are equally entitled to conclude:

3'    The sensible qualities of physical objects are nothing but
      *our* ideas.

That is (for example), the roundness of a certain billiard ball is identical with our ideas (of roundness). And now the falsity of (3)', and hence of (1) or (2), is glaring.

'Our' ideas of roundness means your idea of roundness and my idea of roundness. These, however, are necessarily distinct, whereas identity cannot 'spread' over distinct things. If x is identical with y and x is identical with z, then y and z must be identical with one another. Whence if the roundness of a certain billiard ball were identical with my idea of roundness and with yours, your idea and mine would have to be identical: which is impossible. Nor does the necessary falsity of (3') even depend on there being more than one 'finite spirit'. *I* can have an idea of roundness at two different times, hence I can have two ideas of roundness; but the roundness of a billiard ball cannot be identical with two distinct ideas, even if both of them do happen to be mine.

I call the argument I have just criticized 'the central argument', because in Berkeley's own thought it certainly was so. But it does not seem to have recommended itself to any later idealists: at any rate, I have never met, among those writers, with a recognizable version of it. I suppose the reason is, the argument's premise (1). Surely that was always an *unlikely* way for an argument for idealism to begin? But then Berkeley, unlike most of the later idealists, loved steering as close to the wind of common sense as he could, and (as I said) loved to pretend to be even a defender of common sense.

There are, then, these three arguments for idealism in Berkeley: the Gem, the meaning-argument, and the central argument. I believe that these are also his *only* arguments for idealism.

I could, of course, be mistaken in this, and it is especially doubtful whether Berkeley himself would have agreed with it. But then, he suffered from a peculiar narrowness of vision: John Locke was the only opponent he ever had in his sights. Hence every argument he had, against any element of Locke's philosophy – the distinction between substance and quality, the distinction between primary and secondary qualities, the representative theory of perception, whatever – seemed *to him* to be an argument *for* his own idealism. He was remarkably successful, too, in carrying the later British idealists with him in this perspective. Green sees matters in essentially this way, always proceeding as though Locke and idealism are the only possible alternatives.[9] And even Bradley begins *Appearance and Reality* by – can you remember or guess how? With some Hegelian dialectic? A Kantian deduction, perhaps? Nothing like that: he begins by dragging out the poor old distinction between primary and secondary qualities, for yet another belting.[10]

We cannot be a party to this: it is just packaging together issues which are distinct from one another. If primary and secondary qualities are in the same boat, it is an independent question whether it is an idealist boat or not. Even if physical objects are nothing but their qualities, it is a further question whether they exist 'without the mind'. Our interest is in idealism, and we simply *must* break up the Berkeley package, because we are trying to find out what his arguments *for idealism* were. When we do break up the package, we certainly find the three arguments which I have distinguished above; and I, at least, have not been able to find any other.

In Essay 5 I said that all idealism after Berkeley depended on his arguments, so far as it depended on argument at all. In this essay I have said that he had only three arguments for idealism, and that neither his central argument, nor his meaning-argument, had any significant influence on later idealists. But this leaves only the Gem: an argument so bad (as I said) that it is hard to imagine anyone ever being swayed by it. Can it possibly have been by *this* despicable argument that the West was won for idealism?

This may seem altogether too improbable. It will seem less so, if you recall the execution that has been done in the world by a very similar argument: the one from 'Whatever will be, will be'. to 'All human effort is ineffectual.' Anyway, improbable or not, I say that insofar as the business depended on argument at all, it *was* the Gem, virtually unaided, which made idealism *the* philosophy of the Western world for more than a hundred years. It was the ugliest toad of them all who got the princess and the kingdom.

# III

While its fatalistic counterpart has often been justly and effectively ridiculed, the Gem never has. In fact this argument has never yet met with a serious setback. On the contrary, beginning with Kant, it simply overran Western philosophy, as the rabbit overran Australia. And even when idealism finally died out, it was not because of any general recognition that it had depended all along on the original philosophical sin of drawing interesting conclusions from tautological premises. There *was* no general recognition of this fact. Indeed, there was scarcely any recognition of it at all; there still is scarcely any.

My object in this section is to convince the reader of the enormous prevalence of the Gem in idealist philosophy after Berkeley. But the variety of the historical materials, even more than their volume, threatens to overwhelm me. No one will expect to meet with the Gem, among later idealists, in just the form which Berkeley gave it, and still less in the form which I gave it in the preceding section. In what form, then, *is* it to be looked for? Any argument is a Gem if it pretends to deduce, from a tautological premise about knowledge or thought or consciousness, that the only possible objects of knowledge, or that the only possible objects, are internal or mental or spiritual. But it is sadly obvious that there is practically no limit to the variety of forms which an argument of that kind might take.

Yet clearly, I cannot afford to content myself here with *general* historical remarks. I must display, by nothing short of quotations, later idealists caught *in flagrante delicto*: actually using an argument which is a recognizable form of the Gem. But if I were to give (as I easily could) thirty such examples, I would defeat my own object, by extinguishing the reader's interest in the subject; while if I were to give only (say) four, I could hardly convey the ubiquity of the Gem.

I will adopt a *mixed* strategy. I will give quotations from eight idealists employing a recognizable Gem: this way, my case will at least have some secure foundations. But, to try to give it wide scope as well, I will, before doing that, point out two things which every philosopher will at once recall as having enjoyed enormous currency among idealists after Berkeley, and which are in fact only lightly disguised forms of the Gem. One of these is a certain ambiguous thesis; the other is a certain family of arguments.

Every philosopher has read hundreds of paragraphs, by nineteenth century idealists, about 'the unity of subject and object,' 'the identity of the Ego and the Non-Ego', and so on. Any such paragraph is almost certain to contain the Gem, but most of them contain it only in a state which is too gaseous to enable it to be pinned on the author. But there are other forms of the Gem which are disguised by an opposite characteristic: by being highly *compressed*.

The most important of these is the saying, which idealists repeated so often that they wore it down at last to a four-word slogan, that there can be no object without a subject. This saying, like many other Victorian artifacts which were once in every home, now produces only incomprehension and a dull distaste. Yet it was in fact a triumph of philosophic art. And despite its compression, it is not really hard to detect the Gem in it.

'There can be no object without a subject.' Take it one way – take 'object' to mean 'trees and such' – and the saying is one which is big, in fact bulging, with interest. For then it asserts nothing less than idealism: that there can be no 'trees without the mind', etc. But you can also easily take 'object' to mean 'object of knowledge or thought', and then the saying not only stops bulging, but folds up absolutely flat: into the tautology, that if something is an object of knowledge or thought, then something knows or thinks of it. And here, it will be obvious, there is a Gem argument just waiting to happen, and sure to happen. You first satisfy yourself or others of the truth of the proposition, by taking it in its tautological sense; and then, later, you allow yourself or others to take it in its idealist sense.

Under a dull exterior, then, the slogan 'no object without a subject' concealed a brilliantly miniaturized Gem, which fully deserved its immense popularity. It is, to my mind, easily the most beautiful of all Gems. Think how easy the transition is, from the tautological sense of the slogan to its idealist sense: much easier, for example, than the transition from 'Every effect has a cause' to 'Every event has a cause.' Yet that is a transition which many people can feel no bump whatever in making; even though Hume justly ridiculed it, by comparing it to the one from 'Every husband has a wife', to 'Every man is married'.[11]

To someone already persuaded of idealism, of course, there will seem to be no *equivocation* between 'object' and 'object of thought'. For he *believes* that an object *must* be an object of thought: that is what 'no object without a subject', taken in its idealist sense, *says*. But his problem is that his only *arguments for* this belief are Gems; such as the one from the tautological sense of 'no object without a subject'.

My other general piece of evidence is a certain family of arguments which was even more popular than the dictum, 'no object without a subject'.

The members of this family are so very various, that it is not easy to distil a schema of which they are all instances. But it is not necessary, either, because their family resemblance is so pronounced that, once you have met one member, you will easily recognize any other. The following specimen, though it does not pretend to be a quotation, will, I am confident, be enough to remind the reader of the famous family of arguments I mean:

We can think of things only under the forms of our thought,

So,

We cannot think of things as they are in themselves.

That is too short, of course, to have much historical verisimilitude. It also lacks the owlish pomposity which is needed to invest an argument of this family with any plausibility, and which only idealist professors can provide: indeed, if you want the best, only German idealist professors. For these reasons, the emptiness of the premise here is, no doubt, a shade too obvious.

Even so, I am sure that this specimen will bring, flooding back into the reader's mind, scores of Kantian-and-later idealist arguments: arguments for idealism from 'the presuppositions of the possibility of knowledge', etc., which are not really so very different from the one just given. In fact, contemptible as this argument undoubtedly is, it would take a sharp man to say how it differs *essentially* from the argument which is the sole support of Kant's idealism.

But this family of arguments varies enormously (as I said), both in the details of expression, and in substance. Instead of being about thought, as above, it can be about knowledge; or about consciousness; or about concepts; or about conceptual schemes; and so on. 'Under' can be replaced by 'within', or 'in accordance with', or 'subject to the limitations imposed by', and so on. 'The forms of our thought' can be replaced by 'the categories which are the preconditions of the possibility of knowledge', or by 'the schematisms under which alone the manifold of sense can be brought together in consciousness', etc., etc. It will be clear, then, that the number of possible combinations here, and hence the number of members of this family of arguments, is indeed very large.

Only three things are essential: idealism in the conclusion, tautology in the premise, and pomposity throughout. So, even every little bit of redundancy helps. Thus you never say, for example, 'things as they are', and still less, 'things'. You say 'things as they are in themselves', or better still, 'things and their properties as they exist both in and for themselves'. Never call anything a necessary condition of x: call it a presupposition of the possibility of x. Likewise you do not argue, for example,

> Our thoughts are our thoughts,
>
> So,
>
> They are only our thoughts.

Or again,

> We can know only what it is possible for us to know,
>
> So,
>
> We cannot know anything.

That would never do. You must instead argue more like this:

We can know objects only [if, as, insofar as] they are brought under the categories, which are the presuppositions of the possibility of knowledge,

So,

We cannot know things as they are in themselves.

Or like this:

The properties of physical objects can be given and present to the forms of sensuous intuition only [if, as, insofar as] they appear to the senses,

So,

They cannot be known as they are in themselves.

It was Gems like these last two which became the most popular and respected Gems of all time. But they had a group of cousins which also deserve mention, because they were, for a few decades, almost equally popular. These cousins go like this:

We can know physical objects only [if, as, insofar as] they are related (to us, if to nothing else) (by the relation of being known, if by no other),

So,

We cannot know physical objects as they exist out of relation, in themselves, or absolutely.

Here again, no doubt, I have made the vacuity of the premise a little too obvious. But no one should be disrespectful about these Gems, unless he is also disrespectful about the ones mentioned just a moment before. These ones are simply the Hamiltonian, as those just before were the Kantian Gems. These arguments were, in fact, the sole support of Sir William Hamilton's famous and influential doctrine of 'the relativity of knowledge'.

There was, then, beginning with Kant, a large and influential family of arguments for idealism, the Gem-character of which was disguised only by pompous language. The general schema of these arguments (remembering that they can be put in terms of thought, or of consciousness, as easily as in terms of knowledge) is the following:

> We can know things only if condition C, which is necessary for knowledge, is satisfied,
>
> So,
>
> We cannot know things as they are in themselves.

And after all, that knowledge is possible only where the absence of a necessary condition does not make it impossible, is what nobody can deny.

I end my historical generalities here. What I have said may go some way, even if only a very short way, towards indicating the enormous volume of later idealist argument which reproduced the essential character of Berkeley's little Gem. The fact is, that beginning with Kant, the pulling of fat idealist rabbits out of pompous but tautological hats became *the* occupation of philosophers. The motorless motor-car, which Berkeley had launched with well founded and ill concealed misgivings, became in the next century the only philosophical way to travel.

I now have to support this contention, not by historical generalities, but by actual quotations. Of the Gems which follow, almost half are mercifully clear and short. The others are the opposite, and some of them, while they contain the Gem all right, also mix other things with it. In historical reality, of course, the proportions were not like that: the long, or obscure, or mixed examples were far more common than the opposite kind. Beyond this principle of mercy, though, my examples have not been chosen on any particular principle. There was no need to put them even into chronological order, since I claim only that there was a general diffusion of the Gem after Berkeley, not that it followed any particular lines of descent.

Henri Poincaré is not much remembered now as an idealist. But he was in fact one of those eminent mathematicians and scientists who formed (as I mentioned in Essay 5) a late-nineteenth-century branch of idealism which was more Berkeleian than mainstream-Hegelian. He was not a consistent idealist, but then the only thing that Poincaré was consistent in, was in being determined to shine.[12] Still, he was idealist enough to leave us, on the last page of his book, *The Value of Science*, the following Gem.

> All that is not thought is pure nothingness; since we can think only thoughts and all the words we use to speak of things can express only thoughts, to say there is something other than thought, is therefore an affirmation which can have no meaning.[13]

We have just met the Gem in one of the least representative of idealists. The following example of it is from one of the most representative: John Caird. It is hard to believe that Caird, when he wrote this passage, did not have Paragraph 23 of Berkeley's *Principles* in mind.

> Neither organisation nor anything else can be conceived to have any existence which does not presuppose thought. To constitute the existence of the outward world, or of the lowest term of reality we ascribe to it – say in 'atoms', or 'molecules', or 'centres of force' – you must think them or conceive them as existing for thought; you must needs presuppose a consciousness for which and in which all objective existence is. To go beyond, or attempt to conceive of an existence which is prior to and outside of thought, 'a thing in itself' of which thought is only the mirror, is self-contradictory, inasmuch as that very thing in itself is only conceivable by, exists only for, thought. We must think it before we can ascribe to it even an existence outside of thought.[14]

Henry Mansel, Waynflete Professor at Oxford and later Dean of St Paul's, was Sir William Hamilton's principal lieutenant, and after Hamilton's death, his champion in controversy. He is virtually forgotten now, and always deserved to be. But, as the following quotation will show, he was at any rate a good enough philosopher to *let a cat out of a bag*: a service more useful than any which most of us manage to perform.

> all our knowledge is relative, – in other words, . . . we know things only under such conditions as the laws of our cognitive faculties impose upon us[15]

Hamilton would have objected violently to being listed among idealists. Yet he confessed he was mystified as to how various of his predecessors in European philosophy had managed to stop short of full-blooded idealism: so mystified, in fact, that he could only suggest, not very plausibly, that they had retained their belief in matter only because of a reluctance to contradict the Catholic doctrine of the Eucharist![16] And in just the same way, Hamilton's contemporaries were completely mystified as to how *he* managed to stop short of full-blooded idealism; nor has this mystery ever been solved. Anyway, the general affinity between the following passage and the idealism of Kant, say, will be obvious to the reader.

> From what has been said, you will be able, I hope, to understand what is meant by the proposition, that all our knowledge is only relative. It is relative, 1, Because existence is not cognisable, absolutely and in itself, but only in special modes; 2, Because these modes can be known only if they stand in a certain relation to our faculties; and, 3, Because the modes, thus relative to our faculties, are presented to, and known by, the mind only under modifications determined by these faculties themselves.[17]

The examples from Poincaré and Mansel are too short, clear, and unmixed, to be typical Gems. The Caird example is at least unmixed with anything but the Gem. The Hamilton example is not quite unmixed, but Hamilton's arguments, at least from the propositions he numbers 2 and 3, are still too clear to be typical Gems. To do the nineteenth-century idealists justice, we need an example which is long and obscure, and one in which the Gem is mixed up with other things. We need, in a word, a *German* Gem.

Such an example follows; but it will not be pleasant. Here the reader will even find, for example, the idea that we can know only our own thoughts, confused with the idea that we can know only our own *sense organs*! Still, I think it will be clear enough – though only *just* clear enough – that Schopenhauer's reason for denying that we perceive external objects is that, as he says, perception is '*perception of the perceiver*'.

> 'The world is my representation': this is a truth valid with reference to every living and knowing being, although man alone can bring it into reflective, abstract consciousness. If he really does so, philo-

sophical discernment has dawned on him. It then becomes clear and certain to him that he does not know a sun and an earth, but only an eye that sees a sun, a hand that feels an earth; that the world around him is there only as representation, in other words, only in reference to another thing, namely that which represents, and this is himself. If any truth can be expressed *a priori*, it is this; for it is the statement of that form of all possible and conceivable experience, a form that is more general than all others, than time, space, and causality, for all these presuppose it. While each of these forms, which we have recognized as so many particular modes of the principle of sufficient reason, is valid only for a particular class of representations, the division into object and subject, on the other hand, is the common form of all those classes; it is that form under which alone any representation, of whatever kind it be, abstract or intuitive, pure or empirical, is generally possible and conceivable. Therefore no truth is more certain, more independent of all others, and less in need of proof than this, namely that everything that exists for knowledge, and hence the whole of this world, is only object in relation to the subject, perception of the perceiver, in a word, representation. Naturally this holds good of the present as well as of the past and future, of what is remotest as well as of what is nearest; for it holds good of time and space themselves, in which alone all these distinctions arise. Everything that in any way belongs and can belong to the world is inevitably associated with this being-conditioned by the subject, and it exists only for the subject. The world is representation.

This truth is by no means new. It was to be found already in the sceptical reflections from which Descartes started. But Berkeley was the first to enunciate it positively, and he has thus rendered an immortal service to philosophy, although the remainder of his doctrines cannot endure. Kant's first mistake was the neglect of this principle, as is pointed out in the Appendix. On the other hand, how early this basic truth was recognized by the sages of India, since it appears as . . .[18]

When you have read that, you have read the first page of *The World as Will and Representation*, and you have only 1177 pages to go. But the reference to the Appendix (near the end of the quotation) is worth following up. There Schopenhauer expresses his puzzlement, and regret, that his hero Kant did not, as Schopenhauer himself does, rest his idealism entirely on 'the simple, undeniable truth', which he also called the 'Berkeleian principle': 'no object without a subject'.[19]

It will be a relief to turn from the pathological windbag Schopenhauer to an example from McTaggart. This example is in fact so very brief and bald, that it may not be recognized at once as being the Gem it is.

> If I am to distinguish myself from any other reality, then obviously, I must be conscious of this other reality. But how can I be conscious of it without it being in me?[20]

'In me', indeed! Every reader of Berkeley soon realizes, and of course Berkeley himself knew, that his whole philosophy hangs on one tiny word: 'in', in the phrase 'in the mind'. The whole of later idealism does too. In fact, there is remarkably little, not only in the history of idealism, but in the entire history of philosophy, which does *not* hang on the word 'in'. 'The predicate is in the subject' – what a pregnant old dictum! Our knowledge is in the mind. Secondary qualities are not in the object. We cannot know things in themselves. Centaurs exist in mythology. Value is not 'out there' but 'in here'. . . . The list is endless.

What Bradley's argument for being a monist was, we know, because he was good enough to repeat it about five hundred times. But why he was an *idealist*, is a question which has rightly puzzled very many of his readers. Give him, if you like, that the Absolute is one, is consistent, is perfect, etc.; but why *will* he say that it is also *experience*? This is a part of Bradley's intellectual anatomy which he himself seemed to find distinctly tender to the touch; because, in all of his voluminous writings, he argued for idealism only twice. And the argument was a Gem each time.

The following is one of these two passages, and Andrew Seth rightly said of it that it is 'almost in Berkeley's language':[21] that is, in the words of Paragraph 23 of Berkeley's *Principles*, the Ur-Gem itself.

> When the experiment is made strictly, I can myself conceive of nothing else than the experienced. Anything, in no sense felt or perceived, becomes to me quite unmeaning. And as I cannot try to think of it without realizing either that I am not thinking at all, or that I am thinking of it against my will as being experienced, I

am driven to the conclusion that for me experience is the same as reality. The fact that falls elsewhere seems, in my mind, to be a mere word and a failure, or else an attempt at self-contradiction. It is a vicious abstraction whose existence is meaningless nonsense, and is therefore not possible.[22]


But the other passage in which Bradley argued for idealism is a Gem which is in some ways even more striking, although it is almost never referred to.


On this whole matter, and not specially with reference to religion, it is worth while to consider the position of our philosophy. People find a subject and object correlated in consciousness; and having got this *in* the mind, they at once project it outside the mind, and talk as if two independent realities knocked themselves together, and so produced the unity that apprehends them; while, all the time, to go out of that unity is for us literally to go out of our minds. And when the monstrous nature of their position dawns on some few, and they begin to see that without some higher unity this 'correlation' is pure nonsense, then answering to that felt need, they invent a third reality, which is neither subject nor object but the 'Unknowable' or the Thing-in-itself (there is no difference). But here, since the two correlates are still left together with, and yet are *not*, the Unknowable, the question arises, How does this latter stand to them? And the result is that the Unknowable becomes the subject of predicates (see Mr Spencer's *First Principles*), and it becomes impossible for any one who cares for consistency to go on calling it the Unknowable. So it is necessary to go a step further, and, giving up our third, which is *not* the correlates, to recognize an Identity of subject and object, still however persisting in the statement that this identity is *not* mind. But here again, as with the Unknowable, and as before with the two correlated realities, it is forgotten that, when mind is made only a part of the whole, there is a question which *must* be answered; 'If so, how can the whole be known, and for the mind? If about any matter we know nothing whatever, can we say anything about it? Can we even say that it is? And, if it is not consciousness, how can we know it? And if it is in and for the mind, how can it be a whole which is *not* mind, and in which the mind is only a part or element? If the ultimate unity were not self or mind, we could not know that it was not mind: that would mean going out of our minds. And, conversely, if we know it, it can not be not mind.[23]

Bradley's repeated saying, that we would be 'going out of our minds' if idealism were not true, must not be mistaken for *mere* phrase-making. It is obviously the same thought as Malebranche's, when he said that non-idealists must think that, in astronomy, 'the soul goes for a walk among the stars'[24] – ha ha! Bradley's attempt to *frighten* us into idealism is even more embarrassing than Malebranche's attempt to *joke* us into it, but that is the only difference. Green's often repeated saying, that 'Outside itself, consciousness cannot get,'[25] is, equally obviously, a third version of the same thought.

All these three sayings are things of the same kind as 'no object without a subject': that is, they are miniaturized Gems, necessarily true and even trivial when taken in one sense, and idealistic only when taken in another. For example, that consciousness cannot get outside itself, can equally easily be taken either to mean:

Consciousness can reach only what it can reach,

or to mean:

Consciousness can reach only itself.

And likewise, if Father Malebranche were to insist that it really is necessarily true that the soul cannot walk among the stars, why, we would have to agree with him. In any case, who could grudge him his sad little clerical joke? But if he were tempted to make anything idealistic of it, we in turn would have to insist that it is also a necessary truth that the soul cannot walk even among trees, and that it cannot ride a horse among them either; and that idealism no more follows from either of these two truths, than it does from the first one.

There is another one of these 'no-travel' sayings, and, though it is even more homely than Malebranche's, Bradley's, or Green's, some idealists have not been ashamed to resort to it. It is this: that stars, trees, and the like, with all the qualities they actually have, can hardly be supposed to migrate into our consciousness, and take up residence there, can they? Ha ha.

One could reply, with professional gravity, that it is also necessarily true that physical objects cannot migrate into physical theory
either, but that it does not follow that physical theory does not
deal with physical objects or their qualities. Or, one could reply
that numbers cannot take up residence in our consciousness either,
yet we know quite a lot about numbers: yea, even about numbers
'as they are in and for themselves' – or, as we say in English,
numbers.

But do we really *have* to emulate the owlishness of these
people? We have here, surely, gone beyond the embarassing, to the
disgusting, and the reader might well feel that he is now on a
guided tour of the sewers of idealism. Surely no serious philosopher has even tried to make idealistic capital out of *this* no-
travel saying?

Do you think so? Then learn to recognize the great philosopher
Immanuel Kant.

> I can only know what is contained in the object in itself if the
> object is present and given to me. Of course it is then still inconceiv-
> able how the intuition of a thing that is present should make me
> know it as it is in itself, for its properties cannot migrate into my
> faculty of representation[26]

Anyone who is tempted to think that I have here taken unfair
advantage of a sad little professorial joke, should consider the
following passage from the same author. It clearly echoes the
same reasoning, and it is, equally clearly, a representative passage.

> If we treat outer objects as things in themselves, it is quite imposs-
> ible to understand how we could arrive at a knowledge of their
> reality outside us, since we have to rely merely on the represen-
> tation which is in us. For we cannot be sentient [of what is] outside
> ourselves, but only [of what is] in us, and the whole of our
> self-consciousness therefore yields nothing save merely our own
> determinations.[27]

I do not say that this is the clearest Gem in the world. But it is
prevented from being so only by the cause which is by now all
too familiar: namely, that a proposition such as 'the whole of our
self-consciousness yields nothing save merely our own determi-

nations' is ambiguous, between a tautological meaning and an idealist one. Still, it is clear enough that Kant's real argument is the old one, the everlasting one, the unspeakably contemptible one: that our knowledge is not real knowledge at all, because it is *our* knowledge.

# IV

Beginning with Kant, the Gem conquered all: this is an historical fact. But it is a mystifying fact. How can so bad an argument have passed for a good one with so many powerful thinkers? After all, the argument for fatalism from tautological premises has often been (as I said earlier) not only justly but effectively ridiculed. The argument for universal selfishness from tautological premises met with classic exposure long ago. But the argument for idealism from tautological premises has never met with any similar setback.

Yet suppose someone had argued as follows:

We cannot eat oysters as they are in themselves,

Because

We can eat oysters only insofar as they are brought under the physiological and chemical conditions which are the presuppositions of the possibility of being eaten.

Would this argument have established gastronomic idealism? Only a rash man, or an ignorant one, would bet much money against it, but I do not think it would have. Even at the height of the Gem-craze, and even if Kant himself had been called in to phrase it in his inimitable way, I think that this argument would have deceived no one. Yet it is no worse than the Gem argument on which, in sober historical fact, idealism did depend. So what did that one have which this one lacks? Or rather, what is there *in us* which the Gem appeals to, but this gastronomic Gem does not?

It is easy to see what it is in human nature which carries people over the logical 'hard place' between

Whatever will be, will be,

and

All human effort is ineffectual.

It is our laziness. We often have the ability, and sometimes have an obligation, to make successful efforts. But any excuse, even a tautological one, for shedding these burdens, and innocently doing nothing, is sure of a welcome from our depths.

It is likewise easy to see what it is in human nature which makes people susceptible to the argument from

All a man's interests are interests of his,

to

All our actions are self-interested.

It is our selfishness. We often have the ability, and sometimes have an obligation, to act disinterestedly. But any excuse, however feeble or even tautological, for shedding these burdens, we are always ready to meet more than half-way.

Likewise, one would think, only some powerful emotional element in human nature can ever have sufficed to carry anyone over the hard place between

We can know things only as they are known to us,

and

We cannot know things as they are in themselves.

But what on earth could this element have been? What was the *psychology* of the Gem argument?

A partial answer can be given easily enough. Fatalism and

hedonism, although superficially they are depressing conclusions, are secretly welcome, because they promise us relief from some everyday burdens: the capacity and the obligation to make successful efforts, and to act disinterestedly. Idealism, too, is a superficially depressing conclusion: the conclusion that we cannot go outside (cognitively speaking). But it also has the secret attraction of promising us relief from the burden of an outer-directed capacity and obligation: the capacity and obligation to know things as they are. It *is* a relief, to some extent, to be told that our cognitive claims are not going to be judged by an external and impartial authority. External examiners are never entirely welcome.

But in fact this parallel goes only a little way. Laziness and selfishness are universal and powerful; hence everyone often feels effort and disinterestedness as burdens. But few people ever feel that the external world, just because it decides indifferently the value of our cognitive claims, is a *burden*. Even the few who do, never seem to feel it so outside the walls of their studies.

There must be more than this, then, to the psychology of the Gem. What would seem to be required, in order for someone to find that argument compelling, is what might be called 'cognitive Calvinism'. Calvinists believe in the total depravity of human nature: if an impulse is one of ours, it is bad, *because* it is one of ours. The argument,

Our knowledge is our knowledge,

So,

It is not knowledge of real things,

could seem valid only to someone who felt that any knowledge *we* have could not be the real thing, *because* we have it. But this cognitive Calvinism, whatever else one might say of it, is hardly a *common* kind of feeling. So what *was* the psychological basis of the long ascendancy which the Gem enjoyed over countless philosophers from Kant to Bradley?

I have not implied, and it is not true, that the Gem was accepted by *all* philosophers in that interval, and was never exposed by any. Its weakness was so extreme, that that was hardly possible.

Mill,[28] James McCosh,[29] and the Duke of Argyll,[30] were three critics who did something like justice to the Gem, at least in its Hamiltonian forms. In its Berkeleian-Kantian-Bradleian forms, it was seen through well enough by F. C. S. Schiller,[31] for one. Oddly enough, its feebleness was once pointed out by Green himself;[32] and, odder still, Bradley once made fun of arguments like the Gem.[33]

Still, there was, overall, extraordinarily little contemporary criticism of it: the critics I have just mentioned are, in fact, the only ones that I know of. And even what criticism there was, was as though it were not. I suppose the reason was that nearly all the critics were idealists themselves, of one shade or another. Mill's own metaphysics was much too close to Berkeley's for *him* to be likely to be a searching critic of the Gem. Schiller, for all his long and unscrupulous vendetta against Bradley, agreed with him, in so many words, that 'reality is experience.'[34] Green, having made essentially the right criticism of the Gem, immediately said it was wrong and took it back.[35] What Bradley was doing on the one occasion when he made fun of Gem-like arguments, I do not fully understand. But even popes feel the need for an anticlerical expression now and then, and Louis XIV could not always resist tormenting his courtiers with rude remarks about the institution of absolute monarchy.

Even when at long last the tide began to turn against idealism, with Moore, Russell, and then the American 'New Realists', the situation did not change nearly as much as one would have expected. The Gem was never, as far as I know, singled out for the conspicuous exposure which its unique importance and utter worthlessness entitled it to receive. It suffered many glancing blows: for example, one from R. B. Perry's attack on what he called 'the ego-centric predicament'.[36] But there was, and is, no *classic* exposure of it. Remembering what Bishop Butler did for the argument for hedonism from tautological premises, we may say that the Gem argument for idealism has never yet met with its Butler. The nearest approach to that, as far as I know, is the criticism made of the Gem by A. C. Ewing in 1933, when idealism was dead on its feet. On 'no object without a subject', he makes the admirable remark that 'no author would argue that he had saved his readers' lives, on the ground that without him as author they could not have existed as readers.'[37] But Ewing seems not to realize how far what he does say makes any further comment on idealism superfluous. And then, a little later, he quite unnecessarily concedes some ground to the Gem:[38] as though that argument, like a tiger-snake, was still dangerous even in its death-throes.

This charmed life which the Gem has led only deepens the psychological mystery about it. It has always been obvious (as I said in Essay 5) what the attraction of the idealist *conclusion* was: a congenial universe. But what was it which recommended, and sheltered from exposure, the idiotic *argument* on which that conclusion depended?

Am I too hard on the Gem? On the cosmic scene, consciousness is certainly something exceptional. Is it, perhaps, also something so intrinsically bewildering, that we easily succumb to arguments concerning it which would never deceive us on any other subject? Suppose, for example, that (as Julian Jaynes believes) consciousness originated, not only not before *Homo sapiens*, but only in *historical* times. Then idealism might be an excusable, even if irrational, attempt to adjust to this enormous and disconcerting novelty. Susceptibility to the Gem argument could be part of the cost of 'the breakdown of the bicameral mind'.[39]

Quite apart from the difficulties peculiar to Jaynes's theory, this apology for the Gem and for idealism cannot be right. The reason is, that the connection between idealism and the Gem is not at all as close as this suggestion would require. Idealism depended on the Gem, indeed; but the Gem does not depend on idealism. Far from that: when idealism expired, somewhere around 1940, the Gem argument not only survived it, but was poised to enter upon the most brilliant phase of its career.

The Gem, for example the argument from

We can know things only as they are known to us,

to

We cannot know things as they are in themselves,

is the Calvinistic core, so to speak, of idealism. But this core of argument is far from being peculiar to idealists. It is shared by various groups of people, who hold that we cannot know things as they are in themselves, but who are nevertheless not idealists. Remember the schema of the Gem:

We can know things only if condition C, which is necessary for knowledge, is satisfied,

So,

We cannot know things as they are in themselves.

Idealists put in, as *their* value of the variable C, some mental condition or other; but of course those are not the only possible values of C. Knowledge has or might have any number of necessary conditions, of many different kinds: physical ones, chemical ones, neurophysiological, genetic, historical, cultural, economic... Any such condition is a possible value of C. And, of course, the premise remains a tautology, whatever value is given to C.

There are, then, many different kinds of possible Gem arguments, and most of them would *not* go on to a specifically idealist conclusion after reaching 'We cannot know things as they are in themselves.' Your argument is a Gem if you infer that proposition from the tautology that we can know things only if a certain mental condition M, necessary for knowledge, is satisfied. But it is equally a Gem if you infer it instead from the tautology, that we can know things only if (say) a certain biochemical condition B, necessary for knowledge, is satisfied. Now, of these possible Gem arguments, many have enjoyed actual currency, especially in the last thirty years. Some of them have even acquired enormous popularity. In fact, Gems now lie all about us, for almost any possible value of C, if only we will learn to recognize them.

There are, for example, *biological* Gems. These have not been very popular lately, in fact distinctly the reverse. But even so, all of us must have met, at some stage or other, with the thought that

We can know only what our genes allow us to know,

So,

There is much that we cannot know.

Unfashionable this may be, but it is a 24-carat Gem for all that, and quality (or so the dealers say) is never out of fashion for long.

Likewise, the prudent collector will not part too hastily with a Gem like the following:

> We can know things only under the neurophysiological conditions (neurons firing, or whatever) which are necessary for knowledge,
>
> So,
>
> We cannot know things as they are in themselves.

This is, again, not one of the most brilliant performers. But it is still yielding respectable dividends to two classes of investors who have never lost their faith in it. One is sceptics and cognophobes who recognize the truth of the premise, and who cannot be persuaded that there is not *some* mileage in it. The other is anti-materialists who recognize the falsity of the conclusion, and cannot be persuaded that there is not some mileage to be got out of *that*.

But it is (as was to be expected) the humanities, not the sciences, which are now the most fertile source of Gems. And absolutely all of those which have lately achieved general acceptance come from this source.

The cultural-relativist, for example, inveighs bitterly against our science-based, Europe-centred, white-male cultural perspective. She says that it is not only injurious but cognitively limiting. Injurious it may be; or again it may not. But why does she believe that it is cognitively limiting? Why, for no reason in the world, except this one: that it is *ours*. Everyone really understands, too, that this *is* the only reason. But since this reason is also generally accepted as a sufficient one, no other is felt to be needed.

The Marxist insists that all our knowledge (at least until the day when there is 'a new heaven and a new earth') is inescapably limited and distorted by our own economic-class situation: by our relation to the means of production. You ask him why this must be so. He gives you the following reason, and no other: that knowledge, like any other social product, can come into being, and survive, only under the concrete material-practical circumstances, and in particular only under the economic circumstances, which are its historically necessary preconditions.

The Kuhnian is scandalized if you call a current scientific paradigm 'true' or an earlier one 'false', or if you say that the later one is 'probably nearer the truth' than the earlier. Paradigms are incommensurable, he tells you, and no special authority attaches to one which governs a given field of science *now*. And why must we accept this astounding and sordid democracy of paradigms? Why, just because, in any field, even the best scientific knowledge which is current now, or at any time, is always rigidly constrained within the limits imposed, by the paradigm prevailing at the time, on scientific knowledge.

Thus do all those now in authority in Western humanistic studies speak in Gems; and even (to tell the truth) in precious little *except* Gems. Even the children who come in millions to sit at their feet have learned, even before leaving school, to lisp in little Gems. Their intellectual temper is (as everyone remarks) the reverse of dogmatic, in fact pleasingly modest. They are quick to acknowledge that their own opinion, on any matter whatever, is only their opinion; and they will candidly tell you, too, the reason why it *is* only their opinion. This reason is, that it is *their* opinion. Protagoras is the only philosopher they can warm to.

The Gem argument is very far, then, from being a weakness peculiar to the idealist philosophers. On the contrary, it is common to all the main varieties of cognophobe who now make up the staff of the faculties of arts in Western universities; and none of these is idealistic, even by implication. My reference to Protagoras may also serve as a reminder that the Gem is also much *older* than idealism. In fact it goes back, in a tolerably distinct form, to Aristippus the Cyrenaic, and, in a less distinct form, further back still.[40]

But these facts, of course, not only do not solve the psychological mystery of the Gem: they deepen it. *Why* is there this apparent determination, of idealists, but also of so many others besides them, to deny, not merely on insufficient grounds but literally on tautological grounds, what everyone knows to be true: the existence of human knowledge of the external world? I do not know. I have to confess that the psychology of the Gem is too deep for me. Perhaps only *born* cognitive Calvinists, cognophobes, or misologists as Plato called them, can enter into its psychology. Susceptibility to Gem arguments may be genetically determined.

But on the special case of Gem arguments for *idealism*, I can perhaps throw some light, though not light which penetrates at all deep. So let us return to that special case.

There is, or at least there used to be, a proverbial saying (an unusually baffling one) that whoever drives fat cattle must himself be fat. And connoisseurs of faded positivistic manuals of 'scientific method', 'clear thinking', and the like, may recall reading criticism of what their authors sometimes called 'the fat-cattle fallacy'. This was the belief that a cause must be *like* its effects. It was alleged that this belief was especially prevalent among rationalist philosophers, and also among primitive peoples.

All this may sound superficial enough; and it is. Still, it is undoubtedly true that we all have *some* tendency to think, what is false, that a cause must be like its effects. And this fact may have some relevance to the psychology of Gem arguments for idealism: because it is also true that those arguments shade, not only easily, but imperceptibly, into arguments of the fat-cattle kind.

Berkeley, Bradley, McTaggart and others, as we have seen, argued in effect:

> We can only know what we have in mind
>
> So,
>
> We can know only what is mental.

Now, that argument differs in no important respect from this one:

> We can know only what is intelligibile,
>
> So,
>
> We can know only what is intelligent.

Then, we need only add a little *causal* inflection, and we have:

Only what is intelligible can make itself known to us,

So,

Only what is intelligent can make itself known to us.

And by this time the fat-cattle effect is palpable enough.

It will be worthwhile to give an actual specimen of fat-cattle reasoning from one of the idealists. The following is from Edward Caird, and it occurs, just as one would expect it to, in a setting of more-familiar Gems: 'no object without a subject', and so on. '[T]he world is essentially intelligible, and therefore may ultimately be seen in its unity with intelligence.'[41]

To connect Gem arguments for idealism with our all too familiar susceptibility to fat-cattle reasoning, is not to suggest any *deep* account of their psychology. But I cannot suggest anything deeper. I should add, however, that I doubt whether those arguments actually *had* any deep psychology: whether they ever expressed anything which went beyond the most superficial layer of anyone's mind. The strongest reason for doubting this is the following historical fact. The Gem-*like* arguments for fatalism and for hedonism have always flourished most among men of the world; whereas the Gem argument for idealism has *never* taken root out of doors, but was born, lived, and died as an indoor plant. This fact is indisputable, and to me, at least, it seems to speak for itself.

It can hardly be a coincidence that Kant, who made the Gem argument the foundation of modern idealism, is also the man with whom modern philosophy fell hopelessly into the hands of the professors. Hume was a man of the world, and wrote for a general audience. Even in his most severely philosophical books he said that Berkeleian or hyper-Berkeleian metaphysics, though he played with it for a while, is just too silly to be worth anyone's spending much time on; which is no less than the truth, at that. But with Kant, the audience of philosophy, and with it the whole external world, suddenly vanishes. No chink of daylight or breath of air was ever allowed to penetrate the solitary cell at Königsberg where he sat, forever polishing his Gems, and fuming against the other professors because they stupidly kept mistaking him for an idealist. That *owlishness* which I earlier remarked upon, as distinguishing idealists even among philosophers, presumably owes something to their philosophy having been born in these dark and confined conditions.

## V

Idealism was a long Victorian marriage of philosophy and religion: a marriage of the Carlyle-Mill-Ruskin kind. Its only offspring was a nauseous mixture of obscurantism, spurious consolation, evaporated Christianity, and collectivist zeal. This mixture filled every chair of philosophy in the English-speaking world, and almost every one in Germany. It furnished what is known as 'the great tradition in nineteenth-century philosophy'. Yet an intelligent child of ten might have seen well enough what the idealist professors were up to: raising so much learned dust that no one would be able to see any objection to retaining belief in even the grossest absurdities of the Christian religion. Even Lenin could see this much, though he did not have a hundredth part of the philosophical capacity of the professors on whom he heaped abuse. More surprisingly, he failed to see in them some useful political allies, even when one of them called his particular brand of idealism 'cognitive socialism'.[42]

It would be absurd to ascribe this gigantic farce primarily to the influence of the Gem argument: that would imply an estimate, of the ability of the philosophers in question, so unfavourable as to be flatly incredible. Idealism depended on the Gem *insofar as* it depended on argument; but what we ought to infer is (as I said near the beginning of this essay) that it hardly depended on argument at all. It must have been the powerful attraction of the idealist *conclusion*, which did nearly all the work; not any merit, or even any deep naturalness, in the Gem *argument*, since it had none of either. It was the need for a universe congenial to man which pulled the Gem through; not the other way about.

Anthropocentrism, we saw near the end of Essay 5, was the very essence of idealism. But it was also the essence of nineteenth-century philosophy altogether, though the forms which it took outside idealism were much less subtle.

Marxism is the best-known example. It pretended, and still pretends, to be a philosophy. Yet it has only ever been really interested in one thing: the economic well-being, for the next few centuries, of a particular species of terrestrial mammal. How helpful, even towards *that* end, Marxism has proved to be, it cannot now be necessary to state. But a point of view so extremely narrow and practical has, in any case, almost nothing to do with philosophy. And when this point of view is occupied exclusively and too long, it creates an atmosphere unbearably foetid, like that of dog-kennels, rabbit-warrens, and other over-occupied homes of land-mammals. A long course of reading in Marxism is enough to make anyone, or at least any philosopher, sick of the smell of man. The best antidote is to read something odourless, like astronomy.

The Positivism of Comte was intellectually far more formidable than Marxism, but it became afflicted to an even worse degree with the smell of the human lair. It *began*, of course, as a philosophy austerely scientific, designed specifically for a coming *post*-religious period in the history of the human race. It purported to be the first philosophy which was *not* anthropocentric. Yet it quickly became, at the hands of its founder, not only a religion itself, but, of all things, 'the religion of humanity': a religion more ferociously hostile than any before it towards philosophy, and indeed towards any intellectual activity not totally subordinated to the demands of the human heart. Nor was this amazing metamorphosis due to any peculiarities, pronounced enough though these were, of Comte's personality or circumstances. Frederic Harrison, the most distinguished of the British Positivists, and a writer now undeservedly forgotten, spoke for the whole movement when he wrote, for example, as follows. 'The Positive Philosophy is geocentric in its science, i.e., regards everything outside this earth from the point of view of our Earth, and it is anthropocentric in its moral and spiritual aspect, i.e., its beliefs and its hopes are concentrated on human life.'[43] Phew! Humanity is like garlic: a little goes a long way. A *religion* of humanity would be as unendurable as a religion of garlic.

The idealists, however, were philosophers *pur sang*, and they were rightly contemptuous of such gross anthropocentrism as that of the Positivists and the Marxists. Any of their disciples whom they caught dallying with it, they dealt with severely. Bosanquet, for example, was disgusted, as he should have been, when some of his Italian disciples spoke of 'the human and the terrestrial as the exclusive reality'.[44] Bradley, likewise, more than once had occasion to ask, when some half-taught idealist had blathered upliftingly about 'the future of mind', whether he was referring to *our* unpromising species and planet, or referring instead (as he should have been) to Absolute Mind.[45] If the former, then uplift was an impertinence at best, at worst a cruel irony; if the latter, then there could be no question of the *future*, because the Absolute is not in time. Yet in all such cases, the disciples were being more honest (though more stupid too) than their revered idealist masters. What could Bradley *expect*, when he denied the existence of 'inorganic nature'? What did Bosanquet have to offer, except an anthropocentrism more refined and oleaginous than that which his Italian disciples artlessly embraced?

And all this, let us remember, was going on in the century of Faraday, Darwin, and Maxwell! The idealists, Comte, Marx – these are *the great philosophers* of the nineteenth century! A return to 'the classics of Western philosophy' has lately been called for by some of our wisest educators, as a help for the ills (mortal enough) of our faculties of arts. But these educators themselves usually possess only a moderately close acquaintance with the 'classics' which they commend so earnestly to the attention of others. No doubt their wisdom is shown in this respect too. But the fact of the matter is, that the philosophy of the nineteenth century, unlike its science, is a proper object not of reverence but of shame. A minimum-test of the intrinsic merit of anything written is this, that some non-historical reason can be given why it should be read: a reason, I mean, absolutely independent of the fact that other people *have* read it. Hume's *Dialogues*, for example, easily pass this test; so does Lucian; so does Montaigne; so do the pre-Socratic philosophers. But who can supply a reason, of this kind, why anyone should read Kant, or Green, or Bradley? To ask this question, is to answer it.

What does it all mean, this triumph of anthropocentrism in nineteenth-century philosophy, and of idealism in particular? What *can* it mean, except that philosophy then spoke for human nature, and that human beings, by and large, simply *cannot* reconcile themselves to the knowledge that they are only the most intelligent and capable of known organisms? All human beings have always *had* this knowledge: as I said on the first page of this essay, the Mexicans knew well enough that, until the Spaniards came, *they* had been on top in Mexico. But it has almost always been possible for us to hide this unwelcome knowledge from ourselves. By about 1870, however, the diffusion of astronomical, geological, and biological knowledge had made it impossible to hide the truth from anyone any longer: the secret was out, beyond recall. Idealism, then, and nineteenth-century anthropocentrism in general, was a reaction to the misery of godlessness.

That life is lonely at the top of the organic tree, is a logical truth. To prevent your species from being lonely, there has to be another above it, and if there is a species above you, you are not at the top. *Whatever* species was *in fact* the most intelligent and capable one, then, would always have a strong inducement (as distinct from a reason) to believe that it was not so. And as it happens, *we* are at the top. Then there is the other fact, the significance of which is still unexhausted, despite the 2600 years since Anaximander pointed it out: that in humans the helplessness of the young is both more extreme and more prolonged than in any other species of animals. Perhaps these two facts are all that is needed, to explain the irreparable misery of human beings once they lose their belief in gods.

But whatever may be the explanation of it, that misery is one of the most momentous facts of human life, and it is *the* fact behind nineteenth-century anthropocentrism in general, and behind idealism in particular. It is also the fact behind many other post-Enlightenment historical phenomena: for example, the drug-dependence which has in the twentieth century crippled the Western world. Idealism was, to all the profoundest philosophers from Kant to Bradley, what heroin now is to millions in the West. It can hardly be an accident that Coleridge, who introduced German idealism into Britain, was also the slave of another and less intellectual anodyne.

## Notes

1 See, for example, D. Hume, *A Treatise of Human Nature* (1739; ed. L. A. Selby-Bigge, Oxford, Clarendon Press, 1888; re-ed. P. Nidditch, Oxford, Clarendon Press, 1978), bk III, pt I, sect. i, p. 463; the *Abstract*, p. 653; *An Enquiry concerning Human Understanding*, pp. 163–4. (These last two page references are to the Selby-Bigge edns, re-ed. P. Nidditch, of the *Abstract* (Clarendon Press, Oxford, 1978), and of the first *Enquiry*, (Clarendon Press, Oxford, 1975).

2 J. Bentham, *A Fragment on Government, and an Introduction to the Principles of Morals and Legislation*, ed. W. Harrison (Basil Blackwell, Oxford, 1967), p. 136.

3 J. Locke, *An Essay concerning Human Understanding*, ed. P. Nidditch (Oxford University Press, 1975), p. 620.

4 D. M. Armstrong (ed.), *Berkeley's Philosophical Writings* (Collier Books, New York, 1965), pp. 163–4.

5 Ibid., p. 211.

6 Ibid., p. 137. Italics not in text.

7 *Works of T. H. Green*, ed. R. L. Nettleship (Longmans, Green, London, 1885), vol. I, p. 204. Italics in text.

8 Armstrong, *Berkeley's Philosophical Writings*, pp. 137–51.

9 See his Introduction to *David Hume: The Philosophical Works*, ed. T. H. Green and T. H. Grose (Longmans, Green, London, 1874), *passim*.

10 See F. H. Bradley, *Appearance and Reality* (Clarendon Press, Oxford, 1893), ch. 1.

11 Hume, *A Treatise of Human Nature*, p. 82.

12 Cf. J. M. Keynes, *A Treatise on Probability* (Macmillan, London, 1921), p. 84n.

13 H. Poincaré, *The Foundations of Science* (Science Press, New York, 1913), p. 355. (This is not a book which Poincaré wrote, but a one-volume edition of his three books, *Science and Hypothesis*, *The Value of Science*, and *Science and Method*.)

14 J. Caird, *Introduction to the Philosophy of Religion*, as quoted in Green's review of that book in *Works of T. H. Green*, ed. R. L. Nettleship (Longmans, Green, London, 1889), vol. III, pp. 139–40.

15 H. Mansel, *The Philosophy of the Conditioned* (Alexander Strahan, London and New York, 1866), p. 63.

16 Sir W. Hamilton, *Discussions on Philosophy and Literature, Edu-*

cation and University Reform (Longman, Brown, Green and Long-mans, London, 1853), pp. 198–203.

17   Sir W. Hamilton, *Lectures on Metaphysics and Logic*, ed. H. Man-sel and J. Veitch (Blackwood, Edinburgh and London, 1861), vol. I, p. 148.

18   A. Schopenhauer, *The World as Will and Representation*, trans. E. Payne (Dover Publications, New York, 1969), vol. I, p. 3.

19   Ibid., vol. I, p. 434.

20   J. M. E. McTaggart, *Studies in Hegelian Cosmology* (Cambridge University Press, 1901), p. 21.

21   A. Seth, *Man's Place in the Cosmos* (Blackwood, Edinburgh and London, 1897), p. 146.

22   Bradley, *Appearance and Reality*, p. 128.

23   F. H. Bradley, *Ethical Studies* (Oxford University Press, 1876), pp. 323–4n.

24   The saying is often quoted by idealists; for example, by E. Caird, *Essays on Literature and Philosophy* (Macmillan, New York, 1892), vol. II, p. 315.

25   Nettleship, *Works of T. H. Green*, vol. I, p. 70.

26   I. Kant, *Prolegomena to Any Future Metaphysics*, trans. P. Lucas (Manchester University Press, 1953), p. 38.

27   I. Kant, *Critique of Pure Reason*, trans. N. Kemp Smith (Macmillan, London, 1950), p. 351.

28   See J. S. Mill, *An Examination of Sir William Hamilton's Philos-ophy* (5th edn, Longmans, Green, Reader and Dyer, London, 1878), ch. I, *passim*.

29   See J. McCosh, *The Scottish Philosophy* (reprint by Georg Olus Verlagsbuchhandlung, Hildesheim, 1966, of London edn of 1875), pp. 443–4.

30   See Duke of Argyll, *The Unity of Nature* (Alexander Strahan, London, 1884), pp. 153–5.

31   F. C. S. Schiller, *Studies in Humanism* (Macmillan, London, 1907), pp. 465–6.

32   Nettleship, *Works of T. H. Green*, vol. III, pp. 141–4.

33   F. H. Bradley, *Essays on Truth and Reality* (Oxford University Press, 1914), p. 92.

34   Schiller, *Studies in Humanism*, p. 463.

35   Nettleship, *Works of T. H. Green*, vol. III, pp. 144–6.

36   'The ego-centric predicament', *Journal of Philosophy*, VII, 1(1910), pp. 5–14.

37   A. C. Ewing, *Idealism: a Critical Survey* (Methuen, London, 1933), p. 14.

38  Ibid., pp. 56–9.
39  J. Jaynes, *The Origin of Consciousness in the Breakdown of the Bicameral Mind* (Houghton Mifflin, Boston, 1976).
40  See T. Gomperz, *The Greek Thinkers*, trans. G. Berry (John Murray, London, 1905), vol. II, pp. 229–45; and George Grote, *Plato, and Other Companions of Sokrates* (John Murray, London, 1865), vol. III, pp. 559–61.
41  E. Caird, *Hegel* (Blackwood, Edinburgh and London, 1883), p. 195. Cf. a criticism of Oersted by James Martineau, in his *Essays, Reviews and Addresses* (Longmans, Green, London 1891), vol. III, pp. 108–9.
42  V. I. Lenin, *Materialism and Empirio-criticism* (Martin, Laurence, London, n.d.), p. 193.
43  Frederic Harrison, *De Senectute* (T. Fisher Unwin, London, 1923), p. 173.
44  B. Bosanquet, *The Meeting of Extremes in Contemporary Philosophy* (Macmillan, London, 1921), p. 163.
45  See, for example, Bradley, *Essays on Truth and Reality*, pp. 243, 340.

# 7

## *What is Wrong with Our Thoughts? A Neo-Positivist Credo*

Early in the fourth century Constantine made Christianity the religion of the Roman Empire, and at once had reason to regret his having done so; for now not only the Church but the state was convulsed by controversies about the Holy Trinity. These controversies raged for over two hundred years, after which the bishops found new intellectual outlets, if not more rational ones, for their animosities. But Trinitarian trouble was not dead, only sleeping. The Great Schism of the eleventh and twelfth centuries, which split the Western from the Eastern Church, took place, on its theological side, over a question concerning the Trinity. This was, of course, that most famous of all theological questions, the question of the procession of the Holy Ghost, or of the *filioque*. The Orthodox theory was that the Holy Ghost proceeds from the Father alone. The Western bishops, however, were equally adamant that the Holy Ghost proceeds from the Father *filioque* – '*and the Son*'.

It is obvious enough that these two opinions could not both be right, though both could be wrong. It is equally obvious that both opinions *are* wrong, or at least, that they each have got something dreadfully wrong with them, and the same thing. They both have some fatal congenital defect, whatever the exact nature of this defect may be. And it is equally obvious too, that this defect will also be shared by any other answer to the question, what or whom the Holy Ghost proceeds from. It does not matter much how you answer this question: something has already gone fatally wrong with your thoughts, once you find yourself so much as asking it.

If we go back again to the age of Constantine, and enquire

what the pagan philosophers of that time were thinking about, we expect to hear of something more rational, at least, than questions about the Trinity. And so we do, at any rate among those philosophers who are among the intellectual descendants of Plato. Here is a typical example from the writings of Plotinus, which date from around 260.

> When we affirm the reality of the Real Beings and their individual identity of being and declare that these Real Beings exist in the Intellectual Realm, we do not mean merely that they remain unchangeably self-identical by their very essence, as contrasted with the fluidity and instability of the sense-realm; the sense-realm itself may contain the enduring. No; we mean rather that these principles possess, as by their own virtue, the consummate fulness of being. The Essence described as the primally existent cannot be a shadow cast by Being, but must possess Being entire; and Being is entire when it holds the form and idea of intellection and of life. In a Being, then, the existence, the intellection, the life are present as an aggregate. When a thing is a Being, it is also an Intellectual-Principle, when it is an Intellectual-Principle it is a Being; intellection and Being are co-existents. Therefore intellection is a multiple not a unitary and that which does not belong to this order can have no Intellection. And if we turn to the partial and particular, there is the Intellectual form of man, and there is man, there is the Intellectual form of horse and there is horse, the Intellectual form of Justice, and Justice.[1]

This sort of thing really is, I believe, better than thinking about the procession of the Holy Ghost; although I do not deny that it takes a sharp man to tell the difference. But everyone can tell that, with these thoughts too, as with thoughts about the *filioque*, *something* has gone appallingly wrong; or more likely, several things. Thinking like this is a perfect example of how you ought *not* to think.

It will be a relief, therefore, to turn for comparison to a typical passage from one of the very greatest of modern philosophers. It will also help to give us true ideas of the reality of progress in human thought, and of the speed of it, if we compare Plotinus with Hegel, writing sixteen hundred years later.

This is a light that breaks forth on spiritual substance, and shows absolute content and absolute form to be identical; – substance is in itself identical with knowledge. Self-consciousness thus, in the third place, recognizes its positive relation as its negative, and its negative as its positive, – or, in other words, recognizes these opposite activities as the same *i.e.* it recognizes pure Thought or Being as self-identity, and this again as separation. This is intellectual perception; but it is requisite in order that it should be in truth intellectual, that it should not be that merely immediate perception of the eternal and the divine which we hear of, but should be absolute knowledge. This intuitive perception which does not recognize itself is taken as starting-point as if it were absolutely presupposed; it has in itself intuitive perception only as immediate knowledge, and what it perceives it does not really know, – for, taken at its best, it consists of beautiful thoughts, but not knowledge.[2]

No more cheap jokes, I promise. They are silly anyway, because it would be silly to deny that the long night of ignorance, superstition, and religious or metaphysical delirium, really has by now come to an end. You can see that it has, by comparing the foregoing Hegel passage, the Plotinus passage, and the dispute about the *filioque*, with a representative passage from the writings of a great thinker of the present day: Michel Foucault.

An intrinsic archaeological contradiction is not a fact, purely and simply, that it is enough to state as a principle or explain as an effect. It is a complex phenomenon that is distributed over different levels of the discursive formation. Thus, for systematic Natural History and methodical Natural History, which were in constant opposition for a good part of the eighteenth century, one can recognize: an *inadequation* of the objects (in the one case one describes the general appearance of the plant; in the other certain predetermined variables; in the one case, one describes the totality of the plant, or at least its most important parts, in the other one describes a number of elements chosen arbitrarily for their taxonomic convenience; sometimes one takes account of the plant's different states of growth and maturity, at others one confines one's attention to a single moment, a stage of optimum visibility); a *divergence* of enunciative modalities (in the case of the systematic analysis of plants, one applies a rigorous perceptual and linguistic code, and in accordance with a constant scale; for methodical description, the codes are relatively free, and the scales of mapping may oscillate); an *incompatibility* of concepts (in the 'systems', the concept of generic character is an arbitrary, though misleading mark to designate the genera; in the methods this same concept must include the real definition of the genus); lastly, an *exclusion* of theoretical options (systematic taxonomy makes 'fixism' possible, even if it is rectified by the idea of a continuous creation in time, gradually unfolding the elements of the tables, or by the idea of natural catastrophes having disturbed by our present gaze the linear order of natural proximities, but excludes the possibility of a transformation that the method accepts without absolutely implying it).[3]

Enough. We now have before us four cases in which human thought has gone wrong, not in some superficial or curable way, but in some way which is evidently deep and beyond hope of cure. My question is, what is it that has gone wrong in such cases?

First, however, I need to emphasize what sort of thoughts it is, or rather, what grade of thoughts it is, that I am asking about. I am not interested here (or anywhere else, much) in thoughts of primitive people, or of ignorant or stupid people, or of people of no importance for the history of thought, or of people who are, even by ordinary standards, mad. My specimens above were not drawn from the voodoo religion, for example, or from the medicine of Paracelsus, or from the 'philosophy' of William Blake, or from the 'psychotherapy' of Wilhelm Reich. Indeed, in this essay, I will hardly stray at all 'below the belt', that is, to the rank under-parts of human thought: numerology, magic, lives of the gods, lives of the saints, lives of the demons, necromancy or lives of the dead, astrology, spiritualism, Freudianism, etc., etc. Together, of course, such things as these make up in fact the great bulk of past and present human thought, and there is more than enough that is wrong with them. But my question does not mainly concern them, and would be much less important if it did.

No, my question mainly concerns the thoughts of the world's great thinkers. The examples above are drawn from historically important sources, in the main stream of human thought, and in some of its highest reaches. The disagreement about the procession of the Holy Ghost has occupied profound thinkers and scholars on either side for a thousand years; it has had momentous social, political, and military consequences for the same length of time; and it remains a stumbling-block, at the present hour, to all attempts to reunite Western with Eastern Christianity. The philosophy of Plotinus is, by the unanimous voice of the learned, the fine fruit of Platonism, after it had had the benefit of ripening over the longest period of freedom of thought in all human history: seven hundred years. Hegel is, in the opinion of many philosophers even now, the greatest of all philosophers, and was certainly, at any rate, the most influential philosopher of the nineteenth century. And the writings of Foucault have recently profoundly influenced the intelligentsia, not only of that European nation which prides itself most on thought and learning, but of the entire Western world.

Yet it is also perfectly obvious, when we consider the above examples, that in all of them thought is labouring under some fatal affliction or other. And neither of the conventional evasions will do much good here: that my four examples are so terrible because they have been 'taken out of context', or because they depend on defective translations. In Plotinus, or Hegel, or Foucault, or in Trinitarian disputes, the context of any given passage hardly ever throws any light on it; the simple reason being, that the context just consists of more of the same sort of thing. And when every reasonable allowance has been made for the real difficulty of translating Plotinus, say, or Hegel, into English, this will scarcely even begin to explain what is wrong with the passages above. We cannot understand, indeed, how anyone would come to say the things that Plotinus or Hegel says. But that they *were* saying, in Greek or in German, the same baffling things as they are found saying in good modern English translations, cannot rationally be questioned. (It is a very striking fact, however, that I *had* to go to translations for my three quotations above. Nothing which was ever expressed originally in the English language resembles, except in the most distant way, the thought of Plotinus, or Hegel, or Foucault. I take this to be enormously to the credit of our language.)

My four examples above are, then, sufficiently representative, respectively, of Christian theology, of neo-Platonist metaphysics, of German idealism, and of whatever it is that Foucault represents.

Those four things, in their turn, are sufficiently representative of what human thought, in its highest reaches, has been. My four examples, however, are also examples of thought gone hopelessly wrong. A damning verdict therefore follows, on past human thought: a verdict essentially the same as the one which was pronounced on it by the eighteenth century Enlightenment, and repeated, with even greater vehemence, by the Logical Positivists in the twentieth century.

Of course it is a verdict against *most* past thought, not against all of it. Exempted from it are, for example, Greek mathematics in antiquity, and most importantly of course, natural science in the period since Copernicus: this being the ground on which the Enlightenment in general, and Logical Positivism in particular, took its stand. But both Greek mathematics and modern science are, in the overall historical scene, mere points of light in a boundless and impenetrable darkness. Most of even the highest human thought is what David Hume said religion is: 'sick men's dreams.'⁴ By contrast, rational thought – what Hume called the 'calm sunshine of the mind'⁵ – is historically rare, local, and ephemeral.

From an Enlightenment or Positivist point of view, which is Hume's point of view, and mine, there is simply no avoiding the conclusion that the human race is mad. There are scarcely any human beings who do not have some lunatic beliefs or other to which they attach great importance. People are mostly sane enough, of course, in the affairs of common life: the getting of food, shelter, and so on. But the moment they attempt any depth or generality of thought, they go mad almost infallibly. The vast majority, of course, adopt the local religious madness, as naturally as they adopt the local dress. But the more powerful minds will, equally infallibly, fall into the worship of some intelligent and dangerous lunatic, such as Plato, or Augustine, or Comte, or Hegel, or Marx.

Plato was born of a virgin, after Apollo had appeared to his reputed father in a dream, according to a story which was widely current soon after Plato's death and possibly even before it.⁶ And since he was a lifelong enthusiast for creating popular beliefs which he knew to be false, and beliefs, at that, with rather less to recommend them to him than this one had, who can say with confidence that Plato himself did not encourage belief in this stupid story? Plato – that scourge of the human mind, whom we have to thank for persuading philosophers for 2400 years, and more years to come, that it is a *problem*, how something can be a certain way and something else be the same way! Then, entrust yourself to Augustine's mighty intellect, and you too must agonize, as he does, over the 'problem', for example, whether Jesus is *still* bleeding from hands and feet? Or has he lost by now all trace of the scars of the crucifixion? Or, does he retain some scars but only faint and not-unattractive ones? It is this third alternative, Augustine concludes, which will recommend itself to every rational mind.[7] Auguste Comte simply appointed himself Supreme Pontiff of his new, but final and worldwide religion, the Religion of Humanity. George Hegel thought that his thought not merely discloses, but *is*, the final coming-to-consciousness of the *Absolute Thought*. Marx, too, saw himself as the prophet and architect of a fundamental transformation of the entire human race, and . . . But no! Let us, for pity's sake, as well as for horror's sake, draw a veil. . . But let us never forget, either, as *all conventional history of philosophy conspires to make us forget*, what the 'great thinkers' *really* are: proper objects, indeed, of pity, but even more, of horror.

Now what I would like to know, and what every philosopher ought to want to know, is: what *is* it that is wrong with the thoughts I have been speaking about: for example, with the quotations I gave above? And here I find myself at a loss. The Logical Positivists tell me, of course, that what is wrong with such things is that they are all 'meaningless.' This is not even true, as we will see a little later, but even if it were true, it would be hardly any help. It is hardly more helpful than saying, *à l'Australien*, that what is wrong with the passages in question is that they are 'all bullshit;' or that the authors of them are all mad.

The reason why all such answers are unhelpful is a very simple and obvious, but important and neglected, fact. Namely, that what is wrong with the Hegel passage, say, is quite *different* from what is wrong with the Plotinus passage; that both of those passages are quite different again, in what is wrong with them, from the Foucault passage; and that all three passages are quite different, yet again, from all answers to the question, whom or what the Holy Ghost proceeds from. My four specimens are all profoundly pathological, no doubt; but each of them is pathological in a different way. What we need to know is, what these various ways are. But that is what no Logical Positivist, and still less anyone else, can tell us.

And this is how we are placed in relation to the entire history of philosophy. Whatever it was that went so dreadfully wrong with Berkeley's thoughts about the possibility of things existing 'without the mind', it certainly cannot have been what went wrong with Meinong's thoughts on the same topic. What went wrong with Parmenides' thoughts about how many things there are, must have been very different from whatever went wrong in Leibniz's *Monadology*. The way that Moore's thoughts went wrong about ethics cannot possibly have been the same way as Kant's thoughts about ethics went wrong. How Ryle went wrong about the mind, and how Plotinus went wrong about the mind, must have been very different things. Spinoza's way of getting the relation between the actual and the possible wrong, cannot possibly be the same as David Lewis's way. And so it goes on, right down the line; and we do not know what *any* of those ways of going wrong are.

Our situation is actually a good deal worse than I have just implied. For even in a single paragraph of Hegel, say, there is, presumably, not just one thing that has gone wrong, but half a dozen things which have all gone wrong together; while we are not able to identify a single one of them. And this is after how many centuries of philosophical discipline, books of logic, guides to the perplexed, arts of thinking, rules for the conduct of the intellect, essays concerning human understanding, critiques of reason. . . ?

It is the same story even beyond the pale. For example, no one actually knows, even, what is wrong with numerology. Philosophers, of course, use numerology as a stock example of thought gone hopelessly wrong, and they are right to do so; still, they cannot tell you what it is that is wrong with it. If you ask a philosopher this, the best he will be able to come up with is a bit of Positivism about unverifiability, or a bit of Popperism about unfalsifiability: answers which the philosopher himself will know to be unsatisfactory on various grounds, but which have in addition this defect, that they put numerology in the same boat as, for example, astrology. But numerology is actually quite as different from astrology as astrology is from astronomy. Philosophers do not know this, because, while they often look at the astrological parts of newspapers for fun, they never read a book of numerology. If they did, they would soon find out that the peculiar awfulness of numerology, while clearly quite different from that of astrology, is utterly elusive in itself.

So painfully far are we, from being able to answer the question which is the title of this essay. What is needed in order to answer it, but what we have as yet scarcely the faintest glimmerings of, is a *nosology* of human thought. (A nosology is a classification of diseases.) We will know what is wrong with our thoughts when, and only when, we have identified (for example) all the five different things (or however many there are) which go wrong in a paragraph of Berkeley intended to prove that physical things cannot exist 'without the mind'. Or, when we can write a computer programme which, by combining (perhaps) eleven different nonsense-producing ingredients in just the right ways, will enable us to print out at command a page of pseudo-Hegel which is absolutely indistinguishable from the real thing.

Whatever is wrong with philosophers' thoughts, it is, at any rate, *not* ordinary falsity, or ignorance of empirical truths. Quine argued, with enough plausibility to satisfy some unexacting folk, that philosophy is continuous with empirical science;[8] and Popper once tried to show that philosophical problems regularly have 'their roots in science'.[9] Such a belief can make for better philosophy, (as I remarked in Essay 4 above). The only trouble with it is, it is not true. You need only try it out in particular cases, rather than in general terms, in order to see this. Take any paradigm philosopher: Parmenides, say, or Plato, or Aquinas, or Berkeley, or Meinong. That the thoughts for which they are so famous had gone enormously wrong, is not in dispute. But was their trouble that they were ignorant of, or that they denied, some empirical facts or other, of which we are apprised? To ask this question is to answer it. Or take British idealism of the late nineteenth and early twentieth centuries. Did the idealism of Bosanquet and Bradley depend on ignorance of, or require denial of, anything in Lyell's geology, say, or in Darwin's biology, or in Einstein's physics? Only someone very ignorant of their philosophy could suppose that it did.

Defects of empirical knowledge have less to do with the ways we go wrong in philosophy than defects of *character* do: such things as the simple inability to shut up; determination to be thought deep; hunger for power; fear, especially the fear of an indifferent universe. These are among the obvious emotional sources of bad philosophy. Epicurus was one of the few great philosophers whom anyone but their mothers could love, and he enjoined us to avoid public notice of every kind, and 'live retired;' but Plutarch pointed out that the author of this injunction hoped to be, and was, famous for it.[10] Plutarch was no giant brain, yet if we had twenty contributions to the nosology of philosophy, as good as this little one of his to the nosology of philosophical *character*, we would be a lot further advanced than we are. Still it is, of course, an understanding of bad thoughts that we are after, rather than of bad hearts: of public intellectual effects, rather than of private emotional causes. My question is not, 'What is wrong with us?' (though that is a good question too). When Stephano bawls out in *The Tempest*, 'I am not Stephano, but a cramp,'[11] we know what it is that is wrong with *him*: he is drunk. But it is a different matter, and we do not know, what is wrong with a man's *thought*, when he thinks that he is a cramp; whether he thinks this because he is drunk, or from some other cause.

What is wrong with our thoughts is hardly ever *logical* falsity either, or ignorance of logical truth, or failure to live up to the logical knowledge that we have. This is so, at least, if the word 'logical' is used in its usual sense. Take the controversy about the *filioque*. I have not read any of this literature, but since philosophy in the eleventh and twelfth centuries was, if anything, over-attentive to logic, it is safe to assume that on both sides of this controversy the logic was impeccable. You would search the controversialists' writings in vain for invalid inferences, or concealed contradictions. And the reason is obvious. Logic is concerned only with the relations *between* propositions, but everything that has gone wrong in the *filioque* dispute has gone wrong *inside* propositions: in the terms which are common to both sides, such as 'Holy Ghost,' 'Father,' and 'proceeds.' And this state of affairs is typical. The logicians' net is too coarse-meshed to catch the fish that matter.

If you think otherwise: if you think that it is only, or usually, or even often, by way of *illogicality* that philosophers' thoughts go wrong, then by all means try your skill on the quotations which I gave above. Please display for us Hegel's fallacious inferences, or Plotinus' inconsistencies. What a perfectly farcical idea! Of course the detection of fallacy is sometimes possible, and even important, in philosophy. So it sometimes is in science too. But it is not often possible in philosophy, and even where it is both possible and important, it throws no light whatever on the peculiarly philosophical ways of going wrong.

If what is wrong with our thoughts is not bad science, or bad character, or bad logic, is it perhaps (as some have implied that it is) bad grammar? Obviously not, if the word 'grammar' retains its usual acceptation. The nosology of thought has next to nothing to do with people saying, for example, 'between you and I', or 'I've did that job.' Certain Logical Positivists, in their early days, actually had the cheek to imply that metaphysical statements are defective in the same way as the string of words 'Lenin or coffee how.' What can one say in response to such silliness, except that it is silly? More generally, the Positivists were often justly criticized for calling statements meaningless – 'The Holy Ghost proceeds from the Father alone,' for example – which, quite obviously, you first have to understand, that is, know the meaning of, *before you can tell* that they *have* got something unspeakably wrong with them. Expressed in Turkish, say, the proposition that the Holy Ghost proceeds from the Father alone, would indeed be meaningless to me, and probably to you. But that kind of meaninglessness has clearly nothing to do with the nosology of thought. It is only the proposition, or the thought, that (say) the Holy Ghost proceeds from the Father alone, which is pathological. There is nothing whatever wrong with the English *sentence*, 'The Holy Ghost proceeds from the Father alone,' or with its Turkish counterpart.

That philosophers' errors are usually most intimately connected with their abuses of *language*, I not only do not deny but am most anxious to affirm. Far more often than not, their intellectual crimes and their literary ones are inextricably interwoven.

(Foucault's sentence of twenty-three lines of print, above, is a minor example). The exposure of philosophers' errors, consequently, is likewise often literary as much as it is intellectual. Hume, in his justly famous paragraph about 'is' and 'ought,' brought a fundamental logical truth to light, by complaining of a certain common literary sleight-of-hand.[12] Or, to compare that great thing with a small one, I have shown elsewhere that Popper's philosophical absurdities about science arose entirely from a certain abuse which he regularly practised on words like 'discovery', 'knowledge' and 'irrefutable.'[13] It cannot be an accident, any more than it is an accident that our mental and our bodily powers are extinguished together at death, that thought and language arrive *together*, in Hegel, at the highest degree of corruption of which either is capable. But it is merely ridiculous to try to condense the whole cloud of ways in which language can be abused, into the single drop of bad grammar. Hegel's *grammar* is all right. Why try to convict him on the one charge of which he is innocent?

I have been saying that we need a nosology of thought, and that it would not be – various things. What it *would* be, I have admitted I do not know. My main object, however, is to convince you that no one knows: that the nosology which we need has not yet even begun to exist: that thoughts – as distinct from sentences, or inferences, or character, or information – can go wrong in a multiplicity of ways, none of which anyone yet understands.

It would be impracticable, obviously, to try to convince you of this, by going through the entire history of thought giving longish quotations, as I began by doing. The best thing I could think of to do instead, and what I have done, is to compile a list of propositions which might pass muster both as a kind of epitome of the history of human thought, and as a museum of the pathology of thought – all on a dolls'-house scale, of course. All the thoughts on my list will be ones which have gone fatally wrong, and which you will agree have gone fatally wrong, though each in a different way. But after the first two specimens, you will not know, any more than I do, *in what way* they have gone wrong.

Some of the entries are things which some philosopher has actually believed. Others are caricatures, but very recognizable caricatures, of actual opinions of philosophers. Some are thoughts which probably no one has ever seriously thought; but you can never be sure of that, and if some of my specimens are of that kind, I absolutely defy you to tell where those end and the others begin. The specimens are in some cases so grotesque as to make one feel rather ill; but then a museum of pathology can never be a pleasant place. In case anyone should be so good-hearted, or so ignorant, as to consider my list a libel on the human race, I will give, at the end of this essay, a couple of actual specimens, quotations from one of the greatest of 'great thinkers', which are far more revolting than anything on my list.

The entries are in no particular order, historical or other. But it would be preferable, I decided, if they were given some common thread of subject-matter, however slight; and better still, if that subject-matter were something so homely that no one would think it likely *of itself* to make our thoughts go wrong. I decided on *the number three* for this common thread of subject-matter; but nearly anything else would have done just as well. Here, then, are examples of forty different ways in which thought can go irretrievably wrong, of which we can identify *only the first two*.

1   Between 1960 and 1970 there were three US presidents named Johnson.
2   Between 1960 and 1970 there were three US presidents named Johnson, and it is not the case that between 1960 and 1970 there were three US presidents named Johnson.
3   God is three persons in one substance, and one of these persons is Jesus, which is the lamb that was slain even from the foundations of the world.
4   Three lies between two and four only by a particular act of the Divine Will.
5   Three lies between two and four by a moral and spiritual necessity inherent in the nature of numbers.
6   Three lies between two and four by a natural and physical necessity inherent in the nature of numbers.
7   Three lies between two and four only by a convention which mathematicians have adopted.
8   There *is* an integer between two and four, but it is not three, and its true name and nature are not to be revealed.
9   There is no number three.

10    Three is the only number.
11    Three is the highest number.
12    Three is a large number.
13    Three is a lucky number.
14    The sum of three and two is a little greater than eight.
15    Three is a real object all right: you are not thinking of nothing when you think of three.
16    Three is a real material object.
17    Three is a real spiritual object.
18    Three is an incomplete object, only now coming into existence.
19    Three is not an object at all, but an essence; not a thing, but a thought; not a particular, but a universal.
20    Three is a universal all right, but it exists only, and it exists fully, in each actual triple.
21    Actual triples possess threeness only contingently, approximately, and changeably, but three itself possesses threeness necessarily, exactly, and immutably.
22    The number three is only a mental construct after all, a convenience of thought.
23    The proposition that 3 is the fifth root of 243 is a tautology, just like 'An oculist is an eye-doctor.'
24    The number three is that whole of which the parts are all and only the actual inscriptions of the numerals, 'three' or '3'.
25    Five is of the same substance as three, co-eternal with three, very three of three: it is only in their *attributes* that three and five are different.
26    The tie which unites the number three to its properties (such as primeness) is inexplicable.
27    The number three is nothing more than the sum of its properties and relations.
28    The number three is neither an idle Platonic universal, nor a blank Lockean substratum; it is a concrete and specific energy in things, and can be detected at work in such observable processes as combustion.
29    Three is a positive integer, and the probability of a positive integer being even is $\frac{1}{2}$, so the probability of three being even is $\frac{1}{2}$.

30  In some previous state of our existence we knew the number three face-to-face, as it is in itself, and by some kind of union with it.

31  How can I be absolutely sure that I am not the number three?

32  Since the properties of three are intelligible, and intelligibles can exist only in the intellect, the properties of three exist only in the intellect.

33  How is the addition of numbers possible? Nothing can *make* the number three into four, for example.

34  What the number three is in itself, as distinct from the phenomena which it produces in our minds, we can, of course, never know.

35  We get the concept of three only through the transcendental unity of our intuitions as being successive in time.

36  One is identity; two is difference; three is the identity of, and difference between, identity and difference.

37  The number three is not an ideal object of intellectual contemplation, but a concrete product of human *praxis*.

38  The unconscious significance of the number three is invariably phallic, nasal, and patriarchal.

39  The three members of any triple, being distinct from and merely related to one another, would fall helplessly asunder, if there were not some deeper non-relational unity of which their being three is only an appearance.

40  It may be – though I don't really believe in modalities – that in some other galaxies the sum of three and two is not five, or indeed is neither five nor not five. (Don't laugh! They laughed at Christopher Columbus, you know, and at Copernicus; and even the logical law of excluded middle is being questioned nowadays by some of the sharper young physicists.)

Despite what I said earlier, about the pathology of thought not being the pathology of inference, I have included a few inferences in this list, and some bad ones among them. I did so just for the sake of a bit of verisimilitude. But I have made sure that, in those cases, at least one of the thoughts is bad too, and not just the inference between them.

The list is of tiresome length, but I could very easily have made it more than twice as long. With only a little more trouble, I could have made it deeper too; and anyone with a moderate acquaintance with the history of thought could do the same. But a hundred specimens, while they would have made my point, would have left us all more or less suicidal; while ten would not have been enough to suggest anything like the variety of pathological forms which thought can take. Forty specimens are, perhaps, enough to make the point, without inducing too much depression at the same time.

And now, what does the existing nosology of thought tell us about these forty specimens? Well, we know what it is that is wrong with proposition (1): contingent falsity. And we know what is wrong with proposition (2): that it is self-contradictory, and hence necessarily false. With this, however, our existing nosology falls silent, as far as the above list is concerned. Here, then, are thirty-eight ways for thought to come absolutely to grief, other than by contingent falsity or self-contradiction, and we know absolutely nothing about any of them. We are like physicians who can recognize only two diseases of the human body.

The Logical Positivists, to their credit, at least *tried* to frame a nosology of thought less pitifully inadequate than the common one. They acknowledged *three* ways in which thought can go wrong: contingent falsity, self-contradiction, and meaninglessness. A proposition is meaningless, they said, if it is not a tautology and not verifiable either. Propositions about the precession of the equinoxes, for example, are verifiable, while propositions about the procession of the Holy Ghost are not. And verifiability, they said, consists in standing in a certain logical relation to observation-statements.

But, of course, they never did succeed in making out just *what* logical relation that is, and the story of their successive attempts to do so forms a justly famous episode of black comedy in twentieth-century philosophy. But even if they had succeeded in this, or even if anyone else had succeeded in it since (as no one has), it would help with few, if any, of the propositions listed above. It *might* help with proposition (3), for example, and was, of course, at least *intended* to deal with thinks like (3). But it would not help at all with the grotesque (8), for example; or even with the sordid (13) (which is one of the few slum-dwellers that I have let in). According to Positivism, the only way a proposition about *numbers* could go wrong, apart from being contingently false like (1), is by being self-contradictory. But there is nothing self-contradictory about (8), or (13), or about any item on my list, except (2).

There is no getting away from it: the Logical Positivist nosology too is pitifully inadequate. Hegel just is *different* from Plotinus, and again from Foucault, and so on. Likewise, every specimen from (3) to (40) on my list is different from every other, as well as from the first two. Of course I cannot *prove* that all those things are different from one another, or even that any two of them are different. So if a Logical Positivist chose to dig in his heels, and insist that the ways in which thought can go wrong are all of them comprehended in the three categories of contingent falsity, self-contradiction, and unverifiability – well, I could not prove him wrong. But it is obvious enough that he *is* wrong. There are just more things in hell and earth than are dreamed of in his philosophy; thirty-odd more, at the least.

And yet there are philosophers, and beneficiaries of Logical Positivism at that, who actually propose, not to enlarge the Positivist nosology, but to contract it, to the point where it contains only *one* category! Now I ask you: what ought to be thought of a doctor, even in the most primitive state of medicine, who acknowledges the existence of only one disease? I am referring, of course, to Quine, who wants us to make do just with the category of contingent falsity:[14] an excess of Positivist pedestrianism which deserves (though it will not receive in this book) an essay to itself.

A nosology of human thought, then, like a nosology of the human body, will be hopelessly inadequate if it contains only one or two or three categories. At the same time, adequacy or completeness is not the only desideratum in a nosology. There is also the desideratum of *surveyability*, which must be met if a nosology is to be useful. A nosology *could* be completely adequate *and* completely useless: for example, by containing *too many* categories – a billion, say. In that case the nosology itself would be as unsurveyable as the vast mass of raw facts which it exists to digest for us.

This is the rock that threatens to sink us, if, having realized the inadequacy of the Logical Positivist nosology, we embark on the neo-Positivist project of completing it. Will there not turn out to be just *too many* ways in which thought can go wrong? Tolstoy said that all happy families are the same, while every unhappy family is unhappy in a different way.[15] This is an exaggeration entirely characteristic of its foolish author. You could say with equal plausibility that everyone who goes wrong in philosophy goes wrong in a way all his own: an exaggeration of the originality of philosophers, too ludicrous to require rebuttal. But it *is* true that there are so many ways in which a thing as complicated as a human family can go wrong, and so many human families, that a nosology of the family is indeed doomed in advance to being either inadequate or useless. Long before it was even half-complete, it would be quite as unsurveyable as the combined histories of all the unhappy families. Now the question is, is my neo-Positivist project, of an adequate nosology of thought, doomed in the same way? Must a nosology of thought be either far too short to be adequate, or far too long to be useful?

If the answer is 'yes,' then we must sadly relinquish the project of a complete nosology of thought; if it is 'no,' then, since that nosology certainly does not exist yet, we should cheerfully set about constructing it.

I do not know which answer is right.

But I incline to the sad answer, for two reasons. One is the alarming ease with which a list like the one above can be compiled. At first, indeed, it is not easy at all, quite the reverse: the pathological thoughts will not come to mind. Of course they won't, because you have strong barriers in your mind to prevent them coming. All your life, if you are of the positivistic temperament, or at least all your waking life, you have been trying to think, and talk and write, rationally; but now you are having to try to think either like most people, or like 'great thinkers'. Then, however, you consult your library, refresh your acquaintance with the history of human thought, and at once all those barriers burst. It is like experiencing instant release from the earth's gravity, or from all moral restraints. *Now* the monstrous forms not only come, but come from everywhere. They come in inexhaustible numbers, like the waves coming to the shore, or patients to a socialist medical service – except that these are sick all right. Thus I easily filled my chamber of forty horrors above. And then, remember that I chose my exhibits mainly from the better class of horrors, and for the most part shielded you from the really rough and more numerous element.

The other thing which inclines me to the sad view, that the nosology of human thought would be infinitely or at least unsurveyably long, is an experience less specific, but more extensive. It is the experience of thirty-five years' marking of undergraduate essays in philosophy. Here again I am excluding the worst ones; I am thinking of all *except* the worst and the very best. I do not know whether other people's experience of marking so many of these essays has been the same as mine, but my impressions are these. First, that if I were to write down everything that has gone wrong in a *single typical sentence* of one of these essays, I would finish up writing a book. Second, that if I were to write down everything that is wrong with the *next* sentence, this too would yield a book, but a different book. Third, that, apart from essays submitted by such characteristic products of the contemporary faculty of arts as 'collectives' and plagiarists, no two bad essays are bad to exactly the same degree.

Those are the two things which make me think that an adequate nosology of thought would be unsurveyably long. But as against them, we know of other cases in which phenomena have *appeared* to be inexhaustibly various, and yet this appearance has been proved delusive at last. The history of science furnishes many triumphant examples of this kind, but I will remind you only of the most wonderful one of them all. Nothing could seem more inexhaustibly various than the chemical composition of things; and yet we have the periodic table of the elements. With such an example as that one before him, the neo-Positivist should be, of all people, the last to despair over the *apparently* infinite number of ways in which thought can go wrong.

Accordingly, I do not despair of the idea of an adequate and surveyable nosology of thought. Nevertheless, I do incline on balance to the conclusion that such a thing is not possible. Now, suppose that this pessimistic view is right. What I wish to point out is that, even then, the neo-Positivist is not doomed to ineffectiveness. He might still be able to produce results of the utmost value, and results which no one else could produce.

The reason is simply this, that it might still be possible to carry out the neo-Positivist project with complete success *in particular cases*. Even if the general question, 'What is wrong with our thoughts,' does not admit of an exhaustive answer, still a particular question, such as 'What is wrong with Berkeley's thoughts in such-and-such a key paragraph?,' *might* admit of an exhaustive answer. Someone really might get to the bottom of what is wrong with Berkeley's thought, for example, that the perceptible qualities of physical objects are ideas; *and* get to the bottom of everything else, too, that is wrong with that key paragraph. I am not saying that even this sort of local success would be easy: only that it is still possible, even after we have agreed to abandon the idea of a *complete* nosology of thought. If it were to be achieved, even in a single major case, such as Berkeley's, it would be of great intellectual value. And the only person who could possibly achieve such a thing would be someone fired by the neo-Positivist ambition to understand in detail how human thought goes wrong.

Of course, even if you did achieve such a local success, the chances are discouragingly high that it would be *purely* local. It is better than even money that the next 'great thinker' you turned your attention to would have other ways of going wrong in thought, which all your hard-earned understanding of Berkeley would throw no light whatever on. There is no getting away from this.

There is one factor working in your favour, though. This is the tendency of philosophers to form schools, and of their schools to form sequences. How extremely strong this 'clumping' tendency is in philosophy, is very well known; but the tendency is often strongly at work even in cases where it is not recognized, even by the very people concerned. For example, Kant, and the 'Absolute Idealists' of the nineteenth century, all had a particular detestation of the 'subjective idealism' (as they called it) of Berkeley, and could not emphasize enough their disagreement with it; the reason being, that they owed almost everything to it. (This was an instance, then, of what might be called the Astor effect, after the millionaire John Jacob Astor, who once had occasion to ask, 'Why does that man hate me? I never lent him mony'). So, if we ever *did* get Berkeley's idealism exactly right, the benefit would in fact *not* be purely local, but would extend at least to our understanding of nineteenth-century idealism as well.

This kind of thing – finding out everything that had gone wrong in the idealism of Berkeley, say, or every element which has gone into the making of such a typical pseudo-problem as induction, say, or 'the external world', or universals – this kind of thing is the very most, in my opinion, that any philosopher could ever achieve. This will remind you of a saying of G. E. Moore, which disgusted many people, that he was led to philosophize only by the maddening things that other philosophers said; and it may strike you as a shamefully small and negative idea of philosophy's highest possible achievement. But let it be as small and negative as you like: it is still more than any philosopher ever *has* achieved.

By now, however, some people's indignation will be boiling. 'So that is all that Berkeley, or any great philosopher, is good for, according to you: to fill a show-case in a future museum of the pathology of thought! You say it would be an achievement of great value, to know everything about how Berkeley went wrong: but if he never went right, as you seem to think, where is the value, or the point? No, you would be more consistent if you advised us simply to forget all about Berkeley, and about later idealism too, and about all the rest of it. What your neo-Positivism really tends to, is the *extinction* of philosophy.'

I reply that there *is* another reason for reading Berkeley, apart from the possibility of finding out how he went wrong. It is that he was unusually good at finding out how *other* philosophers had gone wrong: Locke in particular. And this state of affairs is typical, because it takes a philosopher to catch a philosopher. This fact, if neo-Positivism does indeed tend to the extinction of the philosophical profession, will make that profession at least a little harder to extinguish than, say, a priesthood is. Governments and would-be governments will always have a few career-openings for philosophers. Plato, for example, was the ideas-man behind a military attempt to overthrow the government of Dionysius II at Syracuse; but Dionysius also had his own ideas-department, headed by one Philistus, a very distinguished Sicilian don indeed, and dedicated to the intellectual defence of his government.[16]

I must admit, though, that in other respects the case of Berkeley is not typical: he is an unusually favourable specimen of a great philosopher. It seems, by contrast, entirely out of the question that anyone should ever get to the bottom of what is wrong with *Hegel's* thoughts, say. He, then, will never even fill a show-case in a museum of pathology, and there is no *other* conceivable reason for reading him. Hegel could no more tell you where others went wrong, than he could go right himself. And while he is, no doubt, an unusually unfavourable specimen of a great philosopher, he is at any rate closer to the norm than Berkeley is.

What I have just said will only serve to confirm my critic's prognosis. 'It is perfectly clear,' he will say, 'where you are headed. Your neo-Positivism will do to philosophy what a cruder Positivism has already done to religion, in such nightmare states as Sweden and Russia. Think of the Swedish education system, or the Soviet 'Halls of Atheism.' There the docile citizens, purged of all religion, and *en route* to suicide or its vodka equivalent, pause to gaze with mingled horror and envy at some relics of the Christian centuries, and to marvel at a body of thoughts so preposterous that they even possessed the power of reconciling human beings to life. In your museums of the pathology of thought, likewise, they will gaze on some relics of philosophy, and its glorious history. Man, by the time you Positivists have finished re-educating him, will be no more than that trivial bundle of infirmities which at present queues for its food in Russia, and in Sweden has its pornographic videos home-delivered.'

I think that this Muggeridgean critic of mine is essentially right about the social consequences of neo-Positivism. He is wrong only in being too optimistic, because there are in fact two night-mares, not one. One is the present and visible short-term future; the other is the entire past. For that 'glorious history' of philos-ophy to which he refers, what is that? Why, it is that vast repository of sick men's dreams which I began by giving four typical specimens of. It is that never-failing spring of monstrosities which I drew from, in order to prove to you how easily philosophy can create nearly forty different kinds of madness, even out of a theme as small and barren in itself as the number three.

Muggeridge: 'Positivism will deprive man, not only of all objects of religious reverence, but of all objects of the reverence which great philosophers have always, and rightly, received.'

True, Malcolm, except for the 'and rightly' part. In fact the reverence which has been and is accorded, by pre-Positivist man, to such two-legged plagues as Plato, Kant, and Hegel, is merely insane.

Muggeridge: 'Positivist man will be brutish, incurious, untouched by any thought not directed to his comfort, or his control over nature.' True again, Malcolm, or near enough. But then, you know, the alternative is even worse. For when common humanity *does* venture in thought beyond the concerns of common life, it is a thousand to one that atrocity, and not just absurdity, will result. Do the scenes of Tehran, Kabul, Beirut in 1986 disgust and appal you? Then learn to see in them the scenes of Alexandria in 415, of Toulouse in 1218, of Munster in 1535, and all the other famous beauty-spots of your beloved Christian centuries.

Muggeridge: 'Positivist man will be, and will have to live with the unbearable knowledge that he is, trivial.' Most true, Malcolm; but there is another side to the coin. Your 'great thinkers', Plato, Aquinas, Descartes, Kant, flattered and deluded man that he will live for ever; or that he is not really even a part of the physical universe at all; or that he is the whole *point* of the existence of the physical universe; or even that the physical universe depends upon, indeed is constituted by, man's thought of it! Philosophy, take it by and large, has in fact been simply the anthropocentrism of the educated and intelligent, as religion is the anthropocentrism of the others. But, to some of us, farcical flattery is even more disgusting than trivial truth.

For these reasons, I remain an unrepentant neo-Positivist, or an only-slightly-repentant one. I cannot help feeling that rational thought, 'the calm sunshine of the mind', has a right to exist, as well as madness; and even that it has some right to be heard (though I admit that that is more debatable). It is, in any case, a necessity of life for some people. But I agree with Malcolm Muggeridge, that for most people it is not only not necessary, but is an environment as lethal as the inside of a vacuum-tube.

Unlike Muggeridge, however, I do not believe that rational thought *is* a danger to humanity, in the long or even in the medium run. Whether a society of atheists could endure, was a question often discussed during the Enlightenment, though never decided.

If the question is generalized a little, however, from 'atheists' to 'Positivists,' then it seems obvious enough that the answer to it is 'no.' Genetic engineering aside, given a large aggregation of human beings, and a long time, you cannot reasonably expect rational thought to *win*. You could as reasonably expect a thousand unbiased dice, all tossed at once, all to come down 'five,' say. There are simply far too many ways, and easy ways, in which human thought can go wrong. Or, put it the other way round: anthropocentrism cannot lose. The jungle *will* reclaim the clearing (even without heavy infestations of conservationists), darkness will beat the light, not quite always on the local scale, but absolutely always on the large scale.

I therefore believe that the future of the human race is safe in the hands of such typical representatives of it as Colonel Gaddafi, the Ayatollah Khomeini, and the African National Congress. Kant and Hegel, or some other equally 'great thinkers', will still be read with reverence by the most intelligent and educated part of mankind, long after modern science is forgotten, or is confined to a few secret departments of the bureaucracy.

Any student of the history of thought is soon able to say, with Macbeth, 'I have supp'd full with horrors.' To read a book of magic, say, or astrology, is horrible, because the spectacle of steady and systematic irrationality induces depression and nausea. Yet the most horrible book, in this way, that I have ever read, does not come from the underworld of thought. On the contrary, it comes from the dizziest heights of contemporary academic respectability.

The book is the second volume of *Hegel's Development*, by H. S. Harris, of York University, Toronto. It is subtitled *Night Thoughts (Jena 1801-1806)*. It was published in 1983, by Oxford University Press at the Clarendon Press; which is to say, by the best. The book is a colossal monument to the scholarly industry of its author. It is over 700 pages long, and the work of which it is only the second volume must inevitably run into many more volumes. In 1806, after all, most of the publications on which Hegel's fame rests still lay in the future. For Professor Harris, however, no manuscript, no scrap of paper, quite literally no *doodle* even, lacks profound significance, as long as it is Hegel's.

Indeed, all previous instances of philosopholatry, even the one which had Plato as its object and perhaps as its founder, are thrown entirely into the shade by Professor Harris. He does not actually say that Hegel's philosophy can cure wooden legs, but I do not think he would like to hear it denied.

His book is, naturally, full of quotations from Hegel's early writings. In subject-matter these passages range from the astronomical to the zoological. For the examples which I promised earlier in this essay, I have chosen two of the astronomical ones. First:

> In the indifferences of light, the aether has scattered its absolute indifference into a multiplicity; in the blooms of the solar system it has borne its inner Reason and totality out into expansion. But the individualizations of light are dispersed in multiplicity [i.e. the fixed stars], while those which form the orbiting petals of the solar system must behave towards them with rigid individuality [i.e. they have their fixed orbits]. And so the unity of the stars lacks the form of universality, while that of the solar system lacks pure unity, and neither carries in itself the absolute Concept as such.[17]

Second:

> In the spirit the absolutely simple aether has returned to itself by way of the infinity of the Earth; in the Earth as such this union of the absolute simplicity of aether and infinity exists; it spreads into the universal fluidity, but its spreading fixates itself as singular things; and the numerical unit of singularity, which is the essential characteristic (*Bestimmtheit*) for the brute becomes itself an ideal factor, a moment. The concept of Spirit, as thus determined, is *Consciousness*, the concept of the union of the simple with infinity;[18]

I cannot emphasize too strongly that there are in the book *hundreds* of passages like these two, and on the widest variety of subjects. Good as he is on astronomy, Hegel is equally good on gravity, magnetism, heat, light and colour, plants, animals, sickness, human anatomy, the family, and many other topics besides.

Such, then, are the textual materials on which Professor Harris gravely and reverently exercises his profound scholarship for over

700 pages. And never was a philosophical biographer more in tune with this subject. For example, he prefaces the first of the two quotations just given with the following sentence of his own (the italics too being his):

> A fairly clear description of the self-positing of the aether as the 'creation of the world' – first the *fixed* stars as singular *intuitions* and then the conceptual displaying of light and gravity in a 'bloom' with 'petals' that move – is given in the *Natural Law* essay:

Clearly, in Professor Harris, the hour, and the subject, have called forth the man.

And now I ask you: is it not true, as I said earlier, that these two *real* examples of the pathology of thought are far more revolting than any of the invented ones which made up my list of forty pathological propositions? Do you know any example of the corruption of thought which is more extreme than these two? Did you even know, until now, that human thought was capable of this degree of corruption?

Yet Hegel grew out of Kant, Fichte, and Schelling, as naturally as Green, Bradley, and all the other later idealists, grew out of him. I mention these historical commonplaces, in case anyone should entertain the groundless hope of writing Hegel off as an isolated freak. But now, remembering those historical facts, while also keeping our eyes firmly on the two passages I have just given, will someone please tell me again that the Logical Positivists were on the wrong track, and that we ought to revere the 'great thinkers', and that the human race is not mad?

## Notes

1  Plotinus, *The Six Enneads*, trans. S. Mackenna and B. S. Page (Encyclopaedia Brittanica Inc., 1952), Fifth Ennead, VI, 6, p. 237.

2  *Hegel's Lectures on the History of Philosophy*, trans. E. S. Haldane and F. H. Simson (Routledge & Kegan Paul, London, 3 vols, 1892–6), vol. III, p. 550.

3  M. Foucault, *The Archaeology of Knowledge*, trans. A. M. Sheridan

Smith (Tavistock Publications, London, 1972), p. 154.

4　*The Natural History of Religion*, in *David Hume: The Philosophical Works*, ed. T. H. Green and T. H. Grose, Longman's, Green, London, 1882), vol. 4, p. 362.

5　Ibid., p. 360.

6　Diogenes Laertius, *Lives of Eminent Philosophers*, trans. R. Hicks (Loeb Classical Library; Heinemann, London, and Harvard University Press, 1959), vol. I, p. 277.

7　Where I read this discussion in Augstine's works, I cannot now rediscover.

8　W. Van Orman Quine, 'Two dogmas of empiricism,' in his *From a Logical Point of View* (Harper Torchbooks, New York, 1961).

9　K. R. Popper, 'The nature of philosophical problems and their roots in science,' in his *Conjectures and Refutations: the Growth of Scientific Knowledge* (Routledge and Kegan Paul, London, 1963).

10　W. Goodwin (ed.), *Plutarch's Miscellanies and Essays* (Little, Brown, Boston, 1889), vol. III, p. 2.

11　William Shakespeare, *The Tempest*, Act V. sc. i.

12　D. Hume, *A Treatise of Human Nature* (1739; ed. L. A. Selby-Bigge, Oxford, Clarendon Press, 1888; re-ed. P. Nidditch, Oxford, Clarendon Press, 1978), bk III, pt I, sect. i, last paragraph.

13　David Stove, *Popper and After: Four Modern Irrationalists* (Pergamon Press, Oxford, 1982), chs. I, II.

14　See the essay referred to in n. 8 above.

15　L. N. Tolstoy, *Anna Karenina*, the first sentence.

16　See 'Life of Dion', in Plutarch's *Parallel Lives* (*The Complete Works of Plutarch*, Thomas Y. Cromwell, New York, n.d.), vol. III, pp. 342–83.

17　H. S. Harris, *Hegel's Development: Night Thoughts (Jena 1801–1806)* (Clarendon Press, Oxford, 1983), p. 77. The insertions in square brackets were supplied, I take it, by Professor Harris.

18　Ibid., pp. 299–300. The references for these two passages are given by Professor Harris, but need not be reproduced here.

# Index of Persons

Aesop 18
Allen, W. 31, 41
Anaximander 174
Anderson, J. 32
Aquinas, T. 187, 201
Argyll, Duke of 164
Aristippus 168
Aristotle xii, 118
Armstrong, D. M. 53–4, 56
Arnold, M. 117
Astor, J. J. 198
Augustine, St 95, 184–5
Ayer, A. J. 27–8, 143

Bacon, F. 23–4, 135, 137
Balfour, A. J. 107
Barzun, J. 39
Bentham, J. 100, 137
Berkeley, G. ix–xii, 27–8, 64, 66–8,
    93, 97–8, 101–7, 114, 117–18,
    122, 124, 128–9, 139–49, 153,
    157, 169, 186–7, 198–200
Blake, W. 93, 182
Bosanquet, B. 90, 93–5, 97, 104,
    112, 114–19, 121, 124, 130, 173,
    187
Bradley, F. H. 87, 90, 95, 97, 111,
    114, 116–17, 119, 128, 130–1,
    147, 157–9, 163–4, 169, 173–4,
    187, 204
Brougham, H. 23
Butler, Bishop 164
Butler, S. xii, 19, 22, 122, 126

Caird, E. 90–1, 111, 170

Caird, J. 90–1, 154
Carlyle, T. 171
Castaneda, C. 44
Caton, H. 68
Celsus 41
Chalmers, A. 11
Cicero 102, 135
Clifford, W. K. 106
Coleridge, S. T. 89, 174
Collier, J. 102, 109
Comfort, A. 45
Comte, A. 32–3, 88, 172–3, 184–5
Copernicus x, 9, 35, 184
Cortes, H. 82
Cromwell, O. 91, 92

Darwin, C. x, 1, 9, 22, 58, 83,
    114, 173, 188
Darwin, F. 22
Descartes, R. 27–9, 77, 101–2,
    104, 108, 135, 145, 201
Devitt, M. 64–5, 70
Dickens, C. 19
Diogenes Laertius xi
Dostoevsky, F. 11
Duhem, P. 21

Eddington, Sir A. 137
Eddy, M. B. 113
Einstein, A. 188
Epicurus 188
Euclid 58
Ewing, A. C. 164–5

Faraday, M. 173

Ferrier, J. F.  103
Feyerabend, P. K.  10–12, 14, 40, 96
Fichte, J. G.  204
Foster, J.  90
Foucault, M.  181–3, 185, 190, 195
Franklin, C. L.  73–4, 77–80
Frege, G.  130

Galileo  14
Gandhi  44
Gemistus, G.  xii
Gilbert, W. S.  33
Gladstone, W. E.  88
Goodman, N.  viii, x, 30–42, 96
Green, T. H.  87, 89–93, 97, 101, 106, 113–14, 116, 143, 146, 159, 164, 173, 204

Haldane, R. B.  90, 114
Hamilton, Sir W.  97, 102, 135, 152, 154–5
Harris, H. S.  202–4
Harrison, F.  172
Hazlitt, W.  41
Hegel, G. W. F.  xiii, 2, 32–3, 83, 87–90, 97, 101, 105–7, 111, 113–14, 118, 122, 124, 128, 137, 180–1, 183–4, 185–6, 189–90
Hitler, A.  58
Hobbes, T.  27, 135
Hobhouse, L. T.  93
Humboldt, A.  21
Hume, D.  23, 27–9, 41, 50, 56, 66, 87, 90, 107, 130, 135, 150, 170, 173, 184
Huxley, T. H.  21, 58, 88, 106

Ireton, H.  91

Jackson, F.  64–5, 70–1, 75
James, W.  31, 33–5
Jaynes, J.  165
Jevons, W. S.  21
Johnson, L.  58
Joyce, J.  25, 31, 40

Kant, I.  xii, 27, 49–56, 63–4, 87–90, 95, 101, 103–7, 110,

113–14, 118, 122, 124, 128, 148, 151, 153, 155–6, 160–1, 163, 170, 173–4, 186, 198, 201–2, 204
Kuhn, T. S.  8–12, 14, 96

Lakatos, I.  6–8, 10–12, 14
Lambert, J.  91
Leacock, S.  75
Leibniz, G. W.  27, 100–1, 122, 126, 186
Lenin, V. I.  171
Lewes, G. H.  97
Lewis, D.  186
Locke, J.  64, 102, 138–9, 145–6, 199
Lorenz, K.  58, 142
Lucian  173
Lyell, C.  114, 188
Lysenko, T.  2

Macaulay, T. B.  23
Maccosh, J.  164
Mach, E.  21, 106
McTaggart, J. M. E.  87, 95, 103, 115–16, 157, 169
Malebranche, N.  102, 124, 145, 159
Mansel, H.  154, 155
Marcus Aurelius  107
Marx, K.  xiii, 173, 184, 185
Maxwell, J. C.  173
Meinong, A.  27, 186, 187
Melville, H.  x, 61
Mendeleev, D. I.  58
Mermin, N. D.  99
Mersenne, M.  77
Mill, J. S.  21, 23, 39, 97, 106, 164, 171
Milton, J.  91
Mondrian, P.  30
Montaigne, M.  173
Montalembert, Comte de  95
Moore, G. E.  32, 164, 186, 199
Muggeridge, M.  20, 125, 200–1

Newman, J. H.  88, 95
Newton, I.  4, 9, 17
Nietzsche, F.  103
Norris, J.  87, 102

Nozick, R.   vii, ix, 43–59

Oersted, H. C.   115
Owen, Sir R.   22

Paracelsus   182
Parmenides   ix–xii, 186–7
Pearson, K.   106
Perry, R. B.   164
Philistus   199
Picasso, P.   40
Plato   ix–xii, 32–3, 69, 100, 118,
   169, 180, 184–5, 187, 199, 201
Pletho   xii
Plotinus   87, 180–1, 183, 185–6,
   189, 195
Plutarch   188
Poincaré, H.   153–5
Popper, K. R.   vii, ix, 1–25, 50,
   187, 190
Porter, C.   1, 3, 5, 10–11
Protagoras   168

Quine, W. V.   187, 195

Reich, W.   182
Reid, T.   102
Reinhardt, L.   126
Royce, J.   103
Ruskin, J.   171
Russell, B.   73–5, 77, 164
Ryle, G.   186

Santayana, G.   100
Schelling, F. W. J.   105, 204

Schiller, F. C. S.   164
Schopenhauer, A.   155–7
Sedgwick, A.   22
Seth, A.   90, 95, 97, 107, 118–19,
   121
Smith, N. Kemp   66
Sorley, W. R.   95
Spencer, H.   97, 103
Speusippus   xi
Spinoza, B.   100–1, 114, 186
Stalin, J.   58
Stephen, L.   94
Stirling, J. H.   89
Stravinsky, I.   30, 31, 35

Taylor, A. E.   90, 95
Taylor, T.   xii
Tinbergen, J.   142
Tolstoy, L.   107–8, 196
Twain, M.   13, 16, 21

Varro   135
Vane, Sir H.   91–3

Wallace, W.   97
Ward, H.   89
Ward, J.   95
Waugh, E.   19
Whewell, W.   21
Whitehead, A. N.   122, 126
Wilberforce, S.   22
Williams, D. C.   64
Wittgenstein, L.   66
Wolfe, T.   20, 31, 62
Wright, F. L.   20